C. G. JUNG'S COMPLEX DYNAMICS
AND THE CLINICAL RELATIONSHIP

C. G. JUNG'S COMPLEX DYNAMICS AND THE CLINICAL RELATIONSHIP

One Map For Mystery

By

BRENDA A. DONAHUE, ED.D.

CHARLES C THOMAS • PUBLISHER, LTD.
Springfield • Illinois • U.S.A.

Published and Distributed Throughout the World by

CHARLES C THOMAS • PUBLISHER, LTD.
2600 South First Street
Springfield, Illinois 62704

This book is protected by copyright. No part of
it may be reproduced in any manner without
written permission from the publisher.

©2003 by BRENDA A. DONAHUE

ISBN 0-398-07408-9 (hard)
ISBN 0-398-07409-7 (paper)

Library of Congress Catalog Card Number: 2003042673

With THOMAS BOOKS *careful attention is given to all details of manufacturing and design. It is the Publisher's desire to present books that are satisfactory as to their physical qualities and artistic possibilities and appropriate for their particular use.* THOMAS BOOKS *will be true to those laws of quality that assure a good name and good will.*

Printed in the United States of America
CR-R-3

Library of Congress Cataloging-in-Publication Data

Donahue, Brenda A.
  C. G. Jung's complex dynamics and the clinical relationship : one map for mystery / by Brenda A. Donahue.
     p. cm.
  Includes bibliographical references and index.
  ISBN 0-398-07408-9 (hard) -- ISBN 0-398-07409-7 (pbk.)
    1. Jung, C. G. (Carl Gustav), 1875-1961. 2. Complexes (Psychology)
  I. Title.

RC569.5.C68D66 2003
154.2'4--dc21

2003042673

INTRODUCTION

The roads that have led to the writing of this book are the pathways of my own life and my experience as a therapist. My training as a therapist began in the early 1970s. I was a nurse who "assisted" another therapist in group therapy. Part of my role as "assistant" was to do a presentation on each person in the group during supervision and discuss the factors that had shaped his or her life. These presentations included medical and familial history, developmental history, attachment style and ways of communicating. During this same time I also began reading Jung. I was drawn to his writings because he discussed the existence of a "higher power" within each human being and seemed to make room for the operation of that power when he worked with patients. I wanted to learn to make room for that power in my own practice without forcing my patients or myself into a specific belief system or theology. In order to do so I entered the analyst-training program at the Jung Institute of Chicago.

Part of my training as an analyst included learning a new vocabulary based upon Jung's theories. However, as I discussed my patients in supervision I began to discover that there was a split between what I called my "clinical" and my "Jungian" vocabularies. Most of Jung's theories were formed in the early 1900s and although they still applied to the clinical situation, I couldn't find the words to tell my colleagues what was happening with my patients and why. As I continued to study my frustration grew. I felt as if my knowledge decreased as my questions increased. Many of my teachers at the institute encouraged my questions and explorations. This book is the result. It is one attempt to link Jung's vocabulary with modern clinical theories so that therapists can understand his ideas and use them in the clinical hour, while making room for mystery.

The purpose of this book is to evoke questions rather than provide answers. When we ask what transforms people in therapy, we must answer that we do not know. Healing is a mystery. This book is not an attempt to bring light into mystery; rather, it is an attempt to raise questions by providing different viewing points into mystery and to highlight the undeniable fact that mystery appears within the clinical hour. To me, questions are the most important tool in life. They are much more important than answers because they promote observation and introspection during day-to-day experience and are frequently the pathway to the answers we seek.

When I began reading Jung in the early 1970s, I felt as if I had come home. For me, he made space for both questions and mysteries in the study of psychology. He also discussed human experience in terms of patterns, which he called complexes. Gradually I began to understand that complex theory was my bridge over the chasm of "archetypal" vs. "clinical" and it occurred to me that complex theory also might be integrated with modern ideas about human development and relationship. During my training as an analyst I wrote about human development as an archetypal process. My thesis advisor Murray Stein, Ph.D. was both patient and very encouraging. After I graduated from the analyst-training program I continued to write and meet with my friend Peter Mudd, L.C.S.W. who listened, asked questions and gave me helpful feedback. The ideas presented in this book are intended to bridge the gap between "clinical" and "archetypal" as well as link Jung's ideas with modern theories of human development and relationship. In addition, the reader is encouraged to practice the experiential exercises presented in the last chapter to test the ideas presented in the book and develop both questions and clinical skills based upon the material presented.

Jung was not the first to theorize about complexes; Aristotle described them in the fourth century BCE as parts of the physical body and also as partial souls. The first clinical use of the word *complex* appeared in 1893 in a paper written by Josef Breuer and Sigmund Freud. Together they developed the theory that a complex is a cluster of interrelated and usually repressed ideas with a strong emotional content that may compel an individual to adopt abnormal patterns of thought and behavior (Breuer, J. and Freud, S. 1956, pp. 8-13).

About the same time as Freud and Breuer were developing their theory of complex, Jung was exploring similar ideas. He studied with the Parisian physician Pierre Janet, famous for his work with patients who showed symptoms of hysteria, dissociation, and formation of partial personalities. Jung subsequently studied these phenomena and discovered complexes as he developed the *Word Association Test*.

In the *Word Association Test*, patients were given over a hundred stimulus words and time to respond to each word (time to make a personal *association* to the word). An *association* is a linkage of ideas, perceptions, images, fantasies, memories, physical sensations, and behaviors that are linked with certain personal and psychological themes. The main outcome of Jung's studies on word association was proof of a linkage between the associations themselves, affective themes, and the eruption of unconscious patterns of psychic and physical energy. During the *Word Association Test*, unconscious complexes inserted themselves into the subject's reactions to certain words. These reactions included slowing in response time, word replacement, changes in facial expression, laughing, changes in body movement, coughing, stammering, insufficient responses, not reacting to the real meaning of the word, responses in a foreign language, or a total lack of reaction. These responses occurred only with certain words, unique to each person taking the test. The responses took longer than the time allotted and indicated a breach in the flow of consciousness that was caused by the emergence of unconscious material. When the unconscious material was explored, the responses were linked with complexes and the inability to put them into words.

Over time, Jung identified three different kinds of complexes: (1) those related to single, ongoing or repeated events, (2) those that were conscious, partly conscious, or unconscious, and (3) those that revealed strong charges of affect (C.W. 2, 1981, 408-425 and 583-616). Despite the prominent place of the *Oedipus complex* in psychological theory, Freud gradually moved away from the idea of complexes toward drive theory. Jung continued to explore complexes as he developed his own theories.

The idea of *complex* gave Jung a way to think about how human experience accumulates. He observed that as human experience accumulates, it forms into patterns of experience rather than remaining a series of isolated events. As he studied his own and others' dreams, Jung began to believe that an invisible something existed beneath these patterns that structured human experience and behavior into patterns, creating the world as we perceive it. He called these invisible, structuring forms *archetypes*. In the beginning of his studies, he thought of them as psychological patterns of human instinct that were irrepresentable but appeared as numinous images in dreams, fairy tales, and mythology.

Over time, Jung's ideas about the archetype evolved. He began to believe that archetypes were blueprints for human psychic growth and development from the womb on. By 1946, after 44 years of clinical practice, he came to the realization that the archetype was not just a psychological structure; it was a psychosomatic or *psychoid* structure, shaping the patterns that formed both psyche and body which were really two aspects of one reality. Even though archetypes cannot be directly perceived, Jung located them in universally human experiences like falling in love, mothering, fathering, giving birth, dreaming, and dying. He thought of the archetypes as dynamic blueprints that held the potential for the development of human consciousness, maintaining the balance of consciousness through a process he called compensation. Jung did not discuss the archetypal regulation of physical development or homeostasis. However, he implied it when he discussed the psychoid nature of the archetypes.

As Jung developed his theory of archetypes, he began to pay more attention to compensation as it appeared in dreaming, cross-cultural mythology, and fairy tales. He discovered that the ego is not the center of the personality but only the center of consciousness. He hypothesized that the center and the circumference of the entire personality, both conscious and unconscious, is the Self—unknown and unknowable—the innate nature of every human being. Just as every oak tree is unique, each one is part of the greater pattern we recognize as oak. Human beings grow from a small cell. Each cell is unique, and yet each is part of the greater pattern we call human being. The *Self* is the architect of each human being. The *archetypes* are the blueprints of the *Self.*

These concepts are the foundations of complex theory. As Jung grew older, he became less and less interested in complexes and explored dreams, archetypal images and alchemical writings instead. However, the *Word Association Test* and the *Lie Detector Test,* a derivative of complex theory, are still used today even though the theoretical framework they are built on has never been integrated with modern developmental or relational theories.

This book will attempt to link Jung's theories of complex and archetype with: the processes of ego development, Fordham, (1974,1976, 1978, 1985, 1996); the archetypal underpinnings of ego consciousness Stern, (1985) and Tomkins (1981); on human development Erikson, (1950) and Levin, (1974); on human relationship Stern, (1985), and on attachment Ainsworth (1978, 1988), Bowlby (1973, 1980, 1982), Main (1995, 1999) and Karen (1994). In addition, the reader will be introduced to individual and group experiential exercises that can be used to develop clinical skills based upon the theoretical material presented.

ACKNOWLEDGMENTS

I am very grateful to my dear friend Mary Loomis, Ph.D. for spending precious hours of her life editing my manuscript and correcting the figures while she was dying from cancer. I wish to thank Peter Mudd, L.C.S.W. for his willingness to sit and listen to me struggle my way through theoretical muddles, offering many comments and ideas that have become part of the fabric of this work. I also wish to thank Stephen Diamond, Ph.D. for spending time editing my first draft and Jean Tracy, Ph.D. for reading the manuscript and making comments. The first draft of the book was submitted to Ignatius University for my doctoral dissertation in Adult Education. My examining committee, including Anthony DeLuca, Ph.D., Linda Richter, Ph.D., Les R. Greene, Ph.D. and Bertram Schaffner, Ph.D. encouraged me to continue writing. They asked me to present clinical examples side-by-side with the theory. I have attempted to do that and I think the reader will find the clinical vignettes helpful. In addition, I would like to thank Alice Chrismer for the cover and the illustrative figures, and Elizabeth Yoder for the final editing.

CONTENTS

Page

Introduction v

Chapter

1. THEORETICAL FOUNDATIONS: COMPLEX THEORY AND ITS RELATIONSHIP TO MODERN THEORISTS 3

   Complex Theory Rediscovered: Silvan Tomkins 6
   Complex Theory and Daniel Stern 9
   Fairy Tales and Complexes 10
   Archetypes: The Numinous Creators of Complexes 12
   Archetypes: Dynamic Processes 14
   Individuation and the Old Indian Man 16
   Modern Theorists, The Archetype, and Ego Development 18
      Being 20
      Doing 21
      Thinking 22
      Identity 24
      Creativity 25
   Patterns of Mediation of Archetypal Developmental Processes ... 25
   The Process of Ego Development 32
   Creation of a Complex 39
   Summary 40
   Questions 41

2. FORMATION OF A PATHOLOGICAL COMPLEX 44

   The Woman Who Once Walked in Balance 44
   Summary 52
   Compensation 53
   The Self 54
   The Defenses of the Self 55

Operation of the Defenses of the Self 57
Summary of the Defenses of the Self 66
The Evoked Companion 69
The Evoked Companion and the Imago 70
Questions 73

3. MORE VIEWING POINTS INTO THE PATHOLOGICAL
   COMPLEX 76

   The Foundations of Ego Consciousness 77
   Archetypal Structures of Ego Consciousness 79
   Complexes and Aspects of Ego Consciousness 84
   The Medicine Wheel 85
   Summary 106
   The Layered View of the Psyche 107
   The Cycles of Nature 110
   The Cycles of Nature: A Viewing Point into the Pathological
      Complex 113
   Another Look at the Woman Who Once Walked in Balance 115
   Viewing Points into the Pathological Complex 116
   Questions 118

4. PATTERNED FORMS OF ATTACHMENT AND
   PATHOLOGICAL COMPLEXES 121
   Patterned Forms of Attachment 121
   The Formation of Patterned Forms of Attachment 122
   Viewing Points into Patterned Forms of Attachment 125
   Patterned Forms of Attachment and the Components of Ego
      Consciousness 126
   The Imago and Patterned Forms of Attachment 135
   The Ego/Imago Axis 137
   Creating a Transitional Space Between the Patterned Form of
      Attachment and Ego Consciousness 143
   Archetypal Energy and the Imago 148
   The Persona 149
   The Shadow 151
   The Anima and Animus 153
   The Fantasy Bond and the Patterned Form of Attachment ... 158
   Patterned Forms of Attachment and Regression 163
   Summary 173
   Questions 175

5. PATHOLOGICAL COMPLEXES AND DIAGNOSIS 177

Using Complex Theory as an Expansion of DSM-IV 178
Diagnosis Using Clinical Examples 182
Case #1: Jacob and Shirley 183
Case #2: Baby Richard 206
Case #3: Sylvia 210
Case #4: Michael 220
The Benefits of Using Figure 15 With the DSM-VI 228
Questions 229

6. DEVELOPING CLINICAL SKILLS: INDIVIDUAL EXERCISES 231

Individual Skill Development 231
   The Complex Awareness Measure 231
Compensation 243
The Imago 244
Archetypal/Developmental Processes 246
Performing Active Imagination 248
Group Skill Development 248
The Relational Field 249
Triadic Role-Play 251
Focus 251
Listening 252
Facilitating the Development of the Transitional Space 253
Developing the Patient's Awareness of Parts 256
The Imago and Parts Work 258

Appendix 263
Bibliography 273
Author Index 279
Subject Index 281

C. G. JUNG'S COMPLEX DYNAMICS
AND THE CLINICAL RELATIONSHIP

Chapter 1

THEORETICAL FOUNDATIONS: COMPLEX THEORY AND ITS RELATIONSHIP TO MODERN THEORISTS

A man in the early phases of therapy reports a childhood nightmare in which his foot is caught under a railroad tie while a train is coming toward him. At the very last possible moment, he wiggles out of his shoe and barely misses being killed by the oncoming train. He remembers awakening curled up in a ball. He dismisses his nightmare as "one of those silly things kids dream about." As the work proceeds, the man begins to discover that he is terrified of feeling angry. He has moved from job to job and marriage to marriage feeling victimized, misunderstood, and unable to express or define himself. Gradually, he starts to understand that when he finds himself in situations where he must be assertive or speak his own truth, he feels as if he is going to be annihilated, and he would do anything to slither away from any sort of confrontation.

Knowing what we do about this man, let us suppose that his nightmare and his difficulty in defining himself are linked. In broad brush strokes, the linkage for him would go something like this: "When I am required to define myself, I experience something like a train coming toward me. I am stuck and trapped. I feel hollowness in the pit of my stomach, and I break out into a cold sweat. I feel as if I am going to be annihilated. I wiggle out of the situation (my shoe) and slither away so that I do not die."

Here we have the ideas, the physical sensations, the images, the behavior, and the affective tone of his childhood nightmare that appear as a rigidified pattern of reactivity (complex) in his everyday life. The *physical sensations* are hollowness in the pit of his stomach and breaking out in a cold sweat. The *idea* is that he is being asked to do something dangerous (define himself). The *feeling* is that if he does define himself something enormous (a train) is coming to destroy him. The *imago* is the image of the train. This man is operating out of a rigidified set of ideas, physical sensations, images, and behaviors linked together by an *affective theme* of terror. As we see from his history, this rigidified pattern of reactivity is so ready to be stimulated that it makes everyday life a nightmare for him.

How did this complex become so strong? Negative complexes, according to Jungian theory, build gradually, beginning in the womb. They usually have a basis in patterns of personal historical experience as well as an archetypal component. All complexes are patterns of experience, individually unique, yet common to all humans. Complexes are quite natural phenomena, which develop along positive as well as negative lines. Those that are negative are rigid patterns of experience that damage both physical and psychic growth. Those that are positive are open and promote physical and psychological growth. In his article, "A Review of Complex Theory" (*CW* 8, 1981), Jung says two different things about complexes. First, he says that they are "the living units of the unconscious psyche" (101). Second, he pathologizes them by saying that "every constellation of a complex . . . creates . . . a disturbed state of consciousness" (96). Thus, complexes can be both benign and malignant.

Why do people form complexes? Basically all complexes are patterns of experience held together by an affective theme. Jung believed that something existed outside human awareness and experience that formed the human body and psyche into patterns that are interrelated and interconnected. He called these structuring forms *archetypes* and described them as energetic forms that order human experience and perceptions in certain invariant patterns. We could say that all human beings standing with their foot caught under a railroad tie with a train coming toward them would feel exactly the same way this man felt in his nightmare. His terror of death, the image of the train, his inability to define himself, the rigid train tracks, his memory of the nightmare, and his behavior in everyday life are all parts of a pattern that is uniquely his, yet could belong to anyone. The ability to remember; to have physical sensations, memories, and images; to be terrified; and to slip away could be experienced by anyone. All the images in the dream can be connected to universal human experience.

This man does not, of course, really have a locomotive bearing down on him. He has a nightmare that overrides the present reality when he is required to define himself. The archetypal/developmental pattern that underlies his sense of having an identity and being able to define himself as an individual is misapplied. Self-definition is not a life-threatening situation. However, in this man's case, it is *experienced* as life threatening. This distortion does not foster adaptation; instead, it overtakes his consciousness and then is re-enacted in everyday life. His childhood nightmare is a picture of a rigidified complex and an image of what happens to this particular man when life requires that he identify, define, or commit himself. He cannot stand his ground because any time he needs to define himself, the negative complex becomes stimulated. When the outer world demands him to be who he is and to act assertively, his nightmare becomes stimulated. He feels the terror of the train bearing down on him and then slips away from any sort of confrontation. This is what Jung said about complexes in 1934:

> [A feeling toned complex is] strongly accentuated emotionally and is, moreover, incompatible with the habitual attitude of consciousness. This [complex] ... has a powerful inner coherence, it has its own wholeness and, in addition, a relatively high degree of autonomy, so that it is subject to the control of the conscious mind to only a limited extent, and therefore behaves like an animated foreign body in the sphere of consciousness. The complex can usually be suppressed with an effort of will, but not argued out of existence, and at the first suitable opportunity it reappears in all its original strength. (*CW* 8, 1981, 96)

Why would this man have this particular type of complex? After a careful exploration of his history from childhood to the present time, we uncovered experience after experience of avoiding confrontation and the terror it produced as a way to survive. In his family of origin, there was a strong prohibition against his defining himself outside of the authority of his parents. His nightmare tells us how he survived. He slipped out of his shoe at the very last possible moment, and he continues to slip away into the same nightmare. This man's complex is connected with experiences of authority that have been internalized as train-like when he attempts to have an identity. These internalized experiences have stopped him from developing his own inner authority and defining himself. When life requires him to stand firm, he cannot. The anxiety and terror-laden feeling tone of the complex is so powerful and so embedded in his psyche that he regresses into his nightmare when a *perceived authority* requests his opinion, comments on him, or evaluates him. This is an example of how a rigidified or negative complex operates in everyday life in a pathological way.

This is what Jung says about the constellation of a negative complex:

> This term simply expresses the fact that the outward situation releases a psychic process in which certain contents gather and prepare for action. When we say that a person is "constellated," we mean that he has taken up a position from which he can be expected to react in a quite definite way ... the constellation is an automatic process which happens involuntarily and which no one can stop if it is on a course. The constellated contents are definite complexes possessing their own specific energies. (*CW* 8, 1981, 94)

Could the man described above have a positive complex? Yes. In his case, learning and thinking were easy for him. His parents were European immigrants. Their English was not particularly good, and he was a great help in translating for them. He had permission to be bright, to do well in school, and to feel comfortable enough with academic success to acquire several advanced degrees. The ideas, images, behaviors, physical sensations, and feeling tones associated with learning were supportive of this process. The man had pleasure when he was learning and thinking, which was combined with a neutral or positive feeling tone. His parents had supported and nourished his ability to learn. However, when he was required to define himself, the experience was linked with the terror of an overwhelming authority about to annihilate him.

Everyone has complexes. Some are benign and help us in our lives. Others are negative, even pathological, and they interfere with our living full and productive lives. Complexes are psychic fragments that have split off owing to traumatic influences or an incompatibility with ego consciousness (Jung, *CW* 8, 121). I define a negative complex in this way: *A pathological complex is an unconscious pattern of behavioral reactivity linked with rigidified memories, physical sensations, images, ideas, and meaning that is enmeshed with repeated experiences of disintegration that cannot be verbally expressed. The complex is held together by a unique affective theme and is directed by images of primary caretakers, linked with powerful, archetypal forms of energy that are blocked from performing their natural function of supporting adaptation and the continual development of conscious awareness.* What does that mean? What would it look like in the therapeutic hour?

COMPLEX THEORY REDISCOVERED: SILVAN TOMKINS

Jung's theory of the complex, with its accompanying feeling tone, has been substantiated by the research of a professor of social science, Silvan Tomkins. In an article appearing in the *Journal of Personality and Social Psychology* (1981, 306–329), Tomkins outlines a theory of affect, defining it as an invariant of human experience. In Jung's psychology, invariants of human experience are called *archetypes*—unconscious forms that undergird all human perception and functions, forming patterns that eventually become individual experience. Tomkins studied more than 10,000 photographs of infants' facial expressions and discovered nine innate affects: (1) interest-excitement, (2) enjoyment-joy, (3) surprise-startle, (4) fear-terror, (5) distress-anguish, (6) anger-rage, (7) shame-humiliation, (8) disgust, and (9) contempt.

Affect develops from the stimulation of the innate neurophysiological reflexes that human beings are born with: sucking, rooting, startling, and a swaying movement away from the hip being touched when a baby is held in a standing position.[2] The affects named by Tomkins' are related to the innate physical constitution of the child; the frequency, intensity, and duration of stimulation; and the length of time it takes the body to come back to a neutral state (see Fig. 1). Affects combine into patterns with a range that can move between pleasure, discomfort and disintegration.

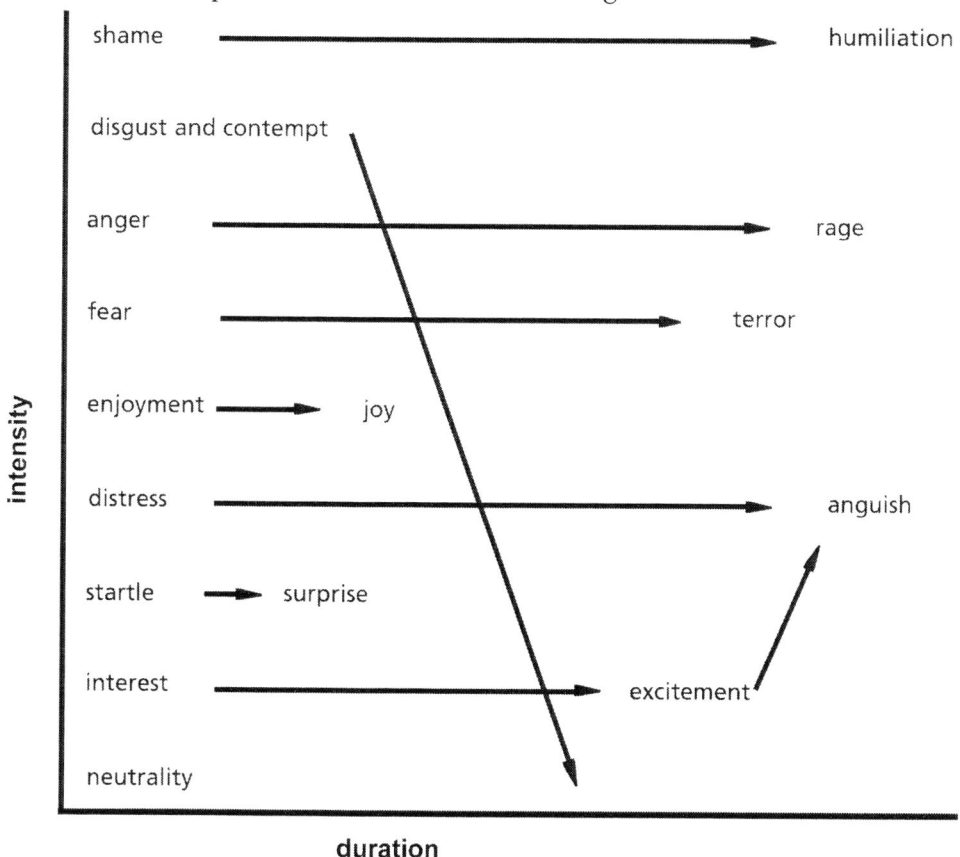

```
intensity
 |
 | shame ──────────────────────────────▶ humiliation
 |
 |   disgust and contempt
 |
 | anger ──────────────────────────────▶ rage
 |
 | fear ───────────────────────────▶ terror
 |
 | enjoyment ─────▶ joy
 |
 | distress ───────────────────────────▶ anguish
 |
 | startle ──▶ surprise
 |
 | interest ───────────────────▶ excitement
 |
 | neutrality
 |_____
                    duration
```

FIGURE 1
The nine innate affects.

In Figure 1, seven of the affects have a range that includes both intensity (vertical line) and duration (horizontal line). Disgust and contempt do not have a range because they are "innate defensive responses" that have to do with hunger, thirst, and smell–taking in the good and defending against the bad (Tomkins 1995, 84-85). In Figure 1, the affects are placed in an order of intensity that extends from neutrality to shame (high level of intensity). This order is based on my own observations of infants, and I am not sure Tomkins would agree with me. However, the higher the level of the individual experience of the intensity of the affect, and the longer the duration of the experience of affect, the more difficult it becomes for the body to endure it. For example, excitement, joy, startle, terror, anguish, rage, and humiliation are prolonged experiences of interest, enjoyment, surprise, fear, distress, and anger. Prolonged experiences of affect are much more difficult to contain, and though they are not negative in themselves, they are more painful to experience than their counterparts. Disgust and contempt have intensity, but they have a short duration. In addition, each of the innate affects may combine with other affects intensifying, reducing, modulating, enmeshing, and suppressing some perceptions and experiences and enhancing others. Shame can also inhibit other affects (85 and 322). Gradually, a unique combination of affects forms itself into an *affective theme* that becomes enmeshed with physical sensations, memories, and images that support certain behaviors and suppress others.

In his theory of affect, Tomkins unknowingly corroborated one of the central elements of Jung's complex theory. As an affective theme develops, it acts like a magnet, pulling affect laden scenes together into an affective memory. Jung would call this a *feeling tone*. Tomkins defined this connection between one affect-laden scene with another as "script theory" (1981, 322). What he discovered is that repetitive experiences of affective amplification (where one affective scene links with another affective scene) create highly individual patterns of reaction. Script theory is another way to describe complexes or patterns of reaction based upon affective amplification.

Tomkins believed that a "script" was formed in the following ways. First, a triggering event or stimulus for a particular affect generates or reaches a certain range of physiological intensity. Second, when that specific range of intensity is reached, an unconscious linkage takes place with previous experiences of that affect, creating a unique blending of affect called an "affective sequence" (1981, 325). Third, when the experience of affective sequencing is reached, there is an unconscious scan of all previous experiences grouped around that particular affective sequence. Fourth, this unconscious scan is followed by an unconscious decision that would be something like this: The situation I am in "safe or not safe" (Nathanson 1993, 546–548). Fifth, based on this unconscious decision, there would be a repetitive reaction to the stimulus (546). These five steps also describe the constellation of a complex.

In the case of the man who had the train nightmare, his "affective sequence" was triggered when an outward situation in his life demanded that he stand firm and speak his own truth. Internally, he would immediately experience himself lying helpless with his foot caught under a railroad tie while a train was bearing down on him. His affective response did not support a fluid and spontaneous reaction to the actual stimulus presented by the environment in the present moment. Instead, an affective theme was constellated, making the present moment physiologically and psychologically unsafe and producing a behavioral reaction (slipping away from the train) that overrode current reality.

How might these complex dynamics appear in a clinical hour?

Patient: "The hysterectomy surgery was really painful. The surgeon laughed and told me I was too old to have children anyway."

Therapist: "That sounds really painful."
Therapist observation: Her voice is raised, her face is red, she is leaning over, and her hands are shaking.

Patient: "My husband didn't want kids even though I did. He and his new wife have two. I have nothing. I am in so much pain. How could he do that to me?"

The patient is discussing her history and the discussion has stimulated the painful affective theme associated with her hysterectomy, her loss of the possibility for having children and her divorce.

COMPLEX THEORY AND DANIEL STERN

In *The Interpersonal World of the Infant* (1985), psychiatrist Daniel Stern creates another version of complex theory by focusing on how a core sense of self develops from lived experience that is formed into patterns that he calls Generalized Event Structures or GERs. A generalized event structure is not a specific memory. It is a pattern formed from averaging lived experiences and is closer to an "abstract representation" rather than to events that have actually happened. Generalized Event Structures create "expectations of actions, of feelings, of sensations, and so on that can either be met or violated" (97). Stern considers generalized episodes (GER's) to be "basic building blocks of cognitive development as well as autobiographical memory" (97). Both Tomkins and Stern discuss human affect and memory in terms of patterns of experience, as does Jung.

Jung began studying complexes in the early 1900s. Even at that time he understood that complexes were patterns. He wondered how the patterns formed. As he observed complexes through the broad lenses of history, myth, art, poetry, ancient patterns of physical movement (e.g., yoga), fairy tales, dreams, and the relentless events of life, birth, death, transformation, love, and desire, he began to believe that something that existed outside of human awareness structured human experience into patterns. He called these dynamic, structuring forms *archetypes*, and he believed that they operated out of the range of human awareness and structured all of human physiology, perception and performance into the patterns that he called complexes.

FAIRY TALES AND COMPLEXES

Fairy tales are perhaps the purest and simplest expression of unconscious human psychic processes. Each fairy tale is a descriptive metaphor for deeply embedded and repetitive patterns of human experience, or complexes. According to Jungian analyst Marie-Louise von Franz (1993), there is a *just so* quality to a fairy tale that transcends logic or feeling; the characters simply expose the underlying patterns and the complexes that order human perception (99–100).

The *Little Match Girl*, written by Hans Christian Andersen is an example of a rigidified complex in operation. In the story, the little match girl (she has no name because she could be anyone), was sent out into the cold world by her parents to sell matches, unprepared, poorly dressed, and hungry. She was not told anything about *how* to sell her matches, but only told not to return home until she did or her father would beat her. Her home was described as cold and empty enough for the wind to blow through. She did not sell any matches the whole day. She finally became so cold that she stopped for a moment to get warm. There were houses and the smell of food all around her. Yet she stopped and huddled in an alleyway between two houses, cold, unseen, and afraid to go home. She did not perceive any way out of her predicament. She was utterly helpless. She lit a match to get warm and had an image of sitting in front of a warm stove receiving comfort. The match went out. She lit another match and saw food. The food moved toward her, but the match went out. All she saw was a cold, thick wall. She struck another match and saw herself sitting under a Christmas tree in an environment where she was warm and wanted. The match went out. Then she saw a falling star and knew that it meant that someone was going to die. The message of the unconscious was very clear, but not to her. It remained a wish not acted upon; and like Freud's notion of the dream, her wish was fulfilled only in fantasy, but never in real life. She needed warmth, food and friends. Without them she was going to die, yet all that the little girl could do was stay where she was. She struck another match and felt her dead grandmother holding her. In order to hang on to the feeling of being loved and wanted, she struck all of her matches. When they went out, she died.

The little girl had visions of a better life, yet she died frozen because she could not choose life. What made her unable to seek help? Why was she unmoved by the compensatory information coming to her in her visions? The answer is given to us in symbolic language. Like the matches, the light of consciousness went out after she had her vision. She saw only a thick, cold wall. There was no door for the little match girl. In her world, there was no way for her to operationalize the images coming to her from the unconscious. During her short life, she had learned that asking for help was dangerous, useless, or destructive; therefore, the possibility of asking for help had ceased to exist for her consciously. Her life was like that of the man who slipped away from the oncoming train. It was a nightmare that overrode reality and the possibility for choice or growth.[3]

In Jung's view, the unconscious balances one's conscious attitude through a process called *compensation*, to maintain psychic equilibrium (*CW* 6, 1977, 340). The compensatory process was operating for the little match girl in the images that came to her; however, her construction of reality could not connect these images with her present situation. She was unable to use the light of consciousness to resolve the problem. In her story, the matches went out. The little girl in the story died because she did not have the capacity to translate the messages from the unconscious into an operational way of relating to the world and everyday life. Her death was a metaphor for a developmental process that failed. All she knew was what she learned in her few years of life. Asking for help was not an option, and there was a thick, cold wall between her and the possibilities offered by life and human relationship.

We could say that the little match girl was pathologically complexed. Her ego consciousness was immature. She could not contain the images of healing she received and learn from them. Healing images emerged from the unconscious. They showed her that she needed to find warmth, food, a loving home, and arms to hold and nurture her. She was unable to use the information to act on her own behalf. The warmth all around her was too far outside her realm of experience. We can assume that, over time, the little match girl did not receive help when she has asked for it. We can even assume that a strong affective prohibition against asking for help distorted her connection to the outer world.

If we think of this fairy tale as Jung might have, we see a child, born with unlimited potential for being, who died because she could not ask for help. What happened to her unlimited potential for growth? We can say that this potential was somehow profoundly narrowed. The little match girl lived in a nightmare that overrode the reality of what was there all around her. The fairy tale was a metaphor for a complex; it described the disconnection between what was perceived and what was actually present. The little match girl is like the man who lives with the perpetual nightmare train: she perceives the outer world through lenses that have tragically limited her ability to adapt and to find options that will help her develop. *The Little Match Girl* is a universally human story in the sense that all humans can become frightened, hungry, and lonely. Her individual problem was an inability to adapt because of a pathological complex.

ARCHETYPES: THE NUMINOUS CREATORS OF COMPLEXES

Complexes are patterns of experience held together by an affective theme. An archetype, as we have seen, forms the basic structure of any complex and makes every complex a pattern of experience. Complexes are not single experiences linked together, they are a pattern of averaged experiences. Every pattern is universally human, yet when filled with life experience, each pattern becomes highly individual. Each human being is a unique individual because of the enormous number of variables that impact the basic structure of each pattern. The reader will discover some of these variables as this book unfolds. All of nature is structured in the same way, uniformly patterned and yet each plant, animal, or piece of earth is highly unique.

We are not able to perceive the archetypes directly. They can be indirectly perceived through somatic intuition, physical sensations that are perceptive or intuitive in nature (Mudd 1990, 131), dreaming, fantasies, visions, images, psychological intuition, history, mythology, and the important events in human life. We know that archetypes are present, not because we can perceive them, but human experience is formed into patterns and these patterns are universal ($CW 9_1$ 1980, 102). For example, we humans can only hear and see within a certain range and our brains, bones, tissues, muscles, and organs are formed in similar ways (CW 3, 1972, 261). The way we are formed makes us people. We also know that archetypes are dynamic because people can continue to learn and become more conscious during an entire lifetime.

The easiest way to experience an archetype is to turn on the television set during a drama, comedy, or action thriller and turn down the volume so that you watch only the body language. You will still understand the story. This is true for foreign language films as well. Body language, like any other normal human capacity, is archetypal or part of being human. *Body parl*, or communicating with the body, is a universal human language. This form of nonverbal language can be used by an actor to convey something quite different from the immediacy of the actor's own internal experience. A great actor is an artist who uses *body parl* to tap into universal, archetypal human experiences in order to convey meaning.

Children with Asperger's disorder are born insensitive to body language (APA 2000, 80–84) and have great difficulty socializing because they are blind to *body parl*. They need to be taught to recognize physical cues in order to have relationships. These children are somehow unable to use a range of perception that is taken for granted by others. Because of their inability, others react to these children in negative ways. The child does not understand what he/she has done to elicit these responses and feels emotional pain.

Gradually these children develop ideas, physical sensations, images, thoughts, and behaviors that increase their sense of being different, making them isolate themselves when approached or noticed by other human beings.

After years of study, Jung finally came to the conclusion that the archetypes have what he called a *psychoid* structure. This means that every archetype has a range of influence that operates between two poles, a physical pole and a psychological pole (*CW* 8, 1946, 215 216 and *CW* 9$_2$, 1973, 3). Psyche and matter are two aspects of the same thing, like particles and waves (Capra, 1991) and they form the patterns associated with both the body and the psyche.

In the case of a pathological complex, there is a problem connecting an archetypal reality with ego consciousness and the archetypal form is prevented from providing a flexible pattern to adapt to a present life situation. In the case of a physical disease or pathological complex, the afflicted person is out of balance and the body and psyche are not functioning according to nature. The symptoms associated with pathological complexes are nature's attempt to restore balance. The little match girl received images from the unconscious that showed her what she needed in order to survive. She was unable to use the images because she didn't know how to ask for help.

The little match girl, the child with Asperger's syndrome, and the man with the train nightmare are unable to access archetypal information to adapt and correct their problems because the archetypal information is unavailable to ego consciousness, distorted, or deleted. They have received strong genetic and/or relational prohibitions against cooperating with their own processes. These prohibitions literally hold the energy of the archetype in the unconscious creating the pathological complex and preventing normal adaptation and conscious development.

Because of the little match girl's inability to perceive options in life, she died. She lived in a drama that has created strictures on her wholeness, curses on her choices, and limits to what she could be, know, and perceive. In the case of the man with the train nightmare, being assertive triggered the experience of being caught on a track with a train roaring down upon him. All he could do was slip away from an oncoming death. In the case of a child with Asperger's syndrome, patterns of rejection with no apparent cause from the child's viewpoint, create rigidified patterns of avoidance in relationships.

In all of these examples there is a problem connecting inner processes of adaptation to outer reality. Outer life demands flexible, receptive, and open responses to experience. When a pathological complex is stimulated, the repetitive pattern of reaction overrides the ability to decode outer reality, halting learning and adaptation, and preventing development. What would this psychological process look like in everyday life?

Imagine a child raised in any neighborhood. The father is gone, and the mother uses drugs and alcohol to anesthetize her feelings. The mother has a new boyfriend who was brutalized by his parents. He and the mother get high on drugs. The two-year-old child needs attention and disturbs their drug-induced stupor. The boyfriend takes a knife and removes the child's entire scalp to teach the child not to disturb people when they are busy. The child is found wandering the streets and is taken to the hospital. The hospital refers the child to the Department of Children and Family Services. He/she is placed in the grandmother's home. Grandmother is an alcoholic. Every evening she ties the child to a chair with an electrical cord while she goes out to spend four or five hours at a local bar. Meanwhile, the Department of Children and Family Services refers the child to an art therapist because of the child's repeated acts of violence when he/she is in daycare.

The therapist sees the child. He/she is unable to speak or use the toilet. He/she draws pictures of monsters with fierce, sharp teeth and red blood dripping from their jaws. The child is telling the therapist that he/she lives in a world where there is only blood and violence. How could that child believe that a therapist would behave any differently from the boyfriend, the mother, and the grandmother? How will this child's nightmare be expressed in the world as he/she grows into an adult? Will he/she become the depicted monster? Will he/she become prey to such monsters? How will he/she nourish and cherish his/her own children?

ARCHETYPES: DYNAMIC PROCESSES

Early in his work, Jung began to notice that there were dynamic, powerful, recurring motifs in his own dreams and in the dreams of his patients. The motifs were dynamic because they produced a strong physical response as well as deep feelings that were inarticulate. Cognitive language failed to describe them; however, the motifs could be partially expressed through painting, sculpture, physical movement; or they could be languaged in poetry, simile, and metaphor. As the motifs were expressed and translated into a new medium, the patient gradually changed. Jung found these motifs in the dynamic myths and symbols that profoundly influenced human beings throughout human history. Gradually it dawned on him that these motifs were not only present in cross-cultural mythology, but they were present in everyday life as significant events that influenced all human beings (e.g., birth, marriage, death, and ritual) and repeated themselves over and over in different ways. They were outside of conscious control, yet always predictable, uniquely human, and deeply moving: "Whenever we meet with uniform and regularly recurring patterns of experience, we are dealing with an archetype" (*CW* 8, 1981, 94).

In order to gain a better internal understanding of the dynamism of an archetypal process, remember yourself as a child. What interested you? What did you most love to do? What did you most enjoy? Where was your special place in nature? What was it like to fall in love with something, with someone? Your memories may contain the attractive, compelling, intense, dynamic, archetypal energy that captured your attention.

Jung confronted the scientific materialism of the early twentieth century by asserting that we humans are composed and directed by mystery, by the archetypes that are both unknown and unknowable. The archetypes form and direct the movement of energy within the human body and the human psyche. They are beyond the control of the conscious mind, and they undergird all human perception and behavior.

If I cut my finger or bump into something and bruise my body, my body knows how to heal itself. It is not something I have to think about; it is an unknown process, something that simply happens. I can observe and describe the healing, but I cannot make the healing happen. My body works according to processes that are outside of my conscious control. These physical principles are the same for every human; they operate through laws that are incredibly complex, interdependent, and interrelated. These laws or archetypes are the blueprints that structure all of human physicality, experience, and performance. Physicists believe that all matter is composed of subatomic particles, which can be viewed as both particles and waves simultaneously (Capra 1991, 67–69). The physical body is matter viewed as particles; the psyche, or what some call the subtle body, is matter viewed as waves. The body and the psyche are different aspects of the same archetypal reality.

Jung observed thousands of dreams and noticed that sometimes symbols spontaneously appeared, transforming a limited, conscious attitude. Symbols are aspects of the archetypes that appear as images in dreams and visions. Jung began writing about symbols in 1911–12 in *Symbols of Transformation*. He described them as being intensely alive and meaningful, appearing spontaneously from the unconscious as an image or images that attract attention and affect, and at the same time, resolve a conflict by providing an entirely new, highly individual way of looking at things (*CW* 5, 1974).

Jung gradually realized that something else, neither conscious nor unconscious, exists at the center of the personality producing symbols and regulating both the form and the dynamic processes of the archetypes. He called this unknowable, unconscious regulating center of the personality the *Self*. He described it as the architect of the body/psyche and author of the blueprints (archetypes) for human development and experience.

The *Self* embraces both consciousness and the unconscious (*CW* 11, 1977, 259) and is the invisible composer of the unique symphony that is each human: the archetypes are the instruments that play the symphony, and our lived experience provides the notes that we alone can create. The interaction between the ego and the Self is a lifelong process of development that Jung called *individuation*. A way to describe this process is to say that something lives inside of us that knows much more than we do about what we need in order to grow, to heal, and to become. The Self lives within each human being as our true nature. The Self is neither good nor bad; it is simply the center and the circumference of all that we are.

The *ego* is a reflection of the Self, and its function is to embody the Self in everyday life. From the moment of conception, the Self begins to shape the developing embryo to become conscious and aware by fostering individuation using archetypal processes. We already believe that growth in the womb takes place through innate biological processes. What Jung is saying is that psychological growth is also taking place, and that the ordering center of these biological/psychological processes is called the Self. What does that mean? The best way that I can explain what it means is by re-telling a story.

INDIVIDUATION AND THE OLD INDIAN MAN

Once upon a time, there was an old Indian man who grew up on the reservation.[4] As a small child, he was taken away from his family and sent to boarding school. He was forced to speak only English. He lost touch with his traditions, his language, and his family. When he grew up, he married and had children; but like many Indians, he developed the disease of alcoholism. Somehow he was able to stop drinking on his own, but by then his wife and children had gone. Life with him was too hard for them.

It took him a long time to create a new life. He remarried, had a job, and felt as if the rest of his life would be all that anyone could want. However, he began having terrible nightmares. He suffered from lack of sleep, and no one seemed to be able to help him. Finally, he ended up going to see an old medicine man, one of the leftovers of tribal life that modern society had passed by. The medicine man told the old man that he was out of alignment with the flow of his own life energy. The medicine man said, "I think the spirit is trying to wake you up because you have work to do here. You must dance your sacred dream awake so that you can give it away to all the people."

The old man worked with the medicine man learning the ancient ways that his people had used in the past to connect with the spirit (the Self), with his sacred dream, and with nature. Finally, the old Indian man felt ready to "pray for a vision." He went into the sweat lodge, purified himself, prayed, and then went up into the mountains without food or water and prayed for a vision. After three days, a hummingbird appeared to him and told him that he was to teach the ways of his people to all the peoples of the world. The people of the world need to open their minds and see the beauty that exists between the shapes and colors of the material world.

The old Indian man came down from the mountain ecstatic and deeply touched. For the first time in his life, he felt a sense of purpose and commitment. He went to the medicine man, told him about his vision, and said, "Now tell me what to do." The medicine man said, "I cannot tell you what to do, the truth of your vision is alive within you. You must let it uncover itself for you over time. I can only be your friend." The old man meditated, prayed, and found no truth. He studied with the medicine man and learned all he could about his native heritage. He went up to the mountain and prayed for his vision each year for seven years. Each time he went he received the same vision along with a powerful urge to do or to create something. He did not know what the something was, yet he felt a painful sense of urgency to create something. As the years went on, this feeling became increasingly painful for him. He suffered because he felt as if he was failing to fulfill his responsibility to the sacred powers that had touched him in his visions. He wept because he kept failing to find the answer. After all this time, he still had only questions. He believed that he would always walk in a never ending darkness, yet he kept on, year after year, praying for a vision and trusting he would find a way to understand it.

The old man worked as a handyman. One day when he was in the general store on the reservation buying nails, there was a man ahead of him in line buying oil paints and brushes. The old man had never seen them; he did not know what they were. But something within him recognized those things and said "yes." Without thinking, he told the cashier that he wanted all of the things the man ahead of him had purchased. He came home with an easel, canvases, turpentine, brushes, palette knife, palette, and paints. He set these things up in his bedroom and waited for inspiration. Nothing happened. Gradually he took his paints and canvases outside and began to paint. He played with the colors and shapes of what he saw behind the reality of the everyday life of the people on his reservation. What he saw was beauty. He painted the beauty that glittered behind, above, around and beneath the joy and the pain of his people. He sold several of his paintings to the manager of the general store so that he could buy more paints.

One day some people drove through the reservation on their way to New York. They saw the old man's canvases and bought them. His paintings were shown in a gallery and purchased almost immediately. Today his paintings hang all over the world as an example of the beauty that beckons us to awaken, to perceive, and to become aware. He painted the beauty that lives in the spaces and the colors of our material world and made the invisible visible in his paintings.

This man's story is an example of an encounter with an archetypal process that led to individuation. We could say that something had been deeply constricted in the process of his development that somehow was released. The old man went through a process of individuation, orchestrated by the Self. The reality of his sacred dream was so far removed from his frame of reference that it could only appear as nightmares. He had no frame of reference to help him develop his creativity. He had to slowly learn to understand his heritage from the medicine man. He was surprised by a meaningful coincidence that offered him the medium he needed to express his creativity. He practiced his painting, and as he did so, the teachings he had received emerged in the canvases. It really didn't matter whether or not he became a famous painter. He danced his sacred dream awake and gave his gift to the people.

Individuation, in the way Jung defined it, demands an alignment of ego consciousness with the intentions of the Self. This concept is not demonstrable or provable, though it can be readily observed in the lives of people who take pleasure and enjoyment from the life they live. It is observable in nature in the processes of growth, movement, change, imbalance, death, chaos, and transformation. It is observable in the study of mythology, comparative religions, dreams, and fairy tales (*CW* 11, 1977, 5–64). All of life is continually evolving into new patterns. In one sense, pathology results in our separation from our own process. When we are not developing in harmony with our own patterns of growth, we are unhappy.

Rigidified complexes restrict the energy of the archetypes, separating a person from the intentions of the Self and hiding their own sacred dream and inner truth. The archetypes are hidden blueprints within the seed and the egg. We humans, like the rest of nature, are dependent upon the right conditions to become ourselves. The old Indian man went through a process that enabled him to express his own innate creativity. One of the purposes of this book is to describe ways for clients and therapists to work together to discover the right conditions that will support individuation.

MODERN THEORISTS, THE ARCHETYPE, AND EGO DEVELOPMENT

Jung's concept of the archetypes as structuring, dynamic forms of physical and psychological patterns of performance has recently reappeared in the psychological literature in several ways: as so-called *self-invariants* that undergird the formation of the ego (Stern 1985, 69–99), as *organizing principles*, which are "the unconscious determinants of developmental processes" (Stolorow and Atwood 1972, 88–99), as processes of ego development (Erikson 1950) and as strictures in the processes of ego development that appear in adults who regress during therapy (Levin 1974).

In 1936, Jung described a series of developmental processes that determine human behavior (*CW* 8, 1981, 114–125).[5] He briefly named these processes–hunger, activity, reflection, sexuality, and creativity–as instincts that are digested and metabolized by the psyche during the lifelong process of becoming conscious. In his typically suggestive way, Jung implied that these processes are archetypal, yet he never carried his ideas further (114–125). It makes sense to complete that connection and think about archetypes as processes that form conscious experience into patterns.

Erik Erickson (1950) and Pamela Levin (1974) have also described ego development as a series of processes. Neither of them connected these processes with Jung's theories of the archetype, and both have thought of these processes as separate entities that begin and are completed within a certain age range. Both Anna Freud (1960) and Melanie Klein (1975) have described developmental growth in infants and children as being linked with psychosexual processes. Dynamic archetypal forms do direct eating, drinking, breathing, and being sexual; and there are reflexes in the body linked with these processes. However, the archetypal/developmental processes are related to the growth of consciousness and flexible adaptation to life. No infant or child would instinctively seek a bottle filled with vodka, be able to eat an eight-course meal, breathe toxic waste without becoming ill, or need to have sexual relations with his or her caregiver.

I have called the developmental themes mentioned by Jung *archetypal/developmental processes*. I believe that these processes are interdependent and interrelated, occurring simultaneously, and in any order throughout a lifetime. Archetypes appear under many different forms and conditions. This book will discuss the archetypes as developmental processes and will be concerned only with their role in shaping ego consciousness, ego development, and the formation of complexes.[6]

It is easier to observe these processes at work in infants and children because their lack of ego development allows these processes to be much more visible. Because the archetypal/developmental processes have a psychoid nature, they influence the development of ego consciousness both biologically and psychologically simultaneously. I have replaced Jung's original words with: *being* (hunger); *doing* (activity); *thinking* (reflection); and *identity* (sexuality) and kept the word *creativity*. The following explanations for each of the archetypal/developmental processes are based on Jung's original work in 1936 (*CW* 8, 1981, 114–125), the pioneering work of Pamela Levin (1974), and the integration of their theories with my own clinical experience.

Being

Jung described this archetypal/developmental process as "hunger" (*CW* 8, 1936; 1981, 114–125). Today, almost 70 years later, we understand that much more is going on within a fetus, an infant, and a child than mere instinctual hungriness. Being, as an archetypal/developmental process, is the foundation for all of human experience. The process of being is easy to observe in infants and toddlers when they are sleeping and playing. *Being* means to have an existence. It is the basic fact of life for human beings to *Be*come and to have *Be*en. Our language describes it well. We talk about being born, being sick, being married, being divorced, being connected or disconnected, being oneself, or just being present. Babies do much more than feed. Even before birth there is a full range of activity around moving, sleeping, eating, gazing, playing, crying, and relating that changes and deepens, supporting the ego to be and to become. The archetypal/developmental process of being can be impaired genetically and/or impaired by caregivers.

When being is in balance, the infant, child, toddler, or adult feels grateful to be alive. The child is nurtured and nourished, and the adult has learned to love his or her life, nurturing and nourishing it. People who are relatively balanced understand that meeting their own needs is important because unless they take care of themselves, they will not be able to care for others. They understand that they can be anywhere and that they can take up space in the world around them. They are happy to be themselves, to move at their own pace, and to love others as they love themselves. They willingly accept love and care from others without asking more from others than those others have to give.

People who are unable to *be* nourishing have not learned to nourish themselves. They may starve their body, overeat, be careless and uncaring of their body, or deliberately injure their body through misuse of food, alcohol, and drugs. When being is not in balance, a person might say, " I can't think or feel, do or remember," indicating that one or more of the archetypal components of ego consciousness may not be operating. The person may have difficulty identifying and/or asking for what he or she needs, or may expect that others will somehow not only "know" what those needs are but automatically fulfill them. When an expectation is not met, the person may feel neglected, resentful, unloved, or rejected. Patients who have difficulties with the archetypal/developmental process of *Being* may be unable to cherish their life. They may continually place themselves in situations where their life or their life energy is endangered or diminished, for example, someone who moves in and out of painful relationships, someone who never has time to have a yearly medical examination or see a dentist, or someone who has no time and no space for him/herself in his or her home. When caregivers neglect, overstimulate, respond sporadically, or abuse a baby, or take care of a baby before it signals a need, pathological complexes are created that are linked with matters of life and death for the baby and/or for others. The archetypal/developmental process of *Being* is intertwined with all of the rest of the archetypal/developmental processes.

Doing

To *do* is to act or to carry forward. To *do* is to explore, to accomplish, to achieve, to affect a purpose, and to perform a task. When we think about the archetypal process of *doing*, we think of exploring something new by going out from a center, doing something, and coming back to that center. When a toddler is doing, the world is full of wonder. Everything is interesting. If you have ever taken a two- or three-year-old for a walk, you will notice that there is no goal, only the interest and excitement of discovering new things along the way and sharing those discoveries with someone. The child needs a familiar, reliable center to return to, protection from harm, and a regular schedule for eating and sleeping. When a baby is blocked in one direction, he or she can continue exploring and doing in another direction. The archetypal/developmental process of doing can be genetically impaired or impaired by caregivers.

Problems occur in *doing* when there is no reliable center to return to or when normal exploration is continually blocked. The adult who has learned to do discovers new things, can perceive people and things from multiple perspectives, and trusts his or her experiences. When the experience of *doing* is good enough, the old, wise child within is permitted to follow his or her heart in life, and work and play are two aspects of the same thing.

Problems with *doing* involve having difficulty initiating an activity or having too many activities. There may be problems with motivation, lack of curiosity, a lack or an excess of physical motion, or an inability to explore new options. There may be difficulties with moving outward into life or moving inward and reflecting on internal experience. There may be difficulties trusting one's own experience. When a caregiver is unable to support exploration and protect the child, or is an unreliable center to return to, the archetypal/developmental process of *doing* is restricted, held down, or derailed. When this is the case, a pathological complex begins forming, which may be composed of a high level of generalized anxiety that is difficult for the person to contain, a need to perform for others while losing the internal center, an inability to explore from the promptings of inner curiosity and interest, and/or a basic mistrust of experience. When this happens, the archetypal/developmental process of *doing* collects more and more material as the child moves toward adulthood, becoming a unique but pathological complex. It is unique because of the number and quality of the caregivers, the genetic predisposition of the child, and the influence of the rest of the archetypal/developmental processes.

Thinking

An infant and a baby begin exercising the mind and the intellect quite early. When we learn to *think*, we learn to test reality, push against boundaries and other people, and learn from experience. When we *think*, we change or affect things by our mental processes. We begin to understand that if we do this, that will happen. Gradually, *thinking* develops and causes something to appear to oneself or to be conceived in the mind. *Thinking* exercises the mind or the intellect. We examine things through introspection and learn to solve problems with cause-and-effect reasoning. Gradually, we learn to think about our feelings and express them in ways that help others understand us. We learn to give up our grandiose, infantile beliefs about being the center of the universe. We learn to develop and maintain boundaries between ourselves and other people. We learn that others may experience life differently than we do.

Thinking is the ability to work toward integrating and communicating our understanding of our experience by connecting emotions, memory, body and behavior. True thinking relates to our own experience and to that of others; it is not mere memorization or mimicking. If a person has a negative connection to patterns of parental caretaking and this archetypal/developmental process, they may be overly adaptive to the ideas of others without developing their own viewpoint, or they may be rebellious and distort or delete the ideas of other people.

If a person does not have a connection to their own internal experience while he or she is learning, the person may not develop the *observing ego*, the capacity to observe themselves at any given moment in time or the capacity to observe others. The *observing ego* is a term developed by Freud in 1940. He described a "split in the ego" that allowed the ego to observe itself through reality testing and perception: "It is the self-observing function that helps to organize and synthesize the experiences of therapy" (Scialli 1982, 388–389).

To think is to find reasons for both internal and external events and to draw conclusions about them. Thinking entails testing boundaries, learning from mistakes, finding out what is and what is not under our control. Thinking means being able to observe and experience our own emotions, change options based on our own experience, set goals, develop choices, check the facts, ask others about what they think, listen to them, and share our thoughts with others. Thinking means to let go and sit with the experience of the KNOWN, the UNKNOWN, and the UNKNOWABLE, like the old Indian man, and to allow these experiences to unfold their meaning over time. Thinking cannot develop without the connection and interactions with all of the other archetypal/developmental processes.

The archetypal/developmental process of *thinking* can also be genetically impaired and/or damaged by caretakers. When caretakers think for a child after he or she is old enough to figure something out for him or herself, when a child is prevented from experiencing the consequences of his or her actions, when a child's ideas are ignored or not considered, or when a child is not given things to think about or stimulated to learn, the archetypal/developmental process of thinking is impaired.

When thinking is not well developed, a person can express an inappropriate sort of rebelliousness or bully other people. Persons who have problems with thinking may think the world revolves around them and feel entitled to do whatever they wish without considering the consequences. Others may feel entitled to think for other people using rules and laws to limit what others can think about. Some individuals may use thinking as a container, constantly reflecting on the linkages between ideas and never truly experiencing life. When thinking rather than the body becomes a container, the connection between the immediate experience of ego consciousness such as memories, feelings, or behaviors may be partially severed. Others who may not have experienced adequate emotional containment may have a tendency to express their emotions much too readily or to mull over problems without ever being able to make a decision.

Sometimes people who have difficulty thinking may mistake words and concepts for experience and live life labeling and categorizing events rather than suffering through actual experience and earning understanding. Other people who have problems with thinking may be rigid, resistant, overly compliant, or rebellious. Some people who have trouble with thinking may have issues with boundaries (the space where one person begins and another person stops), making life a drama about being in or out of power, or whether or not they are in control. Integrating life experience may be extremely difficult for people with underdeveloped thinking because they don't contain, reflect, and learn from their experience. People whose thinking is overly developed may use thinking as a container and not have a sense of being embodied in the events of daily life. Issues of being too messy or too tidy are usually linked with being unable to think. For example, when a person is experiencing a high level of anxiety, it is almost impossible for them to think.

Identity

Identity is an embodied sense of inner authority and responsibility for oneself. When a person has a solid identity, he or she has a sense of responsibility to empower others and a sense of being accountable to a Higher Power. When an infant, toddler, or child is developing a sense of identity, he or she is learning to know that he or she is both like others and separate and unique from others. Playing games, dressing up, pretending, making different kinds of faces, mimicking people, having a hero or heroine, learning this is mine and that is yours are some of the ways we observe infants, toddlers, and children involved with the archetypal/developmental process of identity.

During this archetypal/developmental process, human beings gradually learn what they have power over and what they do not have power over. We learn to define ourselves as being distinct from others. We learn to respect our own experience and the experience of others, by trying to understand them. We learn to acquire information about the world, ourselves and the role our body plays in our preferences as a sexual being. We learn that our behaviors have consequences that have an effect on others and that we have a place in a group. We learn how to exert power to affect relationships. We learn to separate fantasy from reality by engaging in play and by learning how imagination and spiritual experience is different from the everyday world.

When there are problems with the archetypal/developmental process of identity, a person may identify with his or her role or position in life and deny any other kinds of internal or external experience. He or she may feel driven to achieve or afraid to be in a position of power; he or she may misuse or be reluctant to use power. He or she may frequently compare him/herself to others and, in the comparison, may manufacture a fantasy of superiority or inferiority. He or she may want magical solutions to life problems rather than being willing to take responsibility and make the effort to change them. He or she may scapegoat or denigrate others in order to avoid the moral responsibilities that are part of life. He or she may have a tendency to exert control in relationships by engaging in passive aggressive behaviors or manipulation rather than by defining him or herself through communication and actions.

Part of the core of identity is linked with the observing ego. The observing ego is both separate from, and connected to outer and inner experience. It is like a fair witness observing and commenting on the experience of the moment. The observing ego develops from the archetypal/developmental process of *thinking*. It matures through the development of an identity. As the archetypal/developmental process of *identity* matures, a person's observing ego develops the capacity to step outside of his or her experience and observe the activation and movement of a pathological complex. When a person feels as if having an identity is dangerous, he or she may never be able to observe his or her pathological complex.

Having an identity gives a person the ability to be patient and to contain tension produced when there are internal and/or external oppositions so that new information can emerge, enlarging awareness. To have an identity is to be able to receive, remember, feel, and respond to the compensatory messages that come from the unconscious. Identity cannot develop without the interaction and cooperation of all of the archetypal/developmental processes.

Creativity

To be *creative* is to produce a new construction out of existing materials or to cause something new to come into existence. Creativity cannot exist without the action of all of the archetypal/developmental processes. Infants, toddlers, and children are quite creative. They learn through play and enjoy what they do. They practice new skills and learn from mistakes. They watch others do things, repeat what they see and create something new from their observations. As we mature, we learn to exclude other peoples' ways of doing things until we have found our own way. We learn to balance living life and meeting its demands while paying close attention to our own internal promptings, finding ways to express them.

When a person has problems with *creativity*, he or she may function only as a loner or as a member of a marginal group. He or she may not understand the relevance of rules either by being rigidly rule bound without ever questioning the rules, or defying rules without understanding the freedom that rules can give. He or she may be unwilling to examine his or her own values and morals; or need to be king or queen of the hill to control other peoples' creativity. He or she may expect to do things effortlessly without knowing how, finding out, studying or practicing.

PATTERNS OF MEDIATION OF ARCHETYPAL DEVELOPMENTAL PROCESSES

There are seven different forms of mediation of the archetypal/developmental processes I have observed as infants, toddlers, children, and adolescents are parented. It is easiest to observe them as they occur between parents (or caregivers) and infants/children. I have labeled these seven patterns symbiotic, directive, co-operative, confirming, empowering, educating and containing. This list is neither comprehensive nor meant to be definitive. Each of these patterns can be mediated within a range of attunement, or outside the range of attunement of the needs of the child.

Music is a good metaphor for attunement. There is a range of tone within each note that moves from dissonance to perfect pitch. Perfect pitch is the recognition of the perfect vibration of each particular tone. Most of us do not have perfect pitch; however, there is a range of tone that feels harmonic to most of us. When most of the notes (or the communications between the persons within the field) are within a harmonic range, attunement is present most of the time. When most of the notes are dissonant or outside the tonal range, the relationship is not attuned. The quality and timing of mediation of the archetypal/developmental processes can both support or wound the energy of the archetypal/developmental processes as well as the development of ego consciousness.

A *symbiotic* pattern of mediation is one in which a temporary, shared ego unit exists between the child and the caretaker until the child has developed the necessary ego consciousness to function as an autonomous ego unit. The word symbiosis means that two organisms depend upon each other for mutual benefit. A nursing mother depends on the baby to take her milk and the baby depends upon the mother to give milk. This relationship is both a biological and psychological fact. A symbiotic pattern of mediation does not remain static, it is always subject to change. A caretaker can usually understand and fill the needs of an infant and toddler. However, when the infant or toddler is able to begin to identify his or her needs, the process of lending ego functions begins to slowly become a pattern of lending and withdrawing until the child is independent emotionally, financially and can live by him or herself.

Symbiotic patterns of mediation occur during all of the archetypal/developmental processes and can easily be observed in the embryo/infant/child/caregiver relations by noting the ego functions and the archetypal/developmental processes the caregivers are sharing with and carrying for the child. The difficulty with symbiotic patterns of mediation is when to lend ego functions or perform archetypal/developmental tasks (e.g., thinking) for the child and when not to in order to support the child's development. The questions the caretaker must ask are: What does the child need right now? Is the child able to articulate that need or does he or she need help thinking about what the need is? How much can the child do for him or herself right now? How can this child contribute to the family, to the world? There is a range of symbiotic mediation that changes over time. What is appropriate for a baby is not appropriate for a nine-month old. By the time a child is an adolescent he or she has had a great deal of experience with each of the archetypal/developmental processes and is quite mature enough to be included in both life and family decisions.

Symbiotic patterns of mediation also occur in the clinical hour and may be as simple as handing an adult patient a box of tissues without his or her asking for it or thinking for the patient because he or she is so anxious thinking is not possible. When a therapist feels responsible for the patient's being, doing, thinking, creativity, or identity, the therapist is using a symbiotic mode of mediation. There is nothing wrong with using symbiotic forms of mediation as long as both the patient and the therapist have discussed it and agreed upon it.

For example, a patient becomes highly anxious and unable to think during the clinical hour. The therapist, suspecting that the patient is very anxious and upset, asks the patient, "Are you feeling anxious right now?"

Patient: "I am feeling very anxious. I don't know what's wrong with me. How do I stop it so I can figure out what I have to do?"
Therapist: "You do look and sound very anxious. What is it like inside for you to be that anxious?"
Patient: "I have to decide by Friday whether or not I am going to take that job and I am so upset about it I feel as if I am falling apart."
Therapist: "It sounds as if deciding to take that job has so many parts that you are overwhelmed with anxiety. Do those words fit your experience?"
Patient: "Yes, there are so many parts I can't keep track of them."
Therapist: "It sounds as if you are having trouble thinking about all those parts, are you?"
Patient: "I am having trouble thinking and I am so upset with myself."

The therapist has many options to further explore the patient's experience or to become symbiotic with the patient by offering containment and help her with her ability to think.

Therapist (conscious symbiotic response): "Would it help if you told me each of the parts and I wrote them down (containment) so that we could go over them one by one (thinking) and put them in order?"
Patient: "I feel so relieved. I think that would be a big help."

After the patient prioritized her many parts, the therapist and the patient would discuss what the experience of "being helped" was like for the patient and perhaps compare that experience to contents of the pathological complex.

Directive patterns of mediation tell an infant, toddler, adolescent, or adult what to do, how to handle a problem, and what not to do. Being directive has to do with an appropriate use of authority, such as instruction, limit setting, providing consequences for behavior, protection, empowerment and the socializing and disciplinary processes that go on between parents and child. Directive patterns of mediation occur during every archetypal/ developmental process. Directive mediation provides structures for self- care and for socialization. For example, babies gradually learn how to do things within a family structure—toilet training, table manners, dressing and tying shoes, as well as moral principles and social and individual responsibilities.

The patient discussed above is able to name several parts of her problem. However, she remains so anxious that she is unable to think or make a list of priorities about how to manage the problem and the problem needs attention. She may need direction from the therapist to help her begin to relax so that she is able to think about solving the problem. The following dialogue is an example of utilizing a directive pattern of mediation within a clinical hour.

Therapist: "It seems as if you are so anxious you are having difficulty thinking. Is that what you are experiencing?"
Patient: "Yes, I feel so overwhelmed I can't think."
Therapist: "Do you think it might be helpful if I made some suggestions and helped you create your priorities?" "Would it be helpful if I offered some suggestions that might help you decide what to do?"
Patient: "I am just stupid. My father always had to tell what to do. He never said it but I always felt stupid."
Therapist: "It sounds as if you are caught between a rock and a hard place. The rock is your high anxiety that stops your thinking. The hard place is feeling stupid because your father did your thinking for you."
Patient: "I want your help and I don't want to feel stupid."
Therapist: "I don't feel comfortable doing what your father did and somehow repeating your hurt. Would you be willing to learn how to become relaxed when you have this much anxiety?" (The therapist is still being directive. The direction has changed because if therapist thinks for her, the therapist will replicate her father's behavior).
Patient: "I could really learn to relax when I get this way?"
Therapist: "Yes."
Patient: "I would really like to learn that."

There are no mistakes in offering direction when it is done in a dialogue with the patient. There is only the possibility for further exploration.

Cooperative or mutual patterns of mediation are forms of activity where the full ego consciousness of each person is present in the relational field. Cooperative relationships can be observed in play, dialogue, sharing, loving, and certain kinds of work. In cooperative kinds of interaction, two independent personalities (ego consciousness of both) are present to one another.

Cooperative patterns of relating are easily observed in parent-infant babbling, play, helping one another with tasks, and negotiating the appropriate use of power within a cooperative framework with mutual accountability.

Cooperative mediation and communication is the best form of mediation to use in therapy with adults. A therapist is rather like a midwife (Murray Stein, personal communication, 1983) who assists the patient while he or she carries and gives birth to new forms of awareness then learns to support, nourish, and integrate them in everyday life. Cooperation means that the patient and the therapist are accountable to one another for loyalty to the individuation process, respect, honesty, and mutual problem solving. The following example demonstrates these qualities.

Patient: "Last week after I left our session I became upset. I felt as if I am going to be a failure in therapy and that I will make you angry with me."
Therapist: "Please tell me more about that so I can understand your experience and what I may have said to upset you?"
Patient: "You asked to write my dreams down. I hardly ever dream and when I do dream I can't remember them. I am really worried that if I don't dream I won't benefit from the therapy."

Therapist (internal observation): I stimulated her complex. I think our relationship is solid enough to begin to explore it. Part of her complex includes feeling anxious because she is unable to *do* something that someone else *demanded.*

Therapist (to the patient): "It sounds as if I upset you by asking you to do something you are not able to do and you are worried about it."
Patient: "Yes, that's exactly right. I am really worried the therapy won't work."
Therapist: "When I asked you to write down your dreams I think I triggered a painful response within you. It is important that I understand as much as I can about what I triggered and how I did that."

The therapist is taking responsibility for triggering the complex and inviting the patient to explore it at the same time. As the patient and the therapist explore the incident and if possible, link it with the complex, the therapist learns to become more attuned to the patient and the patient learns about his or her complex. After the complex is explored, and observed, it is important for the therapist to retract the demand that the patient write down dreams and educate him or her about the unconscious and how the complex has spontaneously appeared during the clinical hour without a dream.

Confirming patterns of mediation provide an accurate mirror of the child's experience of the world. They support the growing ego consciousness in ways that reflect back an accurate account or image of what is present and what is really happening, in terms the child can understand. When caregivers are confirming, they listen to the child's experience and validate it by the way they explain things to the child. They consider the child's viewpoint when decisions are made that influence the child and the life of the family. They step back and allow the child to experience the consequences of his or her decisions and behavior, while still keeping the child safe from harm. Infants and children are dependent upon confirming patterns of mediation to learn to trust what they are perceiving and experiencing.

Confirming patterns of mediation occur quite often during each clinical hour. Each time the therapist offers his or her total attention, listens, nods, attempts to understand, and attempts to reach an understanding of the patient's experience or how or why he or she did something, the therapist is using a confirming pattern of mediation.

Containing patterns of mediation are ways in which parents help the infant/child maintain inner and outer equilibrium. Containment is performed by parents and caregivers when they: (1) listen to the child's own expression of his or her developing emotions, memories, behaviors, and physical experience; (2) help the child learn to soothe him or herself by not interfering with this process; (3) teach the child regular sleep habits and offer a regular schedule, (4) help the child settle down when he or she is too overwhelmed with affect, anxiety or is too overstimulated to settle him or herself down. Attuned containment helps the child learn to hold his or her experience and reflect upon it in order to gradually integrate it. For example, a child who in the midst of a temper tantrum is communicating that he/she is feeling out of control. What the child needs is settling down, firm holding and warm, nonverbal understanding that he or she is having a difficult time and will get better when he or she is ready. Tantrums often happen in public places like grocery stores, especially to children who are hyperactive or not often exposed to public places. The child is tired and/or frustrated because he or she wants to explore or is attracted to many things all at the same time. The work of the caregivers in this kind of situation is to hold the child gently and firmly and wait until the child stops or remove the child from the situation. When a child or his or her family is going through a change or transition, the child becomes overstimulated much more easily. This is due to an inability to integrate all that is happening. A holding environment is one that gently holds either physically or through a structure like a schedule, an order for tasks or through directive mediation with the understanding that the internal environment is chaotic and ego consciousness is too overwhelmed to integrate and reflect upon what is being experienced. Containing patterns of mediation are used when the child is overstimulated, emotionally out of control, or unable to negotiate change on his or her own.

They support development of reflecting upon personal experience and learning from personal experience.

Containment is one of the most important patterns of mediation that is used in therapy because it makes room for and gently holds the contents that emerge from the unconscious. The fee, the structure for office protocol, appointments and space, as well as privacy, confidentiality and the ongoing presence of a therapist who listens, accepts and attunes, provides a containing structure that can hold what emerges from the unconscious. The use of the transitional space, the place between "not knowing" and "being aware" (or between the pathological complex and the ability to observe, verbalize and interrupt behavioral patterns of reactivity linked with the complex) evolves out of the relationship between the therapist, the patient and the unconscious. The transitional space will be discussed more fully in Chapters 4 and 6.

Educating patterns of mediation empower the infant/child/adolescent/adult to develop answers to their own questions, to become a part of a culture and to become independent and self-sufficient. Therapy has its own language. Part of patient education is helping the patient learn to language his or her experience as the growth of consciousness takes place. It is important that the therapist educate the patient so that he or she can develop an understanding of the operation of the pathological complex and how it interferes with his or her life energy. Questions and answers are a natural part of the therapeutic dialogue and require flexibility and alertness on the part of the therapist. Asking questions may be quite honest or a way for a patient to avoid an encounter with emerging anxiety and/or painful affect. Honest answers and responses given in a way that is attuned to the patient's frame of reference are a form of education and also the foundation of the relationship. Usually, if questions are a defense against experiencing anxiety or affect, the therapist will begin to feel frustrated because the patient does not seem to be able to receive the answer to the question. The patient will simply keep asking more questions. At this time, the therapist can shift into what the patient is experiencing at the present moment and attempt to attune to and understand the patient's experience. When a patient has a question that requires an honest answer from the therapist it is usually wise to spend some time exploring the background of the question so the therapist fully understands what is being asked and can respond in an attuned way.

Empowering patterns of mediation of the archetypal/developmental processes return the numinous energy of the Self to the infant/child/adolescent/adult and are intended to maintain the ego/Self axis. This concept has been developed and discussed at length by Peter Mudd (1990, pp. 125–141).

Encouragement is another word for empowering. It means to instill with courage, to promote hope and support a sense of confidence in another person. Caregivers, teachers and spiritual leaders have a responsibility to empower each individual under their care in order to allow him or her to become a fully responsible, contributing adult. Honesty, respect, belief in the personal needs of the child or the individual, and attunement are the essential components of empowerment. Self-esteem, courage and belief in oneself cannot be given to anyone; the child or the individual must earn them. Empowerment offers hope and belief that the child or individual is able to do the earning. It is especially important in therapy that the therapist trust, support and believe in the patient and his or her experience and at the same time speak with heartfelt and attuned honesty when that is required.

Attunement means that when a fetus, infant, toddler, child, or adolescent lets caregivers know what he or she needs, the caregivers have an understanding of the experience and perceptions of what the need is, and they respond by linking the need with a viewpoint that not only includes the child's experience but also the more mature viewpoint of what purpose the need serves. For example, an infant is fussy, cranky, and doesn't want to sleep. The infant has been fed, changed, and burped–apparently his/her needs have been met. What would an attuned response be? Only the caregiver can decide, based on what the infant is communicating. Is the child overstimulated and needing to be left alone to cry and fall asleep? Is the infant sick–and if so, what are the symptoms? Is a diaper pin open and causing the infant pain? Is the infant colicky? No one can tell the caregiver what the best-attuned response is. There are no rules. The response must be based on what the caregiver understands about what the infant is experiencing and then offer the best possible response he/she can.[8] Mediation must be given and also withheld, which is the incredibly complicated and difficult process of caretaking, especially if caretakers have not undergone attuned mediation themselves. Clinicians carry many of the same burdens that caretakers do.

THE PROCESS OF EGO DEVELOPMENT

Michael Fordham (1970, 1976, and 1985), a child psychoanalyst who studied with Jung, described ego development as an energetic process, a series of ongoing movements of ego consciousness out from and back into the Self called integration, deintegration, and reintegration (1970, 136; 1976, 27). He believed that the Self was central to the formation of ego consciousness. He observed hundreds of children and believed that as human consciousness develops, it begins forming around internal experiences that eventually order consciousness. In addition to his studies with Jung, Fordham was deeply influenced by the work of Melanie Klein and the Object Relations

School. In both his writings and his clinical encounters, Fordham observed and named the presence of the Self, the collective human memory, the individuation process, and the relational aspects of the clinical encounter. He did not write about Jung's theory of complexes or the actual experiences of an infant, toddler, or child with his or her caretakers.

Fordham answered the questions, "Why does ego consciousness develop and how does that happen?" In the beginning of embryonic life and infancy, the ego exists as a potential within the Self in *integration* (1985, 31). He believed that the potential for ego consciousness resided within the Self, "a state without the experience of existing, somewhat akin to sleep" (1978, 136). Integration is described in Figure 2.

During integration, the potential for ego consciousness is stimulated (e.g., the infant feels hungry or hears a loud noise and moves); the potential for consciousness moves from integration into another process called *deintegration* (1976, 55). Figure 2 describes the experience of integration as something like sleep. During integration, the potential for ego consciousness rests within the Self[9] and this experience occurs throughout a human lifetime. It is easier to understand integration when we observe newborns. Nothing seems to happen while a baby is sleeping. Ego consciousness does not develop during integration. However, eventually the baby becomes hungry, cold, or soiled. These experiences are uncomfortable, and the baby wakes up and cries. The process of ego development has moved into deintegration. The baby is uncomfortable and doing something about it: crying. Figure 3 shows the process of deintegration.

The archetypal/developmental processes stimulate deintegration, promoting adaptation through being, doing, thinking, identity, and creativity. The caregivers mediate these processes. Deintegration must occur for ego consciousness to develop (Fordham, 1976, 55). After needs have been met, the infant falls asleep, and the process of deintegration is complete. Ego consciousness moves back into a state of integration, carrying with it all of the experiences gathered during deintegration. This process is called *reintegration* (1976, 16). Reintegration gradually leads to "increasing recognition of external reality and . . . of internal processes and their symbolization" (1976, 27). By the time an infant is ten weeks old, it will have deintegrated and reintegrated more than six or seven hundred times just during the pattern of feeding. The archetypal potentials for ego consciousness begin to gather experience from these interactions, as well as from other interactions, like being cold, wet, colicky, or simply needing to be touched. Gradually, ego consciousness begins to develop. Hunger is only one example of a stimulus for deintegration. Even in early infancy, there are hundreds more that require mediation.

the sleeping infant

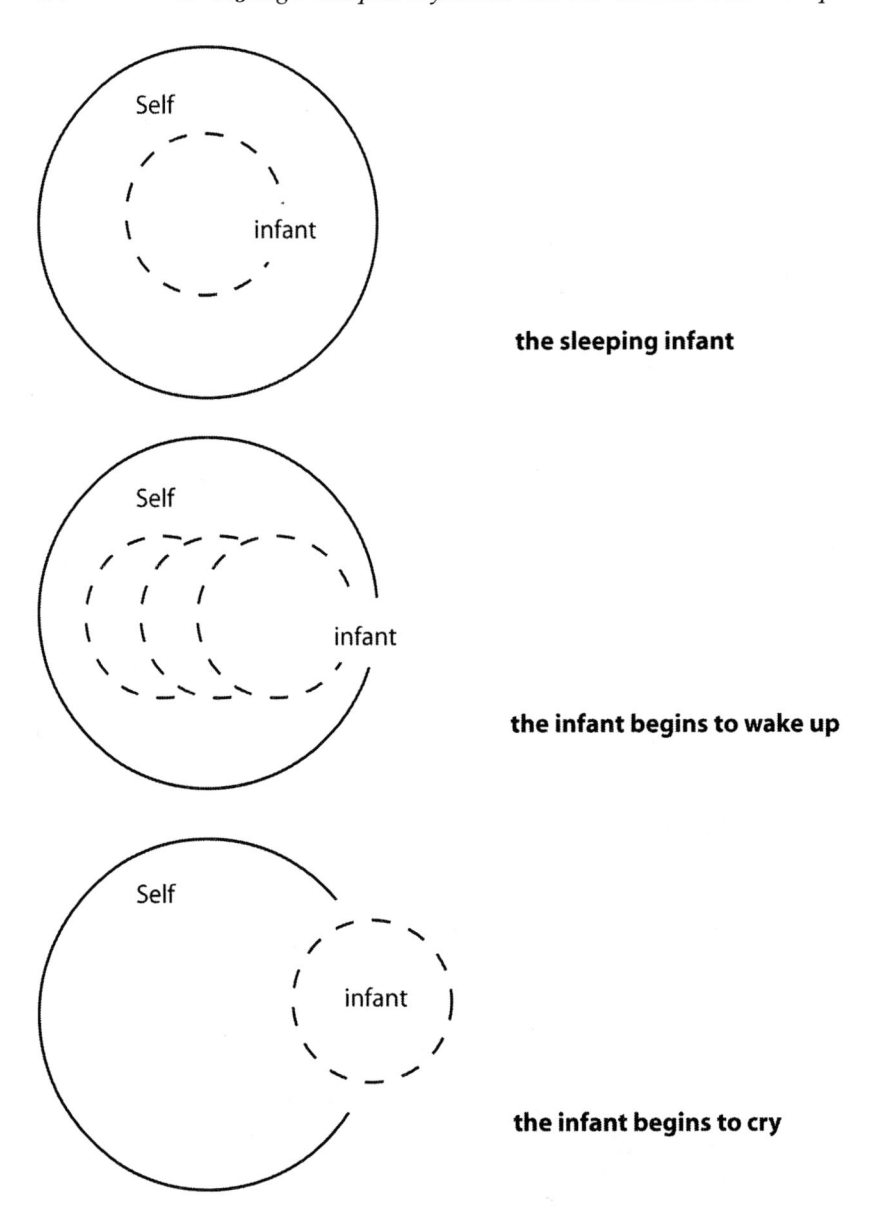

the infant begins to wake up

the infant begins to cry

FIGURE 2
An example of integration and the movement toward deintegration.

Self   infant

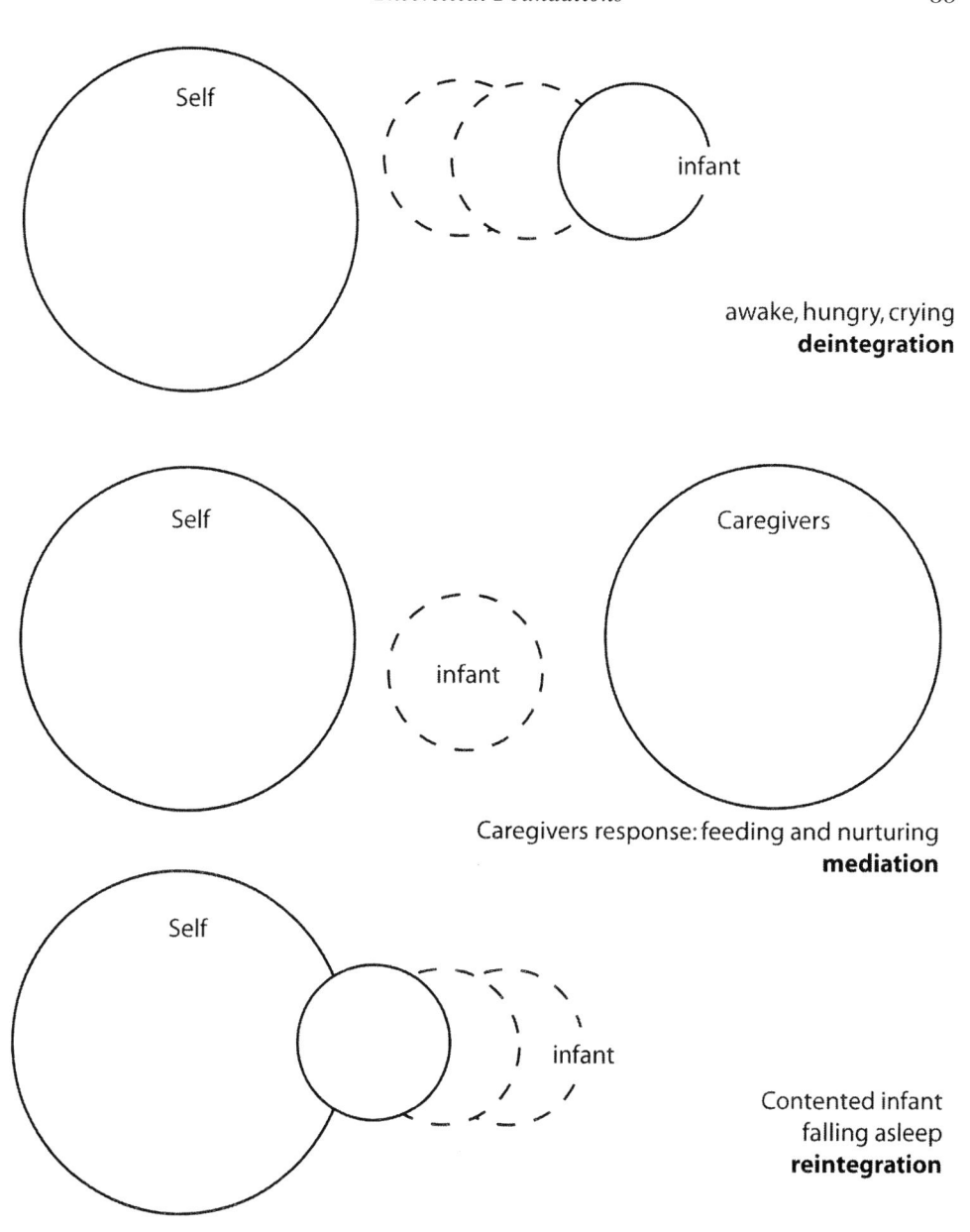

awake, hungry, crying
deintegration

Self   infant   Caregivers

Caregivers response: feeding and nurturing
mediation

Self   infant

Contented infant
falling asleep
reintegration

FIGURE 3
*Deintegration and mediation of deintigration by Caregivers
followed by reintigration.*

As the baby grows older, it will develop the ability to soothe itself from the experiences that have been reintegrated. Infants, toddlers and children to some extent need so much mediation that it is impossible for any one person to mentally or physically provide attuned, total infant care. It is also important to remember that babies are different in their requirements and are quite active and able to indicate their needs during deintegration. It takes many experiences of deintegration and mediation to begin to form the patterns of awareness that eventually become ego consciousness. Integration, deintegration, the archetypal/developmental processes, the patterns of mediation and reintegration are shown in Figure 4.

Fordham's theories were not only brilliant; they were an important step in the evolution of the idea that consciousness grows and continues developing slowly over a lifetime (1985, 212–218). His writings and his clinical work laid the foundation for my own clinical experience and for the inclusion of developmental theory, attachment theory and intersubjective theory within my own clinical experience.

Each time consciousness reintegrates; it carries experiences of mediation of the archetypal/developmental processes. Based upon the constitution of the child, the quality of overall attunement and the intensity of the process of deintegration, experiences are gradually sensed by the body and affects begin to form. The affects begin to combine with one another and begin to attract rudimentary memories. Experiences begin to accumulate into affectively linked patterns, or what Stern (1985, 97) called "generalized event structures." It is important that we realize how very resilient and adaptable human beings are, as well as how many variables influence the development of consciousness and the formation of complexes. Being hungry and being fed represent only one tiny piece of one archetypal/developmental process that contributes to the formation of ego consciousness, complex formation, and the internalization of the patterns of mediation. Each child has his or her own unique genetic structure. There are five archetypal/developmental processes and seven patterns of mediation of these processes, all attached to a range of attunement that is experienced by one fetus, infant, toddler, or child. The interplay of these variables plus the ones we are not yet aware of, create a unique individual. These variables are named in Figure 5.

All of these processes, with their specific differences, foster the development of ego consciousness, adaptation to the demands of the outer world and individuation. Just like the seed, the egg, the cell, and the nut, we humans are dependent on the proper conditions in order to become entities that flourish. In order for individuation to occur, a strong yet flexible ego consciousness must exist. Self-importance, arrogance, disrespect, malice, greed, envy, laziness, or blatant disregard for the rights of others is the result of malfunctions during the development of ego consciousness.

Theoretical Foundations

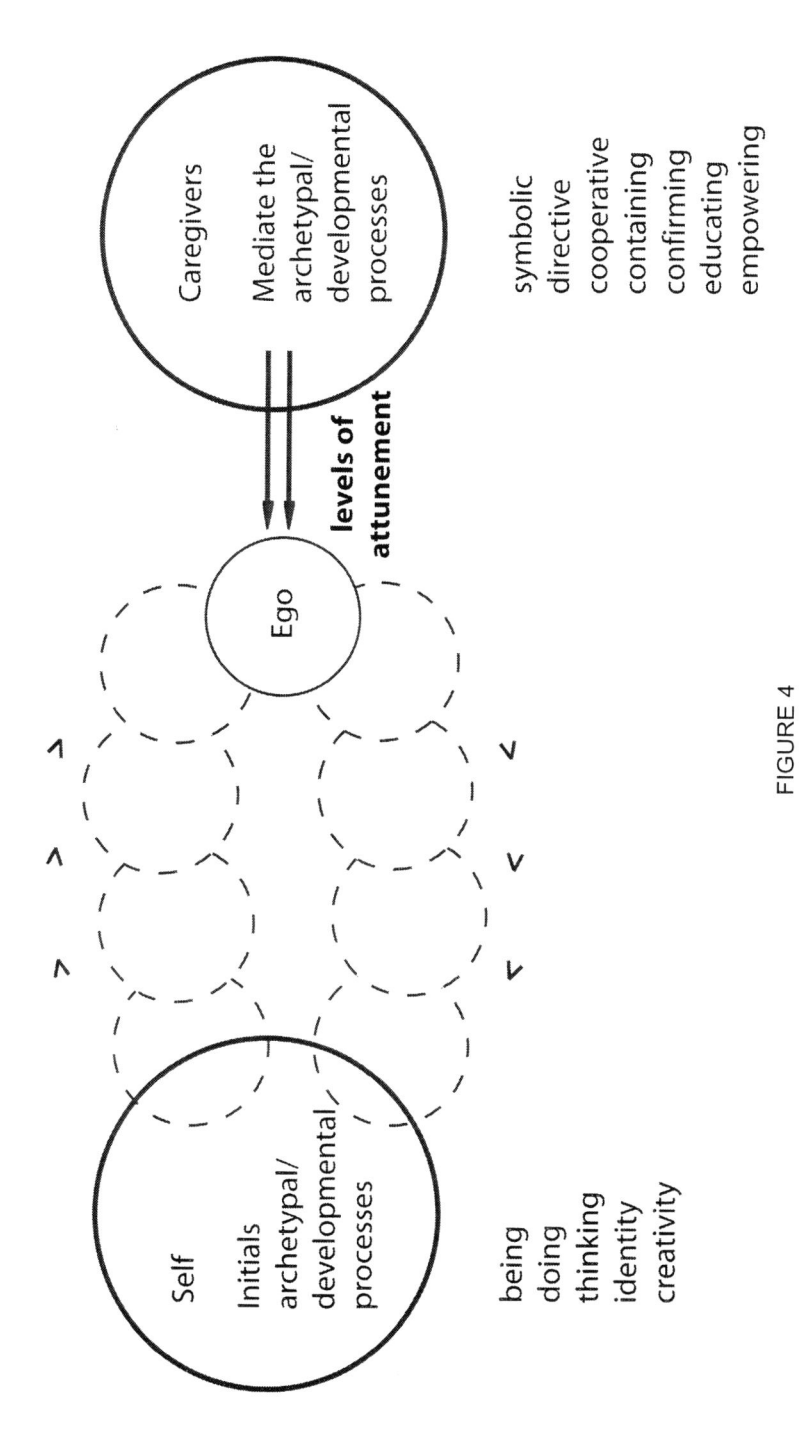

Caregivers

Mediate the archetypal/developmental processes

symbolic
directive
cooperative
containing
confirming
educating
empowering

levels of attunement

Ego

Self

Initials archetypal/developmental processes

being
doing
thinking
identity
creativity

FIGURE 4
The role of the caregiver in deintegration and reintegration.

FIGURE 5

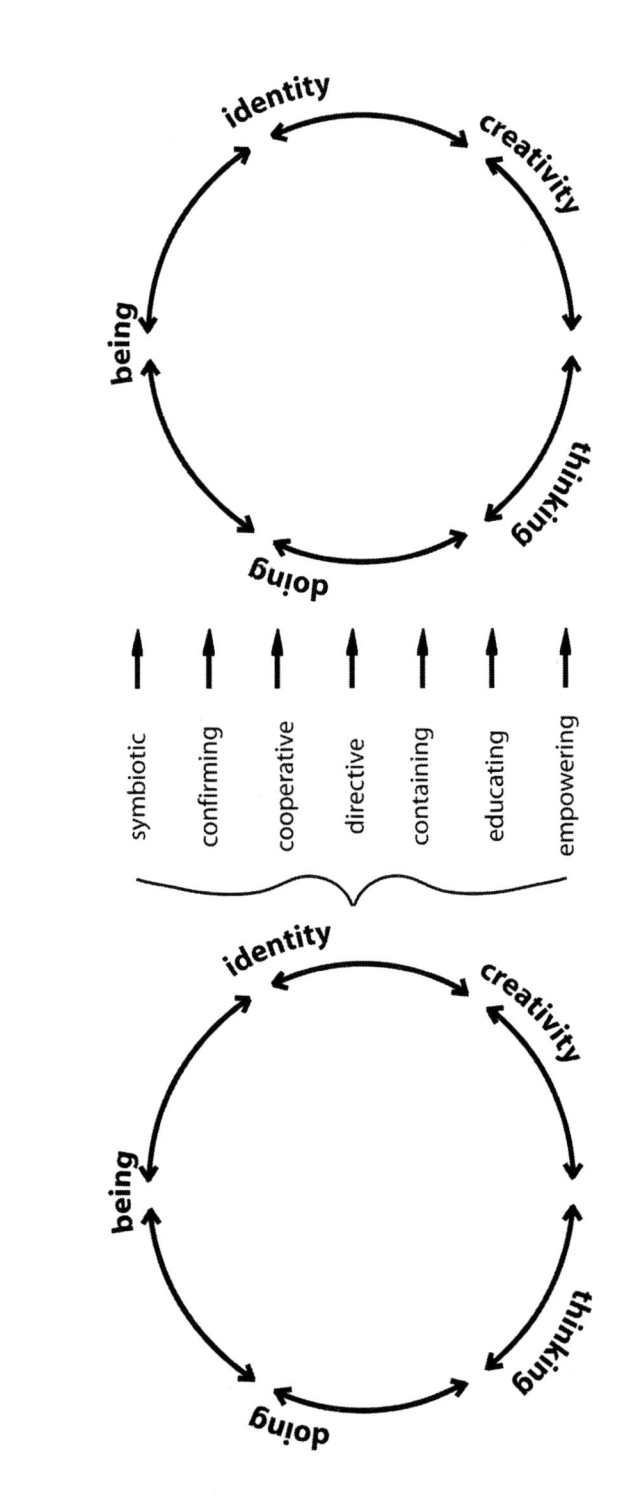

The archetypal / developmental process, patterns of mediation and the formation of ego consciousness.

Fordham described one more process he called disintegration. This is an experience when ego consciousness (or the developing potential for ego consciousness) feels that it is going to be annihilated (1978, 154–157). The experiences of disintegration are gradually reintegrated; becoming located in the foundations of ego consciousness and in the archetypal/developmental processes because of ignorant or abusive patterns of mediation. Pathological complexes form from repeated experiences of disintegration during the process of deintegration.

CREATION OF A COMPLEX

The archetypal/developmental processes are blueprints for both the physical body and the psyche. They are directly linked with the Self, and like the Self are both unknown and unknowable. The archetypes can only be experienced indirectly, appearing as images or as physical sensations. They must be mediated in relationships in order to promote the development of ego consciousness, adaptation to everyday life and individuation.

Human relationship is part of the earth from which ego consciousness grows. We are dependent upon the right conditions to become who and what we are, and on who we can become. Our innate constitution, our human relationships and the quality of help we receive support us as we move from integration, into deintegration and back into reintegration. These processes are a little like our heart filling with energy or blood (integration). As the heart beats, energy is squeezed out into our bodies to be used to nourish, bring life, to create growth and gather the waste (deintegration). The circulatory system responds by sending used energy back into the lungs, which expel waste, take in clean air and fill our heart with new energy thus beginning another cycle (reintegration).

Ego consciousness is not just a genetic structure. Repeated experiences of disintegration can damage ego consciousness, just as the circulatory system can be blocked through a genetic problem, interference, or negligence. If something blocks our heart, the circulation of blood, oxygen and waste does not take place and our organs malfunction. If a baby is hungry and no one feeds or cares for it, the baby's organs and the baby's psyche malfunction. If a pregnant mother is raped, mistreated, or uses drugs or alcohol, a fetus is profoundly affected. All of us are interdependent and interrelated with one another and with what is going on around us. Human relationships can strengthen or damage us as we face everyday life that demands that we continually change, let go, adapt, and endure chaos when it arrives.

The archetypal foundations of ego consciousness are like magnets pulling the iron filings of our experience into patterns of affect, memory, physical cohesiveness, and behavior. The archetypal/ developmental processes shape ego consciousness into certain ways of perceiving and patterns of behavior that are uniquely human. These processes (being, doing, thinking, identity, and creativity) are the movers and shapers of consciousness, energizing the development of the ego. The ego structures and the archetypal/developmental processes must be mediated within relationships that support the ongoing movement of ego consciousness through integration, deintegration, and reintegration. Pathological complexes form because the innate constitution of the child is unsound, or there is a lack of the essential basics that support life, or there are repeated experiences of disintegration during the mediation of one or more of the archetypal/developmental processes, or the archetypal foundations of ego consciousness are damaged, e.g., an infant, toddler, child, adolescent is not allowed to express affect.

When a pathological complex is formed, one or more of the functions of the archetypal/developmental processes is blocked. These blockages are held together by a unique affective theme (Tomkins 1981, 322). A pathological complex has an energy all its own that unconsciously influences the environment in what I call a relational field. This field is shared by all of the members of the family of origin or primary caretakers. Research has already shown that similar complexes exist within family systems. I am highlighting the fact that the pathological complex has an energetic effect on the world surrounding it, creating a unique relational field. Since a family shares this field, any perceptions, ideas, feelings, images, memories or behavioral possibilities that are blocked because of pathological complexes are literally invisible in one way or another to the entire family. This is an important concept for therapists because this field surrounds anyone who has a pathological complex.[10]

A pathological complex is not static; it is subject to change throughout a lifetime. As an infant becomes older the archetypal/developmental processes are influenced and mediated by teachers, friends outside the family, neighbors, playmates, and the surrounding culture (including the heroines and villains in the stories we hear or see on TV). Throughout our lives, our complexes are shaped and reshaped by our daily experience, our dreaming and our relationships.

SUMMARY

Sometimes life is enhanced; sometimes it is crushed, as is true in all of nature. Human development is much more varied and complex than any one theory can address. Perhaps that is why we have so many divergent theories of psychology. When we try to see ourselves, we are unable to step outside of ourselves. We cannot get far enough away to get a good view.

Jung, Stern, and Tomkins have presented differing descriptions of human complexes. When we talk about complex theory, it is important to bear in mind how intricate, individual, and how varied are its parts, how unique and unknown—and to some extent, unknowable—any complex is. Somehow, all of the patterns described above, link together to create adaptation and also form pathological complexes in some cases. There are only 12 notes on a piano, and we have not yet run out of music. I have described five archetypal/developmental processes that influence the development of ego consciousness and seven patterns of mediation of these processes. The patterns I have described above contain so many variables that at this time we are unable to measure them simultaneously. To me, this means that large parts of human experience, including the way pathological complexes function, remain a mystery.

QUESTIONS

1. What is a complex? Can you describe the complex of one of your patients?
2. Draw your idea or create an image of a positive complex; of a negative complex.
3. What are the nine emotions described by Silvan Tomkins? Give an example of the affective theme of one of your patients.
4. What is an archetype? Give an example of an archetype you have observed operating in your daily life.
5. Give an example of how an archetype operates in one of your patients.
6. What are the two aspects of any archetype? Give an example of how both aspects of the archetype have functioned in your daily life.
7. What is the universal human language? Use a mirror and practice the body language of one of your patients.
8. What is the Self? Think back over your clinical experience and give three examples of meaningful coincidences that have surprised you and made you wonder about a higher Power that acts within everyday life.
9. What is *individuation*? Can you remember the dynamic process of individuation from the story of the old Indian man? What do you think about the process he went through? How do you feel about that process? Have you noticed that kind of process operating in your life or in the lives of your patients?

10. Can you give an example from your own personal life or your clinical practice of the operation of an affective theme?
11. How has a pathological complex affected the individuation process in one of your patients?
12. Name the archetypal/developmental processes. Describe one process that is operating in either a negative or positive way in one of your patients.
13. Name Michael Fordham's dynamic processes that energize ego development. Think about how those processes operate in a baby you have observed, and also in an adult you have observed.
14. Describe the process of disintegration and how it operates in a pathological complex. Describe how this process operates in the life of one of your patients.
15. Name the patterns of mediation. Can you identify a misattuned pattern of mediation in a pathological complex of one of your patients?
16. Observe several patients in your practice. How does each one change when his or her pathological complex is stimulated?

ENDNOTES

1. *CW* is an abbreviation for Jung's *Collected Works*. These works contain most of C.G. Jung's theoretical writings dating from 1902 to 1961, the year of his death. The *Collected Works* were compiled in chronological order in volumes 1 through 18. The volume number follows *CW* in the citations. The *Collected Works* were a joint endeavor by Routledge and Kegan Paul, Ltd. in England and Princeton University Press in New Jersey, under the sponsorship of the Bollingen foundation. R.F.C. Hull translated the volumes into English in the late 1950s through the 1960s. Volume 19 (1979) is a bibliography of the *Collected Works* translated into 18 languages. Volume 20 (1979) is a general index covering volumes 1–18.
2. I observed these reflexes in my work as a nurse in pediatrics, labor and delivery, infant intensive care, infant nursery, and premature baby nursery.
3. Jung used the term *individuation* to describe the ability to translate the messages from the unconscious into growth and adaptation. Sister Jose Hobday, a Native American Fransiscan nun describes individuation in a different way. She says, "We are born on Grandmother Earth to dance our Sacred Dream awake so that we can give it away to all the people."
4. Sister Jose Hobday told me this story in 1974. I do not know where she is or how to find her. As far as I know this story has never been published. It has danced in my heart for 26 years. I am sure she would not mind if I shared it with you.
5. The groundwork for the extension of Jung's theories on developmental processes and their connection with Fordham's work was originally developed in 1991 as part of my diploma thesis, "The Way of the Warrior: One Metaphor for

Individuation," presented in 1993 as a requirement for graduation from the Analyst Training Program of Chicago. My thesis advisor was Murray Stein, Ph.D.

6. For those persons who are interested in studying archetypes, authors Marie Louise Von Franz, Anthony Stevens, and James Hillman have written extensively about them.
7. As far as I know Pamela Levin was the first person who described this form of mediation and named it *symbiotic* (1974, p. 25).
8. In the Native American traditions that predate contact with Westerners, infants were kept in cradleboards. It was believed that the infant would let the caregiver know what it needed. When needs were met and the infant cried anyway, the cradleboard was hung from a tree until the infant stopped crying. After the crying stopped, the infant was checked. This kind of mediation did several things. First, it supported the bond between the infant and the Self. Second, the infant learned to signal needs without crying, which was important for the survival of the tribe. The emphasis for the caregivers was on listening well to the communications from the infant and attending to the infant's needs before crying and screaming took place. Maturation occurred in this society much earlier than in our present culture. These people believed that if caretakers held their infants all the time, they would insert themselves into the infant's relationship with Spirit (personal communication Ralph Redfox, Northern Cheyenne elder, 2000).
9. Portions of Figures 1 through 3 were given to me by Peter Mudd to use as springboards to express my own ideas in whatever form I chose. His original figures are published in his article "The Dark Self: Death as a Transferential Factor," *Journal of Analytical Psychology* 1990, 35, 125–141.
10. Emma Furst, M.D. was a member of the staff of the psychiatric Clinic of the University of Zurich and worked with Jung on the Word Association Test and did research on families. Her research showed the similarity of complexes between family members and was published in "Statistical Investigations on Word Associations and on Familial Agreement in Reaction Type among Uneducated persons." Jung cites her essay in the Collected Works, Volume 2 (1981, 466-479, Volume 4, 1979, 136, and Volume 18, 1980, 410-411).

Chapter 2

FORMATION OF A PATHOLOGICAL COMPLEX[1]

The theoretical concepts presented in Chapter 1 need to be grounded in human experience so that they can be understood not only intellectually but in the body and the heart as well. Stories, myths, and fairy tales often provide the basis for that kind of understanding. In the following story that I call "The Woman Who Once Walked in Balance," we can observe the formation of a pathological complex and the release from it. It is a story of one woman's journey (it could just as easily have been a man's) from wounding to freedom. I wrote the story to demonstrate the fact that a pathological complex can be formed at any time in life, that it is an indelible structure that can never be retracted, and that when the archetypal energy held within that complex is gradually released, life can become filled with the peace, balance, and meaning. No matter how young or how old one is, we human beings are dependent upon one another for mediation of the archetypal/ developmental processes. The possibility for growth and the possibility for damage always exist.

THE WOMAN WHO ONCE WALKED IN BALANCE

Ancient she was, old and skinny, wrinkled and white-haired. But she was joyful, and peace flowed around her. We met by chance 25 years ago as I traveled through Mexico. We were together long enough for me to listen to her story. Her wisdom transcended the barriers of race, culture, gender, and time itself. I became the younger woman listening respectfully to the voice of the elder. She was the first warrior I ever met. I will always remember her. Her story has danced in my heart these many years. This is the way I remember the telling:

"The world I remember is gone. The story that could weave the pieces of that lost world together is also gone. I remember only fragments of my life with my people, but not how the fragments fit together. My people were keepers of the balance. In the living of our lives, we wove the threads of chaos together into cycles of harmony. Living and dying, change and movement, were woven together in the daily lives of the people and into all of the life that surrounded the people. The gift of each life was nurtured. Each life contributed to the whole.

"I had seven summers when I was taken from my people. I had already learned to sing in my being with the stone sentinels that guarded our valley. I was learning the language of the wingeds. I could weave cloth patterns that were tight and straight. My grandmothers were teaching me to read the language of the trembling leaves so that I could learn the art of healing. One day I would be Chief as the women in my line had been Chief before me.

"The strangers came by stealth in the night. They had weapons that could kill at a distance. They killed some of the people. They killed my mother and my father. They separated the men from the women and the children. They beat the men. They called the women and children into the center of the village. They told the Chiefs that if all of the women did not submit to rape, they would kill all of the men and all of the children. In our world Life was Sacred. There were only two laws: honor the woman, for all Life comes through her, and do nothing to harm the children. The women stepped forward as Sacred Law dictated and submitted to the men. I watched as those men mounted the women. I waited for the thunder beings to come and destroy them, but the thunder beings did not come. Those men were not human. They had no understanding of what they did and no honor. Lovemaking for them was an act of aggression. I understood while I watched that these people were not human because they were born of women whom they considered as filth.

"I knew with a cold certainty that this was the end of my people. I knew that nothing would be left. They killed all of the elders and all of the children under five. The rest of us were tied to their horses, taken as slaves to sodomize and rape. The warriors who were left behind were killed. The women and the Chiefs were beaten until they were unconscious. The men laughed at the Chiefs, telling them they had no power, that they were only cows to be bred for babies.

"They took us children with them from village to village and people to people. We watched the same scene over and over. Most of the ones taken as slaves died. My soul sank into bitterness and despair. I do not remember much about when they began to handle me. They named me "whore." I had not yet had my true naming. I was not yet a woman. I had not started on my moon cycle. I was too young to do the quest for a vision. I wondered if 'whore' was the only name I would ever know. I felt abandoned by all the Sacred Ones whom I had trusted. I knew they had forgotten me.

"Hate was like a hot knot in my belly. I endured and hoped that I would be able to maim and kill as many of these creatures as possible before I died. Outwardly, I became docile; but inwardly, I began to wait patiently for the time when I would strike them down. I comforted myself with the songs and stories of my people. Gradually the songs and stories began to fade from my mind. I felt numb and dumb. I sank into despair. I was forced to learn to speak with the strangers. I was not allowed to speak with anyone else. If I was not docile and quiet, I was tortured. My body still bears the scars. There was never enough food. They made us fight each other for what little food we received. They would wager on who would win and who would lose. Gradually we lost respect for ourselves and for each other. We lost our ability to keep balanced. I could no longer hear the singing of the stones. I had changed so much that I could not understand the language of leaf or bird. I began to hope for death so that I could be blotted out of existence.

"I began to study the beings that captured us so I could kill as many as possible when I died. When my chance finally came, I killed or wounded more than ten. The others left alive stabbed me in the chest and the back. They left me in the woods to die.

"I woke in a strange place. An old man and an old woman cared for me and nursed me back to health. I begged them to let me die. I tried to explain to them that I wished to be blotted out of life. I tried to tell them that my spirit had been taken from me. I tried to tell them I was no longer human. But they refused to listen to me, and gradually my body began to mend. I could not sleep without screaming. When I awoke, I could not control the shaking of my body when I was surprised by a sound. The old man and the old woman sat with me. They held me when I awoke screaming. They held me when my body shook.

"Gradually I got better. One day they said that they would teach me to become a warrior and learn to regain the balance within myself. They told me that recovering my balance would restore my spirit to me. They explained that although my people were gone, their knowledge lived on. All true knowledge is part of energy as it flows in the universe. Truth can never be lost, only spoken in a different way. I chose to listen to them and to trust their teachings. I could always choose to die if what they promised me did not come to pass.

"The first part of my training was purification. Over and over, I worked to remember all that I had heard and seen and felt. I could barely tolerate my hatred of myself. I wanted to rip out my hair and tear off my skin when I remembered. I kept on remembering, because the only other choice I had was to die. Gradually, I learned to put the rememberings into images, then into words, and finally into a story. Gradually I began to learn to step back and watch myself moving in the story. I could not allow my heart to come too close to the story lest I fall backwards into the darkness of those terrible times. I had to learn to hold the story, yet stay back and observe. I had to stay far enough back to begin to understand what happened there without reentering the darkness. Each time I did this I died a little. As I accepted this little death daily, I began to have an experience of light and life entering the story. As I went over and over the events, the times, the people, and the experiences, I began to see small glimpses of beauty hidden there. The touch of a friend, the song of a bird, sunlight on a leaf, reminded me that even then not all was dark. I wept because I knew then that the Sacred Ones had not abandoned me.

"My teachers listened. Gradually I began to change in the inner part of my being. The part of me that had been locked up and rigid began to move and change. My body often felt as if it were turning to water. I cried most of the time. My teachers gave me work to do that made me sweat; and gradually I began, in the telling, and the telling, and the telling of my story, to understand what bound and constricted my heart. My heart began to let go of the hate and its bindings.

"The process of purification through which these teachers walked with me went on for many, many moons. My story was the Sacred Circle that held the dark seeds of revenge, hatred, and bitterness, sometimes pierced by the light of beauty and wonder. Gradually the numbness lifted from my body and I began again to sense.

"As my emotions began to flow, the second part of my training began. I felt the longing of the Universe to become. I was so open to life and to the feelings of all Creation that I had to learn how to protect myself. I had to learn where I began and where I stopped, while yielding to the energy of all the Creation. This was difficult: relearning to be mentally receptive in my heart, and yet holding all of my experience in order to physically understand that no matter what I experienced I could not lose myself. I had to learn to open and close my being at my own will, not at someone else's.

"I began to learn to communicate again with the world around me. I learned again to allow the stone people to sing in my bones. I learned again to listen to their whispers as I watched the trembling leaves. The old woman taught me movements for my body that opened me to receive energy in my head, in my heart, and in my belly. Gradually these movements allowed energy to move throughout my body. I do not know how long this took. I only know I slowly learned, and as I learned, I began to feel alive again.

"One day the old man told me that I had to learn to speak again with the people who had hurt me. He told me that I would never be free until I had faced them with no fear, no desire, and no despair. He took me to a place called a city, and in that city he taught me how to become invisible. I learned to walk among these people as a child, as an elder, as a cripple, as a man, and as a woman. I walked among them and began to learn their ways. I walked among them and began to see into their hearts. I walked among them and saw how their spirits had been lost because they believed what people told them rather than what they knew. I learned to sense in my body that I was no longer naked and vulnerable when someone looked at me. These people saw only what I chose to let them see. I could meet someone and he/she would see me as an old woman; later I could meet that person again and that person would see me as a young girl. They saw what I wished them to see. I saw their inner chaos. I began to understand that the balance had been lost for all people, not just for my people.

"When I returned to my teachers, I would bring back the pain of the people I met, and sometimes I felt the invisible world of Creation groaning and longing for all the people to return to themselves.

"The old man and the old woman began to teach me to transform the energies that arose within me when my inner chaos arose to overwhelm me. They taught me about the energy that lives in nature and how that energy could heal me. They taught me how to stand and how to breathe so that I could learn to relax, smile, and allow the energy of nature into my being. I stood with my weight on the center of my feet, with hips relaxed, chin tucked in, elbows dropped, and shoulders relaxed. As I learned to relax, the energy of nature taught me to find the places within my body that held constriction and pain. These tight, rigid spaces vibrated with my rage, my shame, and my fear. As I relaxed, I continued to release my pain. Sometimes I stood in the water or sat on the earth, feeling the sun on my skin, receiving the air as I breathed in and out. I allowed myself to smile and feel the warmth and the love held inside all of nature being given to me, in a way that I knew would release and support me.

"I began to experience a transformation. I reviewed each part of my story and opened myself to each part of my experience, allowing the energy of nature to erase the pain. As I did this the stones, the trees, the earth, the water, the sun, the moon, and the creatures of the forest seemed to join me and encourage me to trust in what was happening and to keep on. Transformation took place as a gift of nature, a mystery. The gift of transformation would not have been given if I had not done the work. It took years for me to remember my story, and many more for me to develop compassion. In the end, I was no longer affected by the emotions of others. My body became healthier, and I became younger and stronger.

"The old man and the old woman had kept track of one of the tyrants who had destroyed my people and abused me. They knew that if I could encounter this tyrant and remain balanced, I would be truly free of the limitations of my past. I trusted their wisdom. One day they took me to the place in the city where this man lived and worked. I saw him and I remembered him. He was the one who killed my father and my mother. Now he was a wealthy man, the owner of a large factory where the workers wove cloth. The old man and the old woman said I was free to choose whether I wanted any contact with this man. I knew I would not be free until I chose to submit to that tyrant again to test the strength and the depth of my learning and my healing. I was hired because I looked strong. I cleaned up, moved equipment, and kept the weavers supplied with material and thread. I began to study this man. I learned that he employed women and children who worked long hours and received little pay. Sometimes he abused them. For those he employed, a little was better than nothing.

"When he spoke, people listened. He liked that. They listened because he had so much money. No one knew or even suspected that he was abusing the women and children who worked for him. The people in the community thought that he was a good man who cared for the poor. What people did not know was how he hurt any worker who did not immediately do what he said. The people in the city did not know that there were times when no one was paid. They thought that he treated his workers well and that was why the workers were so efficient. The truth was that he terrified his workers and ruled them with an iron fist. He was wealthy, he was respected, and he was in charge.

"No one in that city would have believed me if I had told the truth about this man. I hated him. I was overcome with hatred. I sat with my hatred and let go of it a little at a time in order to relax into the deep energy of nature. I was overwhelmed with emotion, with memories, with rage and fear. I felt helpless. Again, I wished to be annihilated. I was fearful, shamed, and angry with him. As I felt that pain, I remembered to relax my body and smile a small smile, to allow the deep energy of nature to help me. Again and again that energy came to my aid.

"I began to notice the needs of the people around me, and I began to help them. I listened. I gave them herbs when they were sick. The people began to trust me. The tyrant noticed, and I sensed that he began to fear what he saw as my power. His fear grew; he became less and less balanced. Gradually he moved into a state of constant rage that was terrifying. I worked hard to become better at obeying him. I encouraged the other workers to do the same. I began to understand that the goal of my teachers had been to help me come back into correct alignment and balance. As I practiced learning to relax my body, to remember what had happened, and to smile while the deep energy of nature helped me, the people around me began to ask me to teach them how to balance themselves. They gathered around me at lunchtime or whenever they could. I taught them how to smile and relax. I taught them physical movement to help them come into proper alignment with their own true nature.

"The owner of the factory became more frightened, and he began to act out his rage. He began to abuse the workers. He demonstrated that he was the one in control by becoming more abusive. He created fear in the people and reminded them that he was the one with the power. He began to force me to watch him while he abused the workers, daring me to stop him, showing the people that I had no power. I was overcome by chaos. I could not bear it. But I had to bear it. I felt as if the abuse all around me was my fault. I worked harder to keep myself balanced. I did not react. I looked within. I saw that the outer drama between this man and his workers also existed within my own heart, my own mind, and my own belly. I began to understand that the outer drama was repeated again inwardly in my own soul, my own spirit and my own life energy. Through physical violation and torture, the tyrant had literally forced his way into the very depths of my being, distorting my memory, my feeling, my understanding, my soul, my dreaming body, my behavior, and my spirit.

"I was disgusted with myself. I fell into a deep, dark hole. I was totally incapacitated by the knowledge that my own development could be totally dependent upon the whim of another human, who could use me in whatever way he or she chose. That tyrant lived within me and would always make me remember. In his presence and outside his presence, I could never go away from him, because he was part of me. I was unable to move, unable to think and unable to pray. My heroic journey was at an end. My healing process counted for nothing. I knew that at any time I could remember and experience the wounding again. Outwardly, I continued acting just the way I had before. Inwardly, I felt as if I was dead, embalmed in ice. The agony of finally understanding what had been done to me and then watching it done to others over and over again created an anguish within me that my words cannot convey. I had no words. I let go and allowed the blackness of despair to engulf me.

"I yielded to despair as earth yields to the rain and wood to the fire. In my yielding, I was transformed again. The I who speaks was held by something greater than I, something both unknown and unknowable, something that contained and nourished me. Gradually, awareness dawned like the first tiny rays of morning sun. As the light of consciousness began to illumine my being, I was able to know that this man was deeply connected with me, entwined within my being. I understood that he had contaminated all that was human within me. My experience of him was woven through me; he breathed throughout my being and that experience could feed on my life energy forever, *if I chose.*

"From that place deep within my body where no words are, I understood that I had a choice and that I would have to make this choice over and over.

I could choose to trust the unknowable force that was holding me together and yield to it by smiling and relaxing into it, or I could continue to deny the fact that my experience with this man had created darkness within me. If I fought with him, if I tried to change him, if I did anything to him at all except pray for him, I would remain connected with him. How could I be free of him when he was part of me? Shame overwhelmed me as I felt him alive in my body.

"I chose to rest with the unknowable. I could only hope that the unknowable might be gracious and compassionate. The worst that could happen to me had already happened. I did not have the energy to struggle with what had happened any more. I chose to rest and trust, relaxing into the unknowable as it continued the work of transformation. I felt terrified of what I might become. Repeatedly I relaxed, smiled, and trusted what held me. Gradually I began to feel separate from him and from my experience of him. I do not know how that happened, but as that happened, I began to see into his reality. I saw that he was so afraid of life he had to hurt people in order to feel alive. I saw that he had had many experiences of being victimized, and that these experiences were so painful that he had cut them off from his awareness. There was nothing left of him except his own experience of the actions of his tyrant.

"I was identified with the victim in his drama; he was identified with his own inner tyrant. We were both pushed into roles in a dramatic tragedy that stole our energy and defaced our human nature.

"Slowly, I began to teach the other workers what I was learning, and they too began to trust the unknowable. I waited and I trusted that we would find a way to gain our freedom. The tyrant became more open and more violent in his abuse. He began to make all of us watch as he tortured or abused children. He wanted to frighten us into greater submission, to demonstrate his power over us. I taught my co-workers all I had learned. As I did, the tyrant became more frenzied and less cautious. I was devastated. Part of me felt responsible for all of their pain.

"One day, friends of his came by unannounced. The visit was a blessing. He was not prepared for their arrival. He was abusing a little boy. When I let his friends in, they saw him. They really understood him in the light of Truth. I cannot explain it, but I know that somehow the fact that of all of us were working on ourselves and yielding to the unknowable in order to be healed created the timing for his downfall. We celebrated as he was taken away to prison. I knew the workers would create a better environment for themselves. Together we had learned a great lesson.

"My learning was not yet finished, however. I changed my appearance and began walking around his home, looking into the windows. I was arrested for loitering and looking. They put me in the cell with him since I seemed to be so curious about him.

"I sat patiently and listened. I watched him become crazy, screaming and tearing at himself. I sat with my fear. The guards told him he was overly dramatic and refused to believe he was crazy. They told him what to do and ordered him to clean the toilets of the jail. They made him beg for his food. They spat at him, humiliating him. His sanity reappeared. He attacked the guards and killed three in his attempt to escape. He would not submit to authority. He was the authority; his power had made him feel as if he was a god. That was all he had; there was nothing human left in him.

"I understood how we were alike. I understood that when I became him and killed or maimed more than ten of his friends, I was no longer human; I was only a knot of rage. I was also different from him. The old wise woman and the old wise man had mediated healing to me so that I learned to have a choice in life rather than just a reaction based on the way I had been treated. My teachers had helped me understand and feel the heartbeat that lives in the center of the universe. They showed me how to align my small heart with that great and unknowable heart.

"That man had never learned that there was a power higher than those who had hurt him. He did not care what happened because he felt he was a god. No one could help him except himself. He lived a lie, and his fear of me was his fear of losing this lie.

"I finally understood that if I had not been taught to earn enough energy to make a choice, I would have never understood, never remembered the unknowable nor learned to trust the Sacred Power that held me when I could not hold myself. I could have become him at any time. I also knew that now I had the power of choice.

"When I returned to the old woman and the old man, they celebrated with me and gave me my name. I am called Woman Who Once Walked in Balance. Now when I meet strangers I tell them my story so that others can learn and create change for the better. This is my story. Those people who hear my story and heed it are my people. My people live."

SUMMARY

The story of "The Woman Who Once Walked in Balance" is one way to *feel* our way into the formation of a rigidified, pathological complex and begin to observe what is going on from multiple viewing points. It helps us understand the constriction and loss of freedom that result from formation of the complex, and it provides an opportunity to observe the pathological complex as consciousness increases and the energy locked within the complex is gradually released, increasing life energy. During the time of wounding, our heroine's awareness gradually became a closed system: wordless, unconscious, and impervious to conscious influence: a pathological complex. Her range of consciousness gradually narrowed through repeated experiences of disintegration. Her emotions were locked into terror and rage, her memory disappeared, her physical body held only pain, and her ability to act or assert herself was totally blocked. She internalized these painful experiences because she had no choice in the matter at all. How did she become free? How did she find meaning and understanding? How could anything have been left of ego consciousness after such overwhelming destruction? Yet her consciousness was not destroyed. How did that happen? We will explore these questions by breaking pathological complexes down into multiple viewing points in order to create an understanding of parts because we cannot assimilate the whole. The therapist is someone who helps the patient break things down into meaningful parts and then link with his or her experience with the inner experience of the old wise woman and the old wise man.

COMPENSATION

In the story, the old wise woman and the old wise man are images of the Self that come from the unconscious to restore the normal processes of compensation. Our heroine was left for dead; ego consciousness had been annihilated. The old wise woman and the old wise man balanced death by bringing the hope for life; the unconscious *compensated* the conscious attitude.

Compensation is a process in which the unconscious balances conscious activity (*CW* 6, 1921; 1977, 418–420). This same process operates in the body and is called *homeostasis*. When we drink hot soup or take a hot shower, our body temperature remains normal because of homeostasis. We don't usually notice it, but our body is constantly balancing itself. When homeostasis cannot operate, we develop symptoms and get sick. Physical symptoms appear because the body systems are working together to try to restore balance. Compensation is the psychological equivalent of homeostasis. When compensatory relations between consciousness and the unconscious are blocked, we get sick. The Little Match Girl, the man with the train nightmare, the old Indian man, and the Woman Who Once Walked in Balance are all examples of pathological complexes that have interrupted relations between ego consciousness and the outer world or between ego consciousness and the unconscious.

Pathological complexes are an attempt of the psyche to restore compensation, just as a fever is an attempt to restore homeostasis. Analytical therapy, according to Jung, is a way to make unconscious contents real so that compensation can be re-established (*CW* 6, 1977, 420). Compensation cannot operate when a pathological complex is constellated because the complex has replaced normal ego consciousness. The unconscious keeps providing compensatory dreams that point to the complex, but their messages may be so alien to ego consciousness that they are experienced as nightmares; or, as in the case of the Little Match Girl, the ego simply cannot utilize them because it has no frame of reference. What is behind homeostasis and compensation?

THE SELF

Jung believed that the entire personality is composed of consciousness and the unconscious. He used the term *Self* to indicate both the center and the circumference of the entire personality (*CW* 6, 1977, 460). He reserved the term ego for the center of consciousness (*CW* 12, 1977, 41). The Self is dependent upon the ego for individuation to take place. When a pathological complex is constellated, relations between the ego and the Self are distorted or blocked, interfering with the individuation process and preventing the embodiment of the Self in everyday life.

When Jung discussed the Self he used descriptive terms, metaphors, similes, images, and myths because it is impossible to define it. He described the Self and the archetypes as having both biological and psychological poles. However, he never made a direct connection between the Self, the archetypes and the physical body. Since the body is part of the entire personality, I am carrying Jung's ideas further and saying that the Self is the architect of both the body and the psyche. It is the psychophysical organ that regulates both homeostasis and compensation.

The Self is neither good nor bad; it is neutral like all of nature. It is like the regulating force for the weather all over the world, e.g., volcanoes, high winds, sunny days, flooding, and freezing temperatures. All weather is a manifestation of nature and is part of keeping the balance between the deep earth, the surface of the earth and the heavens. We may experience weather as negative or positive. Weather is not at all concerned with how we perceive it and like the Self it is a force of nature that has both purpose and meaning whether or not we enjoy its manifestations.

Pathological complexes are created by the defenses of the Self in order to protect ego consciousness from annihilation. These defenses are activated when ego consciousness is threatened. They operate unconsciously and are especially active during infancy and childhood because ego consciousness is not yet very developed. The defenses of the Self can operate at any time during life when the intensity, frequency, and duration of disintegration reaches such uncomfortable physical and psychic levels that annihilation seems immanent (as in the story of The Woman Who Once Walked in Balance).

THE DEFENSES OF THE SELF

The defenses of the Self are denial, splitting, projection, introjection, idealization, and identification (Fordham 1974, 192–199; 1976, 93; 1978, 4, 91 and 95; and 1985, 49, 153).[2] Ego consciousness is meant to be incredibly flexible and resilient throughout life. However, mediation of the archetypal/developmental processes that is grossly misattuned, neglectful, or abusive creates experiences of *disintegration* that are experienced within ego consciousness as an imminent sense of annihilation. The defenses of the Self are not pathological in themselves; they are natural mechanisms that protect the tiny growing bud of ego consciousness during fetal life and infancy as well as in maturity. Caregivers who mediate the archetypal processes of development carry the power and the authority of the Self for the child until he or she is strong enough to develop his or her own relationship with the Self. When mediation is good enough, the experiences of disintegration are gradually assimilated and ego development continues throughout childhood free of the negative affective themes of pathological complexes.

When the defenses of the Self operate repeatedly forming pathological complexes, the energy available to ego consciousness is diminished. When more and more material accumulates around the pathological complex, less and less energy is available to ego consciousness, which delays maturation and interferes with adaptation.

In the case of The Woman Who Once Walked in Balance, her parents were killed, her way of life destroyed, and the patterns of mediation that supported the development of her ego consciousness were replaced by patterns of mediation that created continual experiences of disintegration. Her wish for death in the story is a metaphor for an ego consciousness depleted of energy.[3]

In everyday life, the process of the formation of a pathological complex usually happens much more slowly and far less dramatically than in the story of The Woman Who Once Walked in Balance, except in cases of catastrophic events. However, we all experience disintegration from the time we live in our mother's womb until the time we die. Maturity is the ability to endure experiences of disintegration without mobilizing the defenses of the Self.

The process of mediation between the caregivers and the child is a developmental process for the parents as well as the child. In order to attune to the child, the caregivers must re experience and, ideally, repair their own childhood experiences of disintegration to be able to mediate the archetypal/developmental processes in an attuned way. As the child's ego consciousness develops, the child becomes more independent, and parental mediation of the archetypal/developmental processes gradually diminishes. An adolescent can be considered a young adult when he or she is able to live independently of the parents, be financially responsible for his or her own needs, and relate to the parents by understanding and respecting their point of view while maintaining his or her own point of view. Mediation with attunement supports maturation. The parents gain maturity by learning to balance and finally release their authority over the child to support his or her connection with the Self. This is an incredibly difficult and complex process for both the caregivers and the child. One individual's maturity is something like a chain that has been forged generation after generation. Wars, natural disasters, destructive events, and the generally poor treatment of women and children throughout the world for the last several thousand years has interfered with individual maturity. Most caregivers do the very best that they can and are successful if they have mediated the archetypal/developmental processes in better ways than what they received.

Let us return to the story of the Woman Who Once Walked in Balance and further examine the formation of her pathological complex. Almost everything that supported the existence of her ego consciousness was destroyed. Access to what she knew and trusted, and what for her was solid, disintegrated, as did her knowledge of her former wholeness. To me, this is the essence of evil. The villains, who probably received abusive forms of mediation themselves, identified with those destructive experiences, and unconsciously imposed their own nightmare, their own painful reality, their own pathological complexes on other lives, negating any sort of reality belonging to an "other." The villains were locked into their own pathological complexes, *projecting* their own small, helpless parts onto their victims, and *identifying* with their own internal, persecuting caregivers, reenacting their own pathological drama. Unconsciously they inserted their psychic infection into other lives, fully believing that they had the right to do so. As clinicians, it is important for us not only to understand the kind of devastation that produces pathological complexes but also to hope that the experiences of our patients contain the seeds of healing.

In our story, the villains had no regard for the heroine's existence and the damage they inflicted repeated itself internally even after they were gone. In the early 1960s I worked as a registered nurse at a county hospital. The most painful experience I had there was touring the abandoned baby nursery. The children there were left there after birth. This occurred for many reasons: because of a substance-addicted mother's irresponsibility; because the child had a physical defect; because the child was not wanted; or because the child was the painful reminder of rape or incest. The abandoned baby nursery housed 200 children ranging in age from birth to seven months. One nurse and one aide worked there on each shift. That was all the county could afford. The babies received a minimal amount of care and stimulation. And after a time, they did not cry; they did not respond; and they did not move unless they were turned. They were so understimulated (there was only enough help to prop bottles and change diapers) that their potential for consciousness was slipping away before my eyes.[4]

As a nurse, I have seen a great deal of the evil that humans create for themselves: gunshots, stabbings, beatings, and human torture of humans. But I wept only once, there at the abandoned baby nursery. These babies were the innocent victims of other people's wrong choices. They were innocent, and yet they carried the responsibility and the pain of those who had left them there, discarded and forgotten, before they could ever know their own potential. In cases like this, the Self protects the ego by unconsciously mobilizing its defenses to wall off the experiences and protect consciousness. Those babies had so much pain walled off that there was little consciousness left. I have often wondered what happened to those children. Who did they become? Did anyone ever want them or give them a home? Did they ever grow up and have children of their own? How did they treat them? I will never know.

OPERATION OF THE DEFENSES OF THE SELF

As already stated, the defenses of the Self are denial, splitting, introjection, projection, idealization, and identification. It is important for clinicians to have a working, operational knowledge of these defenses in order to understand how they operate within everyday relationships, as well as within the therapeutic hour. The following descriptions are based upon my clinical experience. They operate in ways that are interrelated and interdependent. When they appear in the therapeutic hour they are accompanied by repetitive affective themes, physical sensations, memories, and behavioral reactions. The following descriptions are not comprehensive and it may be useful for you to link your own clinical experiences with what is presented below.

1. *Denial* appears within a clinical hour, for both the clinician and patient, as a feeling of "I don't know" and also as a loss of the sense of safety or mutu-

al connection within the relational field. When it appears there is a heightened anxiety: a sense of falling apart, confusion, not being able to think, feeling numb, finding the other bad and wrong but not being able to discuss it. It also may appear as boredom, sleepiness, mind wandering, agitation, and hatred, negative or positive passion for the other, confusion, fear, or frustration.

The symptoms mentioned above are only a few of the manifestations of denial that might occur within a clinical hour; however, they are the ones I have encountered most frequently. It is important for the therapist to pay careful attention to countertransference reactions; maintaining the boundaries and goals that have been mutually created by both the patient and the therapist; to the patient's stated experience; and to whatever creates a lack of safety, protection, and/or empowerment for either the patient or the therapist.

Clinical Vignette: Denial

Therapist: "You made an agreement with your husband to ask him before you spent over $300. It sounds as if you broke the agreement."

Patient: "I guess I did. I didn't mean to, but the refrigerator was such a bargain and ours is on its last legs. It was such a good price and we really need a new one."

Therapist: "You seem really happy with your purchase. What stopped you from calling and asking him if it was all right?"

Patient: "He is just so controlling about money. He watches every dime I spend. It's not as if we don't need a refrigerator. He's just so tight with the money."

Therapist (internal response): I am really frustrated with this woman. I would really like to tell her she is lying to herself. I must be in my countertransference. I had better slow down, smile, deep breathe and attune to the patient.

Therapist (to patient): "What happens inside you when you think of asking him whether or not you can purchase the refrigerator?"

Patient: "He will just put me down. He'll be angry and think I am stupid. He always acts like an expert on money and he is so tight. If I listened to him all of our money would be in the bank and we would be living in a shack."

Therapist (internal observation): I am still feeling frustration. I can't respond to her from frustration. I will explore the feeling tone, the memories, and the physical sensations. Perhaps it will help us both understand what is going on.

Therapist (to patient): "What is it like inside you when you think about calling your husband and asking whether or not you can spend money for a refrigerator?"
Patient: "He is just like my father, ignorant, male, and controlling. I just ignore him."
Therapist: "What is it like for you when you are ignoring him?"
Patient: "I shut down and just disappear."
Therapist: "Does shutting down and disappearing have a color, a shape, an idea, a feeling?"
Patient: "I don't know. I never thought about it."

Therapist (internal observation): I am feeling really frustrated. I would like to shake her. I wasn't feeling angry when we started the hour. Now I am imagining telling her off because she isn't talking about her own experience.

Therapist (to patient): "What is going on in your body right now?"
Patient: "Well, I feel tight in my neck and jaw and a little angry."

Therapist (internal observation): I feel relieved of some of my frustration. The patient's denial was approached through my own countertransference responses. The denial began to lift when the patient was able to describe her physical sensations and speak about feeling a little angry.

2. *Splitting* can be observed within the clinical hour by listening carefully to what a patient says and does not say. For example, when a patient discusses his or her experience, he or she may criticize or negate it in almost the same breath. Feelings, memories, physical sensations, behaviors, and/or the ability to be, do, think, have an identity, or create may be discounted or the patient may talk about feeling stuck, blocked, or passive. Ambivalence and/or parts are always an indication of splitting. The patient may describe him or herself as feeling stuck, unclear, unable to make a decision, confused, or unable to take in information.

Splitting can also be easily observed by noticing how the components of ego consciousness are present, interrelated, or absent as the patient discusses his or her experience. For example, feelings may be expressed, but the client's body language communicates something different. Feelings may not be expressed at all or the patient might express some feelings but not others. For example, the patient can talk about being fearful but has no awareness of being angry. Memories may be absent or distorted or the patient may have difficulty remembering accurately what has happened in previous sessions.

The patient may have difficulty taking responsibility for his or her behavior or he or she may report that he or she cannot stop reacting from the complex.

Jung was clear that when opposites (splits) were contained a symbol could arise that provided an entirely new point of view that transcended the splitting (*CW* 6, 1977, 478–479). Identifying and working with different parts as they present themselves in the clinical hour begins to destroy one-sided conscious attitudes, creating a felt sense of the opposites for the patient. It is often a relief for patients to find out that they are not crazy when they have different parts with different thoughts, feelings and ideas.

When a patient begins to understand that he or she operates from more than one part, the identification with just one part drops away, giving him or her more psychological space. The therapist can attempt to understand and empathize with each part of the patient's experience, laying the groundwork for the patient's containment and self-reflection.

Clinical Vignette: Splitting

Patient: "You or someone like you was there in my dream. I ignored you. I never ignore you. In the dream I told you to get out of my life. What could that mean? Does it mean I really don't pay attention to you?"
Therapist: "I think it might mean that a *part* of you would like me to get out of your life. Does that feel like it might be right?"
Patient: "You mean I could have just one part of me that didn't like you and the rest of me could still like you?"
Therapist: "Of course. All of us have parts unless we are enlightened–and I don't know anyone who is."
Patient: "I am so relieved. A part of me can dislike you, and the rest of me can like you."

3. *Introjection* is a process that takes experiences of annihilation directly into the psyche in order to contain them. These "introjects" are unconscious parts of the pathological complex and can take over awareness when the pathological complex is constellated. When that happens in the clinical hour, there is a sense that something is not quite right. The patient seems to become someone different. His or her voice, posture, wording, affect, ideation, behavior, and tone may change. Something about the patient's communications or thought processes seems incongruent with his or her usual demeanor. It may seem as if the patient is lying, complaining, covering something up, defensive, or unusually blaming of the analyst/therapist or others in his or her life. The patient may suddenly wish to stop treatment or make decisions that are harmful to his or her own goals for therapy.

An "introject" may be unconsciously transferred to the therapist, who begins experiencing foreign thoughts or unfamiliar feelings that are difficult to dismiss even after the clinical hour is over. The patient may repeatedly come to mind, and the clinician's own complexes may be stimulated, even though usual complex stimulators are absent. The therapist may wish to react in a negative ways toward the patient. It is important for the therapist not to react, but rather to become alert to the experience and contain it. It is important information. Outwardly, the analyst/therapist must assume an attitude of even deeper interest in how the patient is experiencing life events and keep expressing the desire to come as close as possible to experiencing what the patient is experiencing.[5] This sudden lack of attunement in the relational field is difficult to identify and hard to manage, yet it is exactly what must happen for the deepening of an understanding of the pathological complex and one of the main reasons that attunement is so important in clinical work (Racker 1996, 8).

Clinical Vignette: Introjection

Patient: "My dad part hates you. He says he is the one in charge, not you and all your credentials. Those things just taught you to how to play mind games."
Therapist: "Would your dad part be willing to speak with me?"
Patient: "I am afraid of what he would do to you. He really hates you."
Therapist: "He probably has good reason to hate me. What do you think?"
Patient: "I am starting to feel things. It is really hard. I always thought what we did was O.K. Now when I remember things and have feelings about those things. I am beginning to hate him. How could anybody want to have sex with a three-year-old? My dad thought it was fine. My mom thought it was fine. It is so hard to feel all this. They didn't love me."

Therapist (internal response): She sounds terrified, as if she has been abandoned forever. Her anxiety has increased so much she is seeing me three times a week, once in group and she is still really having a difficult time containing what she is feeling.

Therapist (to patient): "How anxious and scared are you feeling right now?"
Patient: "My father told me if I ever talked about this he would have me arrested and put in jail. He put a piece of paper with some of the pictures of us he took in a box and said if I ever talked about what we did he would give that paper to the police and they would put me in jail. I feel nauseous

and so ashamed that I told you. I am so anxious I can't think. I feel like I am burning under my skin. I want to pace and wring my hands."
Therapist: "O.K. Do you want me to pace with you or do you want me to just be here while you pace?'
Patient: "Just be here."

The "introject" is the father and the mother combined with an affective theme of confusion, anxiety, and terror. At this time in the therapy, it was most important to listen to her say her father hated me because we could still maintain our relationship with the parts of her that were not her "introject."

4. *Projection* is an unintentional, unconscious, unperceived transfer of unconscious and preconscious material onto someone or something in the outer world. The person who is projecting feels as if the projected material belongs to whomever or whatever holds the projection ($CW\,9_1$, 1977, 59–61). We don't notice projections until they interfere with our relationships or our daily life. We assume that the world and the people in it are just as we see them; there is no scientific test to prove the difference between projection and reality. However, projection is the only mechanism that could account for the extermination of six million Jews by the Nazis during the Second World War and of nine million women during the inquisition by the Roman Catholic Church (Kramer and Sprenger 1971) and the treatment of Negroes and Native American peoples in the United States during the past 300 years.

Projection occurs all the time. It is present in everyday life. Listen to patients' experiences when they discuss those they love, their family, their friends, and those they consider their enemies. Projections are there in the dramas of daily life, in relationships and in the way the world is perceived. All projections have a "hook" to hold them in place. For example, a patient may project an "introject" onto a spouse, a boss, or the therapist. It is important to remember that the hook for a projection has a truth that holds the projection in place. Exploring the grain of truth locked within the hook will eventually expose the projected material. Becoming aware of projections is a lengthy and delicate process, and the only way we can only become aware of them is by becoming conscious of the discrepancy between the projection and the reality. The space between the projection and reality is filled with parts of ourselves that are lost to consciousness and often too foreign to everyday awareness to be easily understood.

For example, a very timid woman whose father was frightening and physically abusive was married to an alcoholic. She described her husband as angry, unpredictable, and controlling. She felt as if she lived in a continual state of terror and had no space or time to do anything to care for herself. She parented her children with no help from her husband, yet she was as financially dependent on him as she had been with her father. As she explored her relationship with her husband in therapy she gradually became aware that he was not at all like her father and that she assumed that he was angry, unpredictable and controlling and responded to him the way her mother responded to her father. The anger, the unpredictability and the need to control that she attributed to him did not exist.

In therapy, she projected a strong mother onto me and then idealized me. We never discussed the projection or the idealization. Instead, we explored her own potential for developing a strong mother within herself to nourish herself, the way she had nourished her children. Projections must be interpreted in an attuned way and considered as lost and foreign parts of ego consciousness that must be befriended, named, and related to. If a projection is ego syntonic and comfortable, and if it is not interfering with the patient's adaptation or causing pain, it is fairly likely that the projection will remain unintegrated.

5. *Identification* is a normal process in human development connected with the archetypal/developmental process of identity. For example, my three-year-old granddaughter imitates or identifies with her six-year-old cousin in almost everything her cousin says and does. She is developing her identity as a girl, as a member of a family, and as someone who can be, do, think, and create things.

Identification appears clinically through projective and introjective identification. Projective identification is an unconscious blurring of boundaries between one person and another or others, or between one person and a value, a cause, an image or an important figure.

Clinical Vignette: Projective Identification

Husband: "We don't have problems in our relationship, and we don't need to see a therapist. You are the one who has a problem because you're so negative."

Wife: "I am not negative. You're never home. You don't help with the kids, and I am really lonely."

Husband: "You have a good life and lots of money. The kids go to private schools and have everything they want. I am doing the best I can. Stop complaining. Wives are supposed to take care of the kids and the home. Be grateful for what you have. I don't cheat on you. I make good money. I have to work long hours. I wish you would stop criticizing me all the time."

In this vignette, the husband does not "hear" or "see" his wife accurately. He experiences her as critical and ungrateful because he is married to the belief that a wife should be quiet, grateful, and uncomplaining.

Introjective identification is an unconscious identification with those parts of a pathological complex that are linked with the highest levels of affective intensity. When a pathological complex is constellated, both introjective and projective identification are operating.

Clinical Vignette: Introjective Identification in the Couple Described Above

Wife: "Everything he says is true. He is working hard to make money. Why am I criticizing him when he really is doing his best? Why do I feel lonely all the time? I am being negative. What is wrong with me? Our lifestyle is wonderful. The children seem happy. I don't understand why I feel so lonely."

The wife's pathological complex is identified with the introjected shame she felt because of being a poor child in a middle-class school who had holes in her shoes, worn clothes, and no money to join after-school activities. When her husband accuses her of being unappreciative and critical, she identifies with the introjected experience of being shamed and loses her conscious point of view.

Clinical Vignette: Projective and Introjective Identification

Patient: "What draws these nasty, dishonest people into my life? I must be doing something wrong. I wish I knew what it was. Why don't nice people like me?"

Therapist (internal observation): This woman projectively identifies others as "good" and identifies with the introjection that she is "bad." She is unable to accurately evaluate others or herself. This defense operated unconsciously so that she could survive in an alcoholic, abusive, and chaotic family system.

Identification can be recognized in individual therapy when a patient is identified with one of his or her roles in life, e.g., the workaholic, the expert on everything under the sun, the victim, the bully, the nurturer, the gentle man or woman, or the one who is continually overwhelmed. Patients can also identify with the therapist through changes in mannerisms, dress style, use of language or interests. Identification is extremely difficult to explore until the object of the identification surprises, disappoints and/or creates a reaction in the subject that creates confusion and intense affect.

6. *Idealization* is an unconscious defense that makes an object, value, person, or thing much better or much lesser than it really is. Idealization carries an intense affective theme linked to part of a pathological complex. Carol Burnett did a comedy skit on television that is a wonderful way to describe idealization. In the skit, Carol has become a New York celebrity because she has just won the Pulitzer Prize in literature. She returns home to the small town she grew up in to share her good news with her mother. Carol's mother has been very disappointed in her all her life and considers her a failure because she doesn't "beautify" herself with false eyelashes and padded bras. In addition, she thinks that Carol reads too much, is clumsy, and can't even knit. Worst of all, Carol is "deevorced." As the skit begins, Carol greets her mother as a cool, professional and well-dressed woman. She tells her mother that she has just won the Pulitzer Prize in literature. Her mother responds by telling Carol that her chest is still too small and that is probably why she is "deevorced" and not remarried. As the skit goes on, Carol begins to lose her veneer of sophistication as her mother mispronounces Pulitzer Prize and tries to make Carol wear false eyelashes so she can finally "catch a man even though she isn't built right." By the end of the skit Carol is reduced to a stuttering kind of clumsiness, vowing to do better at finding a man. Even though she is a famous writer in New York, at home she is still a flat-chested, clumsy, "deevorced" failure.

Patients reveal idealization by comparing themselves in negative ways with a norm or an ideal of perfection such as physical appearance, health, or wealth. Sometimes they denigrate others in order to build up their own sense of importance. The patient's perception of his or her ability to do, think, be, have an identity, or be creative may depend on what others believe about him. Or the patient may consider herself as "entitled" or "special" and demand more of the therapist than he or she is able to give. The therapist can become "godlike" or "evil," depending on how idealization is used within the transference/countertransference field.

The therapist in turn may idealize the patient by believing that if the patient is only loved enough, he or she will be cured. The therapist can idealize his or her profession by becoming the hero or heroine who will "save" the patient at any cost. The therapist may lock the patient into a diagnostic category and only view the patient through that particular lens. The antidote to the operation of idealization in the clinical setting is the sense of personal choice and responsibility on both the therapist's and the patient's part.

Idealizations always produce issues about power and control because they unconsciously and rigidly deny the reality of another person's existence or experience. Issues about power and control can appear in many ways in the relational field: the patient may continually push the therapist's boundaries by noncompliance, nonpayment of fees, late payments, multiple phone calls requesting immediate attention, or threats of suicide unless the therapist complies with whatever it is the patient wants. The patient may unconsciously feel totally dependent on the therapist who can be, think, do, create, or provide an identity for the patient. In family, group, or couples therapy, the patient may gossip about the therapist in a negative way in order to place the therapist in a one-down position, and never speak directly to the therapist. In any kind of therapy, it is important for the patient to understand in the beginning phases that positive or negative feelings, thoughts, and ideas are food for the relationship and when discussed can deepen the entire clinical encounter.

When a patient idealizes the therapist, there is always a struggle for power accompanying that idealization. Power struggles in therapy make the therapist feel responsible for the patient's well-being. Once the therapist realizes that this is the case, he or she can help the patient focus on redefining his or her goals for therapy and the actions the patient may have to take to reach those goals. The remedy for idealization in the clinical setting is the creation of a cooperative form of relationship between the therapist and the patient. Cooperation means that both the therapist and the patient work together to learn to define problems, set goals, create boundaries, and take responsibility for their own behavior.

SUMMARY OF THE DEFENSES OF THE SELF

The defenses of the Self unconsciously form the pathological complex, creating a closed, unconscious and wordless system that is incompatible with ego consciousness. They are always activated to protect ego consciousness from experiences of annihilation when the pattern(s) of mediation of the archetypal/developmental process(es) create experiences of disintegration within ego consciousness. The operation of the defenses of the Self is normal and material that has been denied, split off, introjected, projected, identified with or idealized can be metabolized back into normal consciousness if caregivers notice what is happening to the child and adjust their mediation.

In cases of ongoing or severe misattunement between the child and the caregivers, the experiences of disintegration collect around the affective theme associated with the experiences and are stored in the unconscious by the defenses of the Self. The affective theme keeps operating and widens the range of experiences that are experienced as disintegrating, further stimulating the defenses of the Self. Eventually this material collects forming the pathological complex.

The way I have described the operation of the defenses of the Self is based upon my own working experience. It is not all-inclusive, rather it is meant to stimulate observations and questions in those clinicians reading this book. It is important for you the reader to observe the operation of the defenses of the Self within the clinical setting and refine your own observations as you develop your clinical experience.

When the defenses of the Self are operating within the clinical hour because a pathological complex has been stimulated, the relationship between the patient and the therapist is distorted, interfered with, or lost. This mutual and painful experience is a reflection of the unconscious enmeshment between the therapist's and the patient's complexes. At that time, the best techniques the therapist can use with the patient are mirroring back to the patient what he or she is saying, validating the patient's experience, containing (through mirroring, validation, and empathy) the patient's painful affect, and exploring each part of the patient's experience with him or her in order to better understand it. The therapist must contain his or her own need to react so that there is enough space for the patient to observe his or her experience and eventually begin developing the *observing ego*.

The most important tool the clinician has is the willingness and patience to explore the patient's experience of the pathological complex and to feel his or her way into that experience. By "feel" I mean more than a cognitive or sensual experience; I mean to experience as closely as possible what the patient experiences and be able to pull back and observe that experience from multiple viewing points. As the clinician aligns as closely as possible with the patient's experience and responds to it, the patient unconsciously responds by beginning to accept the contents of the pathological complex. When this occurs it is important for the therapist to continue confirming the patient's experience and at the same time stretch the range of attunement by switching viewing points into the pathological complex. This kind of attunement helps the patient expand his or her awareness.

Clinical Vignette: Example of Stretching Attunement and Adding Another Viewing Point

Patient: "I don't understand what is happening to me. I feel as if I am falling apart. How can you just sit there week after week and take money from me? I need real help like money and a job. My husband is gone with his pregnant, thirty-year-old secretary. I am 57 years old. My children are raised. I am alone in that big house. I supported him and helped him build a career. I have nothing left for myself. You have got to call him and make him come back. He won't listen to me."

Therapist (internal reflection): This woman is in strong denial and she is immobilized. She has not seen an attorney, she has not told her children what is going on, and she has told no one, including her husband, that she needs money. It seems as if she has lived her entire life as a caretaker. Now she is being forced to care for herself, and she doesn't know where to start. She chose me as a therapist because I am married, have children, and still am able to work and be independent. She is also very angry with me for the same reasons that she chose me as her therapist. Before she can take care of herself she has to identify what she needs and then ask for help.

Therapist (to patient): "I believe you when you say you are 'falling apart.' You are going through something that is terribly painful and you want the pain to stop."
Patient: "I want things back the way they were. I just can't stand the way they are."

Therapist (internal reflection): I cannot support her denial or her fantasy that he may come back.

Therapist (to patient): "He has told you that he is in love with another woman and wants to be with her. It is worse pain for you if you begin to believe that he will come back."
Patient: "He is not coming back. I know. I know he is not coming back. How can I live with the way things are? How could he do this to me?"
Therapist: "It is a really cruel thing to do, to break your life, choosing to live or choosing to let go. Will you let his cruelty destroy your life and your children's lives?"
Patient: "No I will not be destroyed or destroy myself. But how could he do this to me?"

Therapist (internal reflection): This is a vicious circle that we have walked around each of the eight times she has seen me. I would like to see whether or not she is ready to step off the circle and if she is willing to stretch.

Therapist (to patient): "The real question for me is, how are you going to decide to go on with your life? How do you want to make a new life and how can I help you create a new life?"
Patient: "I feel better. When I imagine him coming back and things going back the way they were, I feel awful. I know that cannot happen. He is not doing anything except living with his mistress instead of living at home. I keep waiting for him to serve me with papers, and I know he won't. He knows he is doing a cruel thing to me. When he doesn't do anything, I start to fantasize that he might come back. He is dead to me isn't he?"

Therapist (internal reflection): With every statement of the truth she seems to be more grounded and less anxious.

Therapist (*to patient*): "Yes, I think he is dead to you. Only this is worse than if he really died because he is alive and yet still dead to you. That is the pain, don't you think?"

Therapist (*internal reflection*): The patient's denial is beginning to dissolve and she appears to feel safe enough in the therapeutic container to begin to allow that process of death and loss to begin. I will wait to ask her about her anger with me until she begins to stop the circle of denial.

THE EVOKED COMPANION

Daniel Stern (1985) observed thousands of infants and noticed that memories are made up of patterns of experience that are preverbal, generalized episodes of what has happened. Generalized Even Structures or GERs are the basic building blocks of cognition and memory (97). Archetypes form human experience into patterns and I believe that the Generalized Event Structures that Stern and others observed replicate Jung's discovery of the archetypes. As Stern observed the formation of the Generalized Event Structures, he noticed that they were accompanied by patterns of interpersonal experiences, or averaged experiences of relationship, that he called Representations of Interactions that have been Generalized or RIGs (97). The RIGs are unconscious, preverbal patterns of interactions with others that provide a sense of *being with* another (97–99). The GERs form the core sense of self and the RIGs form the core sense of *other*.

Whenever a RIG is activated the infant experiences the evoked companion, a pattern of "experience of being with, or in the presence of, a self-regulating other" (Stern 1985, 111-112). "It is my belief that the evoked companion is linked with mediation of the archetypal/developmental processes. The evoked companion functions to evaluate specific ongoing interactive episodes . . . slowly updating RIGs by current experience" (Stern 1985, 112–113).

The *evoked companion* is a preconscious, psychosomatic *instructional image*,[6] based on the innate constitution of the child and the child's experience of caregivers as they mediate the archetypal/developmental processes. I believe that the evoked companion becomes the core sense of *other* and acts as a bridge between the core sense of self and the experience of the outer world.

Even if the infant is . . . alone, the infant is being with a self-regulating other . . . (in or out of awareness). . . ." (114). In the relationship between RIGS, ego consciousness and the evoked companion, the core sense of self and other is never breached (115). The relationship is felt as an I-experience with another . . . it differs from internalizations in that [it is] experienced as internal signals (symbolic cues) rather than as lived or reactivated experiences. . . . At some point in development there is no longer the necessity to retrieve the evoked companion and get a dose of the lived experience. The attribute alone serves as a cue that alters behavior, without a reliving of the generalized event. (Stern 1985, 115)

What happens to the *evoked companion* when the experiences of mediation produce repeated experiences of disintegration activating the defenses of the Self?

THE EVOKED COMPANION AND THE IMAGO

Jung first introduced the word *imago* in 1911–12 (*CW* 5, 1974, 44). He used the term to describe a preconscious and unconscious structure that contained patterns of experiences with the actual caregivers enmeshed with archetypal energy. Over time, he linked the imago with the complexes that he discovered during his experiments with the Word Association Test (*CW* 4, 1979, 133–138).

It is my belief that the imago is a numinous aspect of the evoked companion and develops from the patterns of mediation of the archetypal/developmental processes by the caretakers. The imago is a much more powerful structure than the evoked companion because it is also linked with the numinous energy of the archetypal/developmental processes and in cases of a repeated pathological complex it is also linked with the numinous archetypal energy of the defenses of the Self. Because the imago is composed of raw archetypal energy (*CW* 11, 1977, 259), it infuses the actual experiences of the caregivers with godlike qualities.

When the defenses of the Self operate, ego consciousness is also affected. Small portions of ego consciousness involved in repeated experiences of disintegration are denied and split off, forming a partial consciousness within a pathological complex. For example, the core sense of self of the Woman Who Once Walked in Balance receded until her consciousness was so limited it contained only the desire to kill the other and be killed by the other. Every other part of ego consciousness except raw affect was lost in the unconscious.

Sun, soil, heat, cold, wind, and rain are impersonal forces that may or may not provide the proper conditions for an acorn to become an oak. Very few acorns become oaks. Just so, the archetypal/developmental processes, the components of ego consciousness, the Self, the defenses of the Self, and the imago are impersonal forces of nature. They are neither good nor evil. Because an infant is dependent upon caregivers to mediate the raw, unconscious, impersonal energy of the archetypal/developmental processes, he or she has a much better chance of survival than an acorn. When mediation of the archetypal/developmental processes is fairly attuned,[7] the impersonal power of the archetypal energy is metabolized in a way that eventually fosters consolidation of ego consciousness, adaptation, maturation, and finally facilitates relations between the ego and the Self. Attuned mediation is not only dependent upon the caregivers; it depends on the innate constitution of the child and on the affective intensity and duration of the experiences of mediation of the archetypal/developmental processes during deintegration. When there are repeated experiences of disintegration during deintegration, the imago eventually replaces the Self, creating an ego/imago axis that blocks the individuation.

The evoked companion portion of the imago is like the tip of an iceberg–preconscious, yet not too difficult to remember. The unknown, unknowable, and numinous energy contained in the imago is far outside of consciousness and functions independently to grant both blessings and curses that support and/or threaten the survival of ego consciousness. It is *daimonic* and has the power to take over ego consciousness.[8] This daimon may love or hate; it may care about life or not, it can do whatever it wishes. The imago is intended by nature to be a transcendent power that is independent of human will or intention. The numinosity and authority of the imago functions to promote the survival of ego consciousness until it can become mature enough to metabolize and become conscious of the pathological complex.

It is natural for the parents to become imagoes and to be deified by unused archetypal/developmental energy. Part of parenting is restoring the archetypal energy embedded within the imago to an infant, toddler, or child little by little, over time. The parents can only return the deified energy if the child is ready to assimilate it. Effective mediation has taken place when the maturing child is connected to and trusts the inner authority of the Self and is able to move in alignment with his or her individuation process in spite of any external stimuli that might demand another kind of response.

The innate constitution of the infant, toddler, child, adolescent, or adult along with the experiences of mediation of the archetypal/developmental processes ideally form and reform an ego consciousness that has the capacity to contain and reflect upon experience, to act in service of individuation (spiritual development) to experience affect, to develop a sense of the meaning one's life (soul) to remember, to dream, and to recall the images from the collective unconscious that serve the individuation process of that particular individual.

When a pathological complex is formed, the I (core sense of self, ego consciousness) is diminished and the other (the imago) is inflated, creating an ego/imago axis that rigidifies and maintains the pathological complex. When the imago becomes the center of the entire personality, it acts like a power station, redirecting the flow of archetypal energy into channels that support the complex. Jung called this process *canalization of the libido* (*CW* 8, 1981, 41). This means that the imago transforms and converts the libido or psychic energy[9] into the rigidified patterns of experience that eventually become the pathological complex.

When a pathological complex is stimulated it unfolds, overwhelming ego consciousness and replacing reality with the experiences belonging to the complex. This process is directed by the imago.

It is important for clinicians to understand how much energy is bound up in a pathological complex, how unconscious the complex is, and how the complex inevitably limits the adaptation of ego consciousness. *A pathological complex has a pathological imago that limits and distorts the archetypal/developmental processes and individuation in order to preserve ego consciousness.*

The imago can censor the ability to be aware somatically, to imagine, to experience affect, to remember, to dream, to know, to find meaning in life or to act in service of individuation. In the story of the old Indian man, the imago impaired the relationship between consciousness and the potential for creativity. It appears as a structure in fairy tales in the form of the wicked stepparent. In 1946, Jung discussed the importance of the imago in therapeutic work.

> This operation [withdrawal of the projection of the parental imago from external reality] is one of the most difficult tasks of modern psychotherapy. At one time, it was optimistically assumed that the parental images could be more or less broken down and destroyed through an analysis of their content. Nevertheless, in reality that is not the case. Although the parental imagoes can be released from the state of projection and withdrawn from the external world, they continue, like everything else acquired in early childhood, to retain their original freshness. With the withdrawal of the projection, they fall back into the individual psyche, from which indeed they mainly originated. . . .[10] As we know, the parental imago is constituted on the one hand by the . . . acquired image of the personal parent, and on the other hand by the archetype . . . which exists a priori in the pre-conscious structure of the psyche. (*CW* 16, 1966, 96)

The imago wields the power of the Self because it is wielded by the defenses of the Self. It directs every movement of the particular affective drama connected with the pathological complex, creating life experiences that repeat themselves in never-ending emotional tragedies that experience life events like a gerbil on a treadmill, going nowhere.

As a patient in therapy gradually begins to observe his or her internal and external processes, the pathological complex and the imago begin to be exposed. This occurs in several ways: (1) through the patient's containment of his or her behavioral reactivity; (2) through dreams; (3) through the emergence of symbols from the unconscious; (4) through meaningful synchronistic coincidences that occur within the analytic/therapeutic hour and in the patient's everyday life, and (5) through all of the ways the patient and the therapist connect in the relational field. It is important that patients learn to observe those events that stimulate the pathological complex and their own individual experience when that event occurs. The story of the Woman Who Once Walked in Balance is really the story of what happens when a person is willing to confront that pattern through observation, learn from it, and then release it.

It is essential that as therapists we learn to endure our own and our patient's anguish, created not only by wounding but by the healing processes as well. It is terribly painful for consciousness and new life to enter the constricted spaces within us so that they can be recovered and reborn. In order to confront the mystery of a pathological complex, it is important to learn to *see into the mystery of the complex from multiple viewing points*. The aim of this book is to create and clarify multiple viewing points in order for therapists to observe the patterns that support individual pathological complexes. The viewing points into the pathological complex that have been presented so far have been the Self, the archetypal/developmental processes, the patterns of mediation of the archetypal/developmental processes, the defenses of the Self and the imago.

QUESTIONS

1. What did you learn from the story of The Woman Who Once Walked In Balance?
2. What is the Self?
3. What are the defenses of the Self?
4. How do they operate?
5. Think of one patient you are seeing presently in therapy who has a pathological complex. Name how the defenses of the Self operate in this particular patient's pathological complex.
6. What is an evoked companion?
7. How does the evoked companion operate in your life?

8. What is the imago?
9. Think of one patient who has been in therapy with you and has abruptly terminated the therapeutic process. Describe that patient's imago.

ENDNOTES

1. I wish to acknowledge the following authors for their contribution to my understanding of complexes: Toni Wolf, "On Complexes" (unpublished manuscript, 1912); Jolande Jacobi, *Complex, Archetype, Symbol* (1959); and Hans Dieckmann *Complexes: Diagnosis and Therapy in Analytical Psychology* (1999), translated by Boris Matthews.
2. Fordham (1996) identified three types of defenses in 1974. The first are called *ego defenses* and are linked to repressed contents of the unconscious that can be made conscious. These defenses are displacement, passivity, symbolization, compensation, conversion, and reaction formation. The second set of defenses that Fordham identified are linked with compulsion (obsessional) states. He called them *isolation* and *undoing* and defined them as defenses that prevented containment and reflection on conscious affect. The third set of defenses, the defenses of the Self, are unconscious, primitive defenses against a bad object and can reach a level of annihilation (139–140). For clinical purposes the two categories of ego defenses are indistinguishable.
3. Elisabeth Kubler Ross would call this a "little death" (personal communication, 1979). Examples are events like the death of a child or a loved one, loss of a significant relationship, divorce, trauma, retirement, sudden severe or chronic illness, and being fired. The person has not actually died, yet the ego has experienced a loss that is significant enough to be experienced as a kind of annihilation. Little deaths are often experienced before a person enters therapy.
4. Rene Spitz (1945) developed the idea that babies in the hospital developed depression because they had no nurturing contact from a consistent caregiver (53–74). In 1962, Mary Ainsworth supported and clarified Spitz's findings. She divided the concept of "maternal deprivation" into three categories: lack of maternal care, distortion of maternal care, and discontinuity in maternal care; and she "did a better job of defending Spitz than he had done himself (Karen 1998, 123–124).
5. My thanks to Richard Erskine Ph.D. for demonstrating methods of working with introjects and attuning to them in order to defuse the potential for wounding and misunderstanding.
6. Peter Mudd developed this term in 1990 as we discussed the evoked companion.
7. Other theorists, such as D. W. Winnicott and Bruno Bettelheim, have come to the same conclusions about "good enough" parenting.
8. The word *daimonic* does not mean demon. It is a term developed by classical scholars such as Homer, Hesiod, and Plato as a synonym for a god or the personification of a god. "The daimon was the spiritual power that determined one's destiny . . . and manifested as a sort of [fate] that spurred one on toward good or evil" (Diamond, *Anger, Madness and the Daimonic*, 1996).

9. Jung used the words *libido* and *energy* interchangeably (*CW* 6, 1977, 456) and did not confine the terms to sexual energy but considered libido as a form of life energy that is neutral in character (Samuels 1986, 53–54).
10. As the projections of the imago are gradually withdrawn from the external world and fall back into the individual psyche, the archetypes of the collective unconscious become activated and begin appearing in dream images, waking visions, and active imagination to promote and support the individuation process. Jung discusses this concept when he describes regression of the psyche to the prenatal phase, where the imago does not yet exist (*CW* 5, 1974, 181).

Chapter 3

MORE VIEWING POINTS INTO THE PATHOLOGICAL COMPLEX

A pathological complex is much more powerful than ego consciousness and cannot be confronted directly in therapy. However, every complex is made up of parts. These parts emerge spontaneously during the clinical hour. When they are identified, they can be attended to and made conscious, weakening the entire structure of the pathological complex. These small movements toward consciousness allow the patient to develop enough conscious space to begin to interrupt, contain, and observe the patterns of reactivity associated with the complex. This chapter will focus on the components of ego consciousness, the layered view of the psyche, and the cycles of nature.

Daniel Stern (1985) observed thousands of infants, and as he watched them develop, he noticed four "invariant forms" that gradually organized experience into a core sense of self. He named these invariant forms self-affectivity, self-history, self-coherence, and self-agency (76–77). When Stern uses the term invariant forms, he is talking about basic structures that undergird the ego consciousness of all humans. Jung used the word *archetypes*, which has the same meaning as "invariant forms." Archetypes are irrepresentable, bio-psycho-social invariant forms that structure human experience and perception into patterns of experience. The terms are different, but the meanings are quite similar.

I will attempt to integrate the theories of both men in the following pages in order to develop the idea that the components of ego consciousness (personality and core sense of self) can become diagnostic indicators for pathological complexes.

THE FOUNDATIONS OF EGO CONSCIOUSNESS

I am going to replace Stern's words with the words *memory* (self-history), *sensation* (self coherence), *affect* (self-affectivity), and *behavior* (self-agency) in order to simplify the description of the foundations of ego consciousness. My own terminology appears in bold print below and in Figure 6.

self-history
memory

self-coherence
body

Ego
Consciousness

self-agency
behavior

self-affectivity
affect

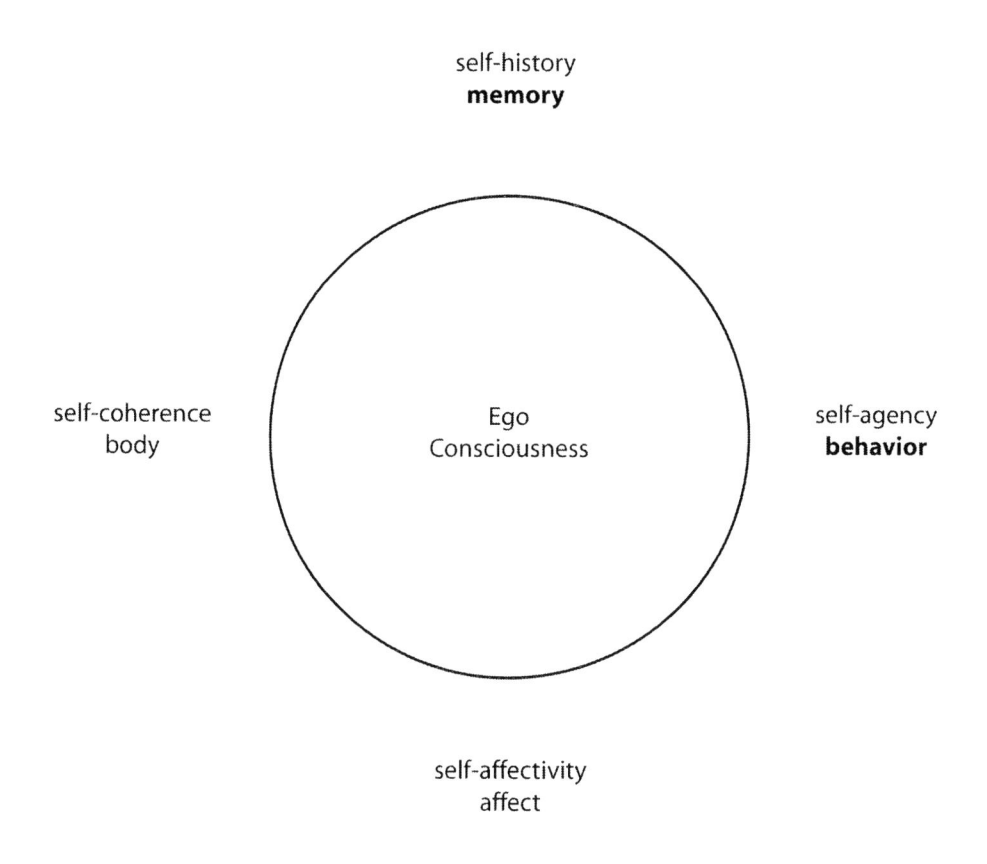

FIGURE 6
The four Physical aspects of ego consciousness.

1. **Behavior** is an action authored by an individual (Stern 1985, 76) and can be broken down into three components: a sense of will or intention that precedes an act, sensual data that occurs during the act, and the consequences that follow an act. Volition, the presence of sensual data, and consequences following an action are directly related to human behavior, according to Stern (76–82).

2. **Body** is the sense and sensation of being a physical entity that has boundaries. Stern discusses several experiential factors that establish a sense of being embodied: a sense of being in a place, the cohesive experience of motion, temporal structure, intensity, and (physical) form (82–89).

3. **Affect** is the capacity to recognize a characteristic constellation of emotional experiences. The experience of affect is composed of sensations from particular muscles, especially those connected with the face, the vocal apparatus, and breathing (89–90).[1]

4. **Memory** is the sense of continuity of experience. Continuity of experience has three sources: motor memory, physical sensations, and affective experience (90–94).

Unless there is some sort of genetic impairment, each human being has an ego composed by the same archetypal structures; body, memory, affect, and behavior. These structures attract experience and as more and more experiences accumulate around them, an individual ego consciousness begins to develop. These same components are also present in pathological complexes because of the activity of the defenses of the Self.

The structures that undergird ego consciousness are not individual they are archetypal, or universally human and all consciousness forms around them. These structures are given. However, the development of an individual ego consciousness is dependent upon the genetic heritage; the action of the archetypal/developmental processes; the experiences acquired during integration, deintegration, reintegration, and disintegration; and the quality of mediation of the archetypal/developmental processes. Life experience creates an individual ego consciousness. Healthy ego consciousness is quite flexible and is capable both of growth in awareness and of regression to early experiences of development in service of play and parenting.

When there are repeated experiences of disintegration during mediation of the archetypal/developmental processes, the defenses of the Self are activated and the components of ego consciousness are affected. What is affected and how it is affected depends upon the enormous amount of variables involved. However, when denial and splitting operate repeatedly, portions of the components of ego consciousness involved in the disintegration are also denied and split off ending up in the unconscious complex giving the complex qualities of a partial, primitive personality.

This statement raises a number of questions that are very difficult to answer: (1) What components of ego consciousness are more likely to be affected by the defenses of the Self? (2) How do the components of ego consciousness function in a healthy ego consciousness and how do they function when they are located in a pathological complex? (3) How can the components of ego consciousness be used to diagnose a pathological complex?

ARCHETYPAL STRUCTURES OF EGO CONSCIOUSNESS

The four components of ego consciousness: body, memory, affect, and behavior are archetypes. All archetypes have a psychoid structure and are connected with both biological and psychological experience at the same time (*CW* 8, 1946; 1981, 215–16). This bipolar structure is similar to the structure of light, a bipolar phenomenon that can be perceived either as a particle or a wave and is really both (Capra 1991).

Jung described the archetypes as having two poles, one pole linked with the physical body and one pole linked with the psychic or subtle body. Figure 7 separates the four archetypal components of ego consciousness into their bipolar aspects, the "Infrared" or physical body pole and the "Ultraviolet" or subtle body pole. Affect, body, memory, and behavior constitute the *physical* body because each of these components can be measured in some way. It is not possible to measure the components of the *subtle* body. However, they are present in the history of human literature, art, ritual, and belief. They are also present in the clinical hour and in pathological complexes. Figure 7 shows four components of ego consciousness with eight aspects.

The **physical body** is linked with the **dreaming body**. The moment-to-moment awareness of ongoing physiological processes in both the physical and dreaming bodies are unknown. Modern science understands very little about the balance of the body's ecology, how mental and physical health is related, or the purposes and the effects of dreaming upon physical and mental health. In this sense, body in both the physical and the dreaming senses is relatively unknown.

Memory is directly related to the **collective human memory** or, as Jung called it, the "collective unconscious." Individual memory gives a person a sense of the continuity of experience and is known in the sense that it can be measured. The collective unconscious is the memory of the human race. This memory appears in dreams and fantasies as images and symbols of human experience that can be located in myths, fairy tales, and cultural and religious beliefs across history.

Affect and **soul** are deeply related. Affect is or can be made conscious, and when affect is contained and reflected on, it is metabolized into soul. Soul is that aspect of human experience that distills meaning from affective experience.

Behavior is directly related to **spirit**. Behavior is an individual act. The effects of any human action on the bio-psycho-social system are unknowable. When human actions are in harmony with the individuation process, the ego/Self axis is operating and spirit is developing. Spirit is the unknowable

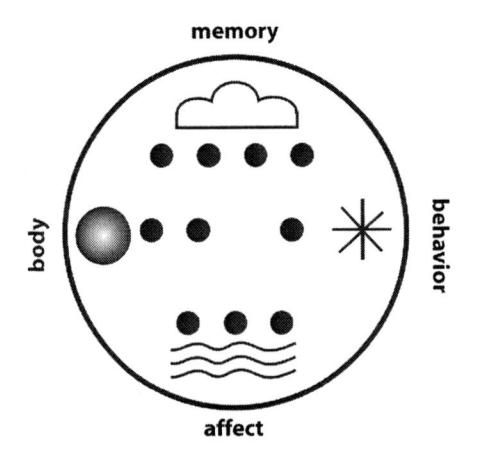

'INFA-RED POLE'

The Physical components of ego consciousness.
The vibrational elements of the Physical Pole are visible to the naked eye.

The experience of the Physical Body at any given moment in time is largely UNKNOWN in terms of current, ongoing physiological processes.

The effects of any behavior and the ramifications of that behavior when considered within a bio-psycho-social system are UNKNOWABLE.

Affect and memory are known in the sense that they may be made conscious.

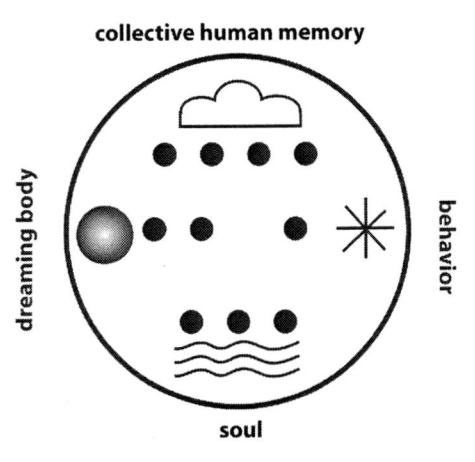

'ULTRA-VIOLET POLE'

The Subtle Body components of ego consciousness.

The vibrational elements are invisible to the naked eye. The Subtle Body is a perceptive conglomerate as the body when we dream.

The experience of the body in dreaming and its linkage to current, ongoing physiological processes is UNKNOWN. Rapid eye movement can be observed, brain waves can be measured, but the how or why of the dreaming body remains a mystery.

The effects of the movement of the individual spirit and the ramifications of that movement are UNKNOWABLE.

FIGURE 7
Summary of the Archetypal compomemts of ego consciousness.

"higher power" that lives within each one of us. The word *spirit* is synonymous with the Self.

When caretakers mediate the archetypal/developmental processes during deintegration, that mediation affects both the physical and subtle bodies of ego consciousness. When there are repeated experiences of disintegration that stimulate the defenses of the Self, small portions of ego consciousness involved in those experiences are denied and split off becoming part of the pathological complex. As material accumulates in the pathological complex, these small bits of ego consciousness attract more and more experience eventually creating what Jung called the "splinter personality" of the complex.

This "splinter personality" is not at all like the separate identities that are present in dissociative identity disorder. In dissociative identity disorder, different identities with distinct personal histories and self-images appear as two or more distinct identities that recurrently take control of behavior and are accompanied by an inability to recall important personal information (DSM-IV, 526–527). The "partial or splinter personalities" that are part of a pathological complex are not distinct identities with distinct histories. They are primitive, "partial personalities" and can be observed when the patient unconsciously communicates experiences that contain only parts of experiences or opinions that conflict with one another.

Clinical Vignette: The Splinter Personality of the Complex

Patient: "I feel like I am falling apart. I am so upset. I am all feelings and anxiety. Why am I feeling like this? Why won't it just go away? I want it to go away."

Therapist (internal observation): The patient is presenting parts of experience. There is one part of the patient describing the experience, another part being described as the experience of falling apart, and a third part judging the experience and trying to make it go away.

Therapist: "Can you say a little more about what this is like for you?"
Patient: "I feel like I am being shaken apart. I don't know why this is happening. I don't know if I can go to work this way. I feel nauseous and like something terrible is going to happen, like I am stuck back on those nightmare train tracks and I can't get away. Why is this happening? I quit work and started a new company. I am successful. Why is this happening now?"

Therapist (internal observations): His complex is constellated and he is all the parts associated with it as well as the affective theme. He can feel the affect (a partial personality), while another part of him is observing his experience of the affect and another part does not want him to experience the affect. This is the first time he has ever come in to therapy with uncontained high anxiety, nausea, and the sense of immanent danger. We have discussed his childhood train nightmare often. He has developed a frame of reference so that he is aware when he reacts by "slipping away" from a perceived authority. This is the first time he has experienced the affect hidden beneath his reactive behavior. He is overwhelmed. His "slipping away behavior" acted as a container to prevent him from feeling the affect associated with the pathological complex. He has stopped reacting. When he was overwhelmed and anxious he did not receive the containing mediation he needed, which is how the complex formed. The part of him that is saying, "I want it to go away" may be the way he was treated by caregivers when he was overwhelmed and anxious.

Therapist (to patient): "Yes, I see that you are really anxious and upset. It looks as if you are barely breathing (confirming mediation). Let's breathe together to begin to give you a sense of control over your anxiety" (directive, cooperative, and containing mediation).

Therapist (internal observations): Deep breathing will slow the experience of anxiety and give him a sense of control so that he can develop a frame of reference for the affect and begin to learn to accept and work with it. While he is learning to repeatedly experience the affect he will gradually develop containment as he and I move into different ways of exploring his experience of the affect.

As therapists we are taught to focus on the physical aspects of ego consciousness. Dreaming, experiences of the collective unconscious, soul, and spirit are largely ignored in the literature and in research. The idea of a subtle body is split off from mainstream psychology in two ways: (1) experiences of the subtle body are thought to be strange, taboo, mystical or an indication of pathology, and (2) they are considered to be part of a religious experience, and people who have these experiences are referred to religious experts who may or may not have an understanding of psychology or have had clinical training. However, the "splinter personality" of the complex often contains aspects of the subtle body aspects of ego consciousness as well as physical aspects.

Clinical Vignette: An Encounter with the Collective Unconscious

Patient: "When I was little I was always frightened. Sometimes I felt spirits around me talking to me and comforting me. I talked to them. Once my father heard me talking to them and told me to stop it. He said I was going to go crazy and he hit me in the back of the head really hard while he called me "stupid" and "crazy" over and over. I got scared of the spirits and ignored them. I feel really scared of going crazy just like my mother. Am I going crazy?"

[The patient's mother was an untreated schizophrenic with paranoid ideation. The patient was encouraged to educate herself about mental illness and eventually forced her family to hospitalize her mother and have her placed on medication. At the time the patient discussed having visions of spirits her mother had been hospitalized and was doing well on medication.]

Therapist (internal observation): This woman has been in therapy for a year. She has common sense, holds down a full time job, and has friends and a good marriage. She came into therapy because she was having strong dreams that she wanted to discuss. She has a history of post-traumatic stress disorder and has difficulty asserting herself. I believe her when she says she "saw spirits" as a child, and I think she is asking me to confirm her experience.

Therapist (to patient): "What is crazy about seeing spirits?"
Patient: "You mean you don't think seeing spirits is crazy?"
Therapist: "No. I don't. Do you?"
Patient: "Sometimes they come around my bed at night and I just lie there with my eyes squeezed shut and shake. I don't know what to do."
Therapist: "Can you say a little more about not knowing what to do?"
Patient: "I want to open my eyes and look, and I am terrified if I do I will be a schizophrenic like my mother. She hears voices when she is really sick. Then she can't eat because she is so agitated she can't do anything."
Therapist: "Part of you is terrified. Part of you is afraid to open her eyes. A third part of you is labeling your experience as crazy. How afraid are you right now?"
Patient: "Yes, I am at about an eight with ten as the highest."
Therapist: "A level eight of fear is really high for you. What is going on in your body as you really feel the fear?"
Patient: "My chest is really tight. My head feels muddy, and my back hurts where my father used to hit me when he called me crazy."
Therapist: "Can you draw that?"

The patient draws her physical experience of fear with colored markers. As the patient repeatedly experiences her fear in the clinical hour and then draws it to make it visible, she is creating a container for her fear. Eventually she would be able to open her eyes and look at the spirits who visited her and finally begin a dialogue with them. Her daily life, her marriage, her work, and her friendships remained the same. As the dialogue continued over time, her frame of reference and her sense of meaning began to change. The spirits also seemed to change as they led her through the devastation and despair of childhood physical abuse. They led her into places of death and transformation, and they led her into a new career that had more meaning for her. Her relationships deepened. The spirits were powerful images from the collective unconscious that wanted to speak with this woman. The therapeutic process took four years and deeply affected both the patient and the therapist.

Ego consciousness does not mean self-importance, bullying oneself or others, greed, lust, laziness, anger, cruelty, ignoring responsibilities, manipulating others to fulfill one's basic needs, or lying to oneself or others. In spiritual disciplines, these qualities are attached to the word *ego*, and then ego is made into something to transcend or destroy. This kind of mislabeling is confusing and serves to maintain the split between treating the physical body aspects of ego consciousness and the subtle body aspects of ego consciousness.

The subtle body aspect of ego consciousness is that part of a human being that remembers dreams and allows images of the collective unconscious to emerge in order to dialogue with them, allows affect to deepen precious life experience into meaning, and bows to the will of the "higher power" (the Self) within. By many therapeutic standards, the "old Indian man" was doing well because he was in recovery from his alcoholism. However, his recovery was only the first step in his process of individuation. Without his recovery his nightmares and his vision would not have happened. They had a prospective function that totally changed the way he viewed the world and lived within it. Without his nightmares and his visions he would not have become who he was.

COMPLEXES AND ASPECTS OF EGO CONSCIOUSNESS

When a patient is operating out of a pathological complex, one or more of the aspects of ego consciousness are affected. How might this appear in a clinical hour?

A middle-aged man enters analysis/therapy. He is wealthy, successful, happily married, and his children are becoming wonderful human beings.

He has everything he thinks can make him happy. He is physically healthy, assertive in a gentle way, and intelligent. However, he is depressed, lonely, and on the verge of an affair with a woman his daughter's age.

He has no memories of childhood until playing baseball in third grade. His affective tone is one of sadness mixed with fear. He believes that something is terribly wrong with him because he finds no pleasure in anything and feels very isolated. He finds church boring and says "life has no meaning for him." He describes himself as being very unemotional, and although he really doesn't care about the impact of his behavior upon other people, he is ethical both at home and in his business. He does not remember his dreams. However, he does remember one terrible recurring childhood nightmare. In the dream, something slipped out from a tiny crack in the bedroom floor and oozed toward him. He always awakened from the nightmare with feelings of the terror of being smothered, mixed with disgust at the ooze trying to smother him. He cannot remember how old he was when the nightmare started, what was going on in his world, or how many years he had the nightmare.

This man seems to be missing a connection to his early memories and to the collective unconscious. His affect appears to be frozen, and he has no connection with any sort of meaning in his life (soul). Although he is physically healthy, he is aware that he feels "constricted and tight" in certain parts of his body. The individuation process appears to be depressed, and the process of compensation that balances the one-sided attitudes of ego consciousness does not appear to be operating. He is suffering from dysthymia, a longstanding, low-level depression (APA 2000, 376–81), and because portions of the components of ego consciousness are unavailable to consciousness, the pathological complex reinforces the ongoing pattern of depression.

The information about this patient identifies problem areas in some of the aspects of ego consciousness. However, in order for this information to become more useful clinically, we need to know more about the eight aspects of ego consciousness and how they function.

THE MEDICINE WHEEL

I discovered this information in a most unlikely place, an ancient Native American Medicine Wheel that has an oral tradition of more than 5000 years and was first written down by Hyemeyhosts Storm (1994). Figure 8 is one version of the Medicine Wheel. It has four directions, each linked with one of the four components of ego consciousness: affect/soul, memory/collective human memory, physical body/dreaming body, and behavior/spirit. When

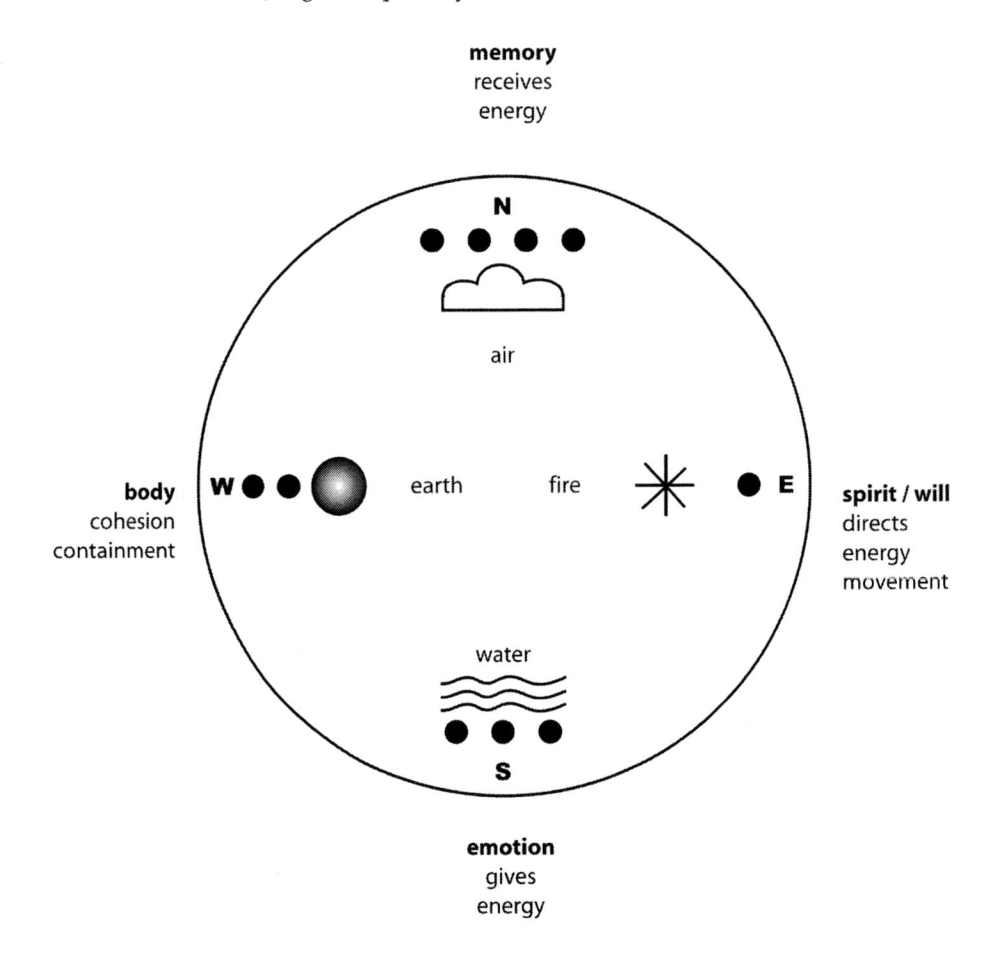

FIGURE 8
The Medicine Wheel with the four directions, the four elements of nature and the four aspects of ego consciousness.

the information contained in the Medicine Wheel is integrated with the four archetypal components of ego consciousness, a diagnostic template is created that provides another viewing point into the operation of a pathological complex.

The ancient culture that developed the Medicine Wheel used the circle to indicate the dynamic movement of life and nature. The particular wheel that I am using is called the "Four Powers of the Human Self" (Storm 1994, 202) or the "Powers of the Four Directions" (Loomis, 1991, 5). Figure 8 is a circle with four directions: south, west, north, and east. Each direction is linked with one of the four powers of the self: the giving of energy, the containment of energy, the receiving of energy, and directing the movement of energy.

The center of this wheel is empty to indicate the void, or the womb of nature that holds endless possibilities for growth and evolution. The wheel identifies parts of the archetypal components of ego consciousness as "powers of the human self" and describes their function and also the element of nature with which each function is linked. Emotion or affect/soul's function is to give energy. The physical and dreaming bodies provide containment and cohesion. When memory and the collective human memory are functioning correctly, energy is received. When spirit and behavior are functioning correctly, the life energy is directed toward growth, development, and individuation.

The patient described above had no connection with either his affect or his soul. They were not giving him energy, so he was depressed and found no meaning in life. His physical body was strong, which gave him a sense of cohesiveness and containment, but his childhood nightmare about being smothered and feeling both terrified and disgusted indicates that he may have difficulty experiencing and containing his experience. He had no memories before third grade, and he never had an experience of the collective unconscious. This indicates that he may have difficulty being receptive. His depression is a symptom of blockages in the function of some of the aspects of ego consciousness, which indicates the presence of a pathological complex. He is on the verge of having an affair because he wants to find relief from his ongoing depression.

Each direction described in Figure 8 is one viewing point into two of the aspects of ego consciousness. And although it is very ancient, the wheel is quite sophisticated and very subtle.[2] It demonstrates that everything within nature, including the components of ego consciousness is in relationship with everything else on the wheel. No one direction can exist by itself because each direction is balanced by every other direction.

For the ancients who developed the Medicine Wheel, life was a school, a place of training to develop and increase energy in alignment with the four directions presented on the Medicine Wheel (individuation). Sacred law was very simple: honor the woman, for all life comes from her, and do nothing to harm the children. These ancient laws focused on developing the consciousness and life energy of each infant, toddler, child, adolescent, and person. They were very practical. If a woman was respected, nourished, and allowed to develop; if the sexual act between a man and a woman was performed with respect, mutual pleasure and delight; if the woman was supported and helped with the bearing and raising of children, the children (both male and female) automatically carried a high level of energy and were able to maintain it. No one person or two persons could adequately birth and care for a child; the work was too demanding. What was important was the level of awareness and development of those raising the child. It was important that these caretakers be filled with trust and innocence, have the ability to contain their experience and learn from it, possess wisdom and knowledge, and be on the path of illumination and enlightenment in order to nourish the life of the child.

Unfortunately, the world we live in is not that way. The overvaluation of the nuclear family, along with the splitting of the extended family through divorce and relatives moving away, the energy expended in the necessity for continual focus on earning money, relatives moving away from the family, and the prejudice against those who might have become the elders has replaced the concept of a community of people who are invested in the development and maturation of a child.

Figure 9 shows the eight archetypal aspects of ego consciousness linked with the parts of nature they are related to: water with affect/soul, earth with body/dreaming body, air with memory/the collective unconscious, and fire with behavior/spirit. The ancients who developed the Medicine Wheel believed that human beings are the caretakers of all creation and that we are directly linked with the four basic elements of nature.

Affect: Soul: Water

Water gives energy to nature. It flows. It is constantly changing. Affect and soul are like water. They are the water of life that gives energy to nourish the growth of awareness, deepening it into a sense of meaning, carving the individual beauty out of life being lived fully. When we learn to allow ourselves to be moved by the waters of our emotions, they flow, passing quickly, shifting and changing all the while. This is easy to observe in healthy infants and toddlers who are filled with trust and innocence. The experience of an affect such as sadness, anger, fear, or enjoyment has a level of intensity and a duration that begins and ends briefly.

The flow of affect can be blocked when affects are wound together and locked into the *repetitive affective themes* associated with pathological complexes. An affective theme is a combination of affect entwined with other affects. These themes are locked together into repetitive levels of intensity and duration that can move from simple numbing to high levels of anguish that can be as short as several hours or last for days, months or years. When affect is flowing like water, the experience lasts for a short time and the experiences that accompany it deepen, becoming shaded with meaning.

The affective themes associated with the pathological complex give energy to the complex, continually attracting new material and increasing its size

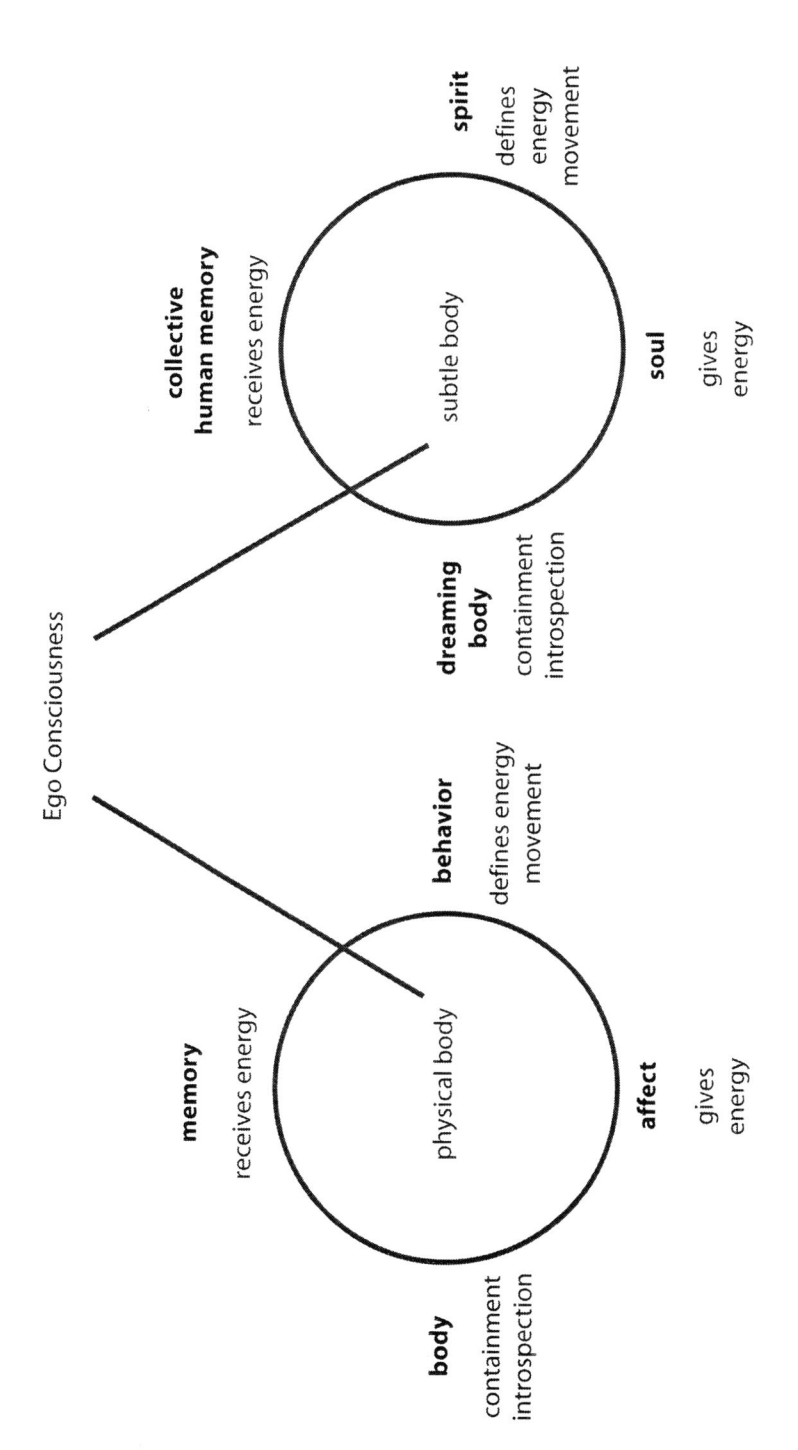

More Viewing Points Into The Pathological Complex 89

FIGURE 9
The eight archetypal aspects of ego consciousness.

and scope. As the material contained within the pathological complex increases, there is less and less affective energy available for the growth and development of ego consciousness.

Traditional Chinese medicine teaches that there are seven affective themes that create disturbances in the flow of life energy when they continue to operate over long periods of time. The physical and subtle bodies become imbalanced, creating both physical illness and mental disorders (Veith 1972). Chinese Medicine is another ancient framework that is based on the idea of human health and the way human energy appears when the physical and subtle bodies are functioning well. The Chinese believe that illness occurs because of blockages in the circulation of life energy due to emotions held in the body and that herbs, acupuncture, and massage of energetic points in the body gradually reduce these blockages, allowing both the physical and subtle bodies to gradually return to a state of balance or health. This concept appears in Buddhist, Taoist, Hindu, Native American, and Confucian traditions and supports the idea that blockages of affect interfere with human health and development.

The "seven emotions" of Chinese medicine are quite similar to seven of the nine innate affects described by Silvan Tomkins (1981).[3]

1. *Startle-Surprise* is indicated by overexcitability, impatience, and irritability and affects the heart and small intestine. Developing a sense of internal silence through meditation, cultivating patience, and being careful of becoming overstimulated creates balance when this affective system is operating.

2. *Sadness-Grief* is indicated by guilt and a sense of deep regret, affecting the lungs and large intestine. Courage and endurance create balance.

3. *Joy-Enjoyment* is indicated by excessive joy and hypomania, which tires and depletes physical energy. Exhaustion creates mistrust, frustration, and resentment. All of these experiences affect the heart and small intestine. Emotional balance involves developing a sense of contained pleasure in what is going on in the here and now.

4. *Fear-terror* is indicated by hate, spite, malice, and holding grudges. It affects the kidneys and the bladder. To create emotional balance, face fear, and relax through it into calmness.

5. *Interest-Excitement* is indicated by excessive concentration, anxiety, worry, and weariness. It affects the spleen, pancreas, and stomach. To create emotional balance, one must develop empathy and the ability to perceive things from more than one viewpoint.

6. *Anger-Rage* is indicated by physical and mental agitation, constriction, vexation, feelings of frustration, and helplessness. This affects the liver and gall bladder. In order to develop balance, we must nourish ourselves, be kind to others, and not give more than we are able.

7. Shame–Humiliation is indicated by anger and rage toward oneself and/or others because of deep wounding and inner sorrow produced by painful events that have happened that are outside a person's control. Shame/humiliation affects every organ system in the body. It is the most toxic of all of the affects and may cause death of one or more of the components of ego consciousness, death of one or more of the archetypal/developmental processes that foster human development, and may be the affective basis for those who murder and torture others.

These gradations of affect confirm the work of Silvan Tomkins (1981) and can be identified when some of them appear as different strands bound together into the unique affective theme of the pathological complex.

In Asian medicine, it is believed that emotional balance can be regained slowly by using herbs, acupuncture, and physical movements such as Qi Gong, Yoga, and Tai Ji. These special movements are supposed to be performed slowly, as if one were moving in water, and are used along with special ways of breathing that release impurities and blockages through the skin and the respiratory, digestive, and urinary systems. In a very broad sense, Asian medicine develops the physical body as a container that assists in the transformation of affective themes. In Western psychotherapy, the relational field is the container for "work" of dissolving affective themes in order to allow the emotions to flow.

The affective intensity that holds a pathological complex together is reinforced by the defenses of the self. Painful patterns of mediation are unconsciously introjected along with the painful affective theme associated with them, so that when the complex is constellated the patient re-experiences the misattuned and painful mediation associated with the generation of the pathological affective theme. The intensity of the affective theme of a pathological complex depends on the innate constitution of the child; the intensity of the experiences of attunement during parental mediation of each of the archetypal/developmental processes; the intensity and duration of the affects that form the affective theme of the complex; cultural rules and laws about emotional expression; and the example of the caretakers and their own pathological complexes.

Affective themes are made up of many strands of affect wound together in a unique pattern. When patients begin to feel safe and contained within the clinical hour, some of these strands begin to unwind and the patient begins to experience parts of the affect connected with the affective theme. When this occurs the patient may feel overwhelmed, disoriented, anxious, and/or frightened. It is important for the therapist to communicate to the patient that this is part of the healing process and that the therapeutic "work" the patient is befriending and containing the emerging affect.

What is important to understand is that the level of intensity of emerging strands of affect coupled with the incapacity to contain and observe them is part of a normal ongoing healing process. The greater the intensity of affect and the more unmanageable it feels to the patient, the more responsible the patient becomes to learn to work with the affect. The therapist's work is to attune to the patient and provide an ongoing *safe enough* container for the "work." If he or she is trained, the therapist can assist the patient to express affect through the use of bodywork,[4] sand play, drawing, painting, journaling, moving to music, expressing the affect in poetry or assisting the patient to create an image of the affect and beginning a dialogue with it. Some of the techniques for learning how to do this "work" are discussed in Chapter 6.

Clinical Vignette: Affect

Patient: "This is too much pain. Everything I thought was real about my life is a lie. I am unloved and unwanted from before I was born. My skin hurts. I want to stop existing. That is better than burning with pain."
Therapist to patient: "Terrible pain."

Therapist (internal observation): He has always moved away from this place into activity. I think it is important we be in this place together in silence. If we can hold the experience for just a little bit. If he can just hold for a minute it will be easier for him next time. I am scared. Is this too hard for him? Am I bringing more hurt to him?

Patient: "I don't have words."
Therapist: "It is good to just be without words."

Silence.

Patient: "I want to do something, anything to make it go away."
Therapist: "Be with the pain and trust it. You are birthing yourself the way your wife birthed your son."
Patient: "It is too much all at once, too much."
Therapist: "I believe you. What is the color, what are the shapes of your pain?"
Patient: "My skin is burning, and someone is scraping my skin off over and over. I am a black hole of pain, a black hole, a nothing."

Therapist (internal observation): I want to protect him and take all this away. I feel nauseated. I had better begin to deep breathe.

Therapist (to patient): "Take my hand and listen to me breathing in and out. Let yourself drop into the hole that's there beneath your skin."
Patient takes my hand and begins deep breathin): "It's black and whirling and the backdraft sound is following us. I have to breathe myself back here and feel my feet on the ground and your hand in my hand." *Patient deep breathes for several minutes then opens his eyes.* "I am here now."
Therapist, still holding patient's hand: "I see you. You are here."
Patient: "Something happened. I have no words."
Therapist: "Someday the words will come, just not today." *The therapist lets go of the patient's hand)*
Patient: "I can breathe and I feel like there is cool on my skin and I went through a door, but that's all I know."

The patient spends the rest of the hour between silence and describing his experiences to the therapist. The therapist listens carefully and confirms his experience.

The relational field—the regularity of visits; the rituals such as time, space, and fee; and the ongoing commitment to the analytic/therapeutic work by both the patient and the therapist—create a safe container to hold the emerging affective strands of the complex as they begin to unravel and affect begins to flow. When affect is allowed to flow from moment to moment, the world becomes four dimensional because it is filled with meaning, as in the following example.

Clinical Vignette: Soul

Patient: "I came back to see you because I got depressed again this fall. I have everything to be happy about. I simply can't believe that I feel down. Really it's only a part of me that is down, the rest of me is happy with my life. I have done all the things I do when I get depressed and nothing has relieved it. I thought I would come back in case it gets worse."

[The patient gives the therapist a history of her life since the last time they met four years ago. Her predominant symptom is stomach pain. She has had a thorough physical examination by her primary care physician. The patient believes the physical pain has to do with something she has to let go of. She does not know what that is.]

Patient: "I know it's something from my childhood in Europe, something I have to let go of. I just don't know what that is."
Therapist: "Let's go back together. Tell me whatever comes to your mind and make the images so clear I can see them too."

[The patient and the therapist spend about half the hour reviewing the patient's memories and the images associated with them. Finally this image comes to the patient.]

Patient: "I lived in my grandmother's small village on the weekends and with my mother in the city during the week. I think I will talk about my grandmother. Her village was one of the oldest in our country. It was walled in and every hour all day and all night the watch blew the horn to tell the village it was safe from attack. My grandmother was very old. She taught me to knit, crochet, and tat. She told me stories of olden times in her village, and I loved her and I loved the stories. Then one day my grandma got sick. Her breathing was really loud. They sent me to the other room. A woman came and put her mouth over my grandma's mouth. She didn't know I saw her. My grandma died and she killed her. I should have stopped her."

The patient talked about how guilty she felt for not helping her grandmother. She never told anyone about what she had seen. We discussed the event and I asked the patient to do some research on what had happened. I thought that the woman who put her mouth over the grandmother's mouth was a midwife who took the last breaths of the dying person into her body in order to transmit the soul back to the womb of the goddess. The woman checked with her mother and the village midwife did perform this function, though the reason why this was done was not known. The patient's stomach pain stopped after she shared her story.

The Physical and the Dreaming Bodies: The Earth

The physical and dreaming bodies are like the earth, holding us together making us both flexible and strong. Just like stones hold the heat of the sun and the cold of the ice, the physical and dreaming bodies contain our experience so that we can reflect on it and learn from it. Looking within and reflecting on experience takes time, just as the movement of the earth creates time. As the physical and dreaming bodies contain experience, time and space are created for being, doing, thinking, identity, and creativity. Containment and time for introspection foster the evolution of awareness both within nature and within ego consciousness.

According to traditional Chinese medicine, the physical body is composed of an invisible substance called *qi* (pronounced chee), which circulates throughout the body in channels and meridians that are similar to the body's circulatory system and the flow of blood. When the flow of blood or *qi* is blocked, the result is physical and/or mental illness. Several ancient traditions (including the Druid and Cheyenne Native American) teach that the earth has an energetic circulatory system like *qi*, with points of power above the ground that are connected with the moon, the sun, and certain constellations. There are channels and meridians throughout the earth that function just like the channels and meridians within the human body. The points of power above the earth are sacred places of containment for the earth's own awareness,[5] just as the chakras[6] of the human body are thought to influence human development.

When the physical and subtle bodies are balanced, a person is able to contain his or her experience and reflect on it. Without containment and introspection we cannot learn; we can only react to situations as they occur. The development of ego consciousness and its maturation is dependent on our ability to contain and reflect rather than react. Nurturing the physical body through exercise, proper diet, resting, and taking care of our material existence, and, at the same time, nourishing our subtle body by paying attention to our dreams and fantasies fosters cohesiveness, understanding, and the evolution of consciousness.

When we are physically ill or so reactive that we cannot contain, observe, and learn from our experience, our ability to remain cohesive diminishes and imbalance is produced. Sickness is not always bad. Many doctors, family members, and nurses are aware that when people are very sick or dying, they report visionary experiences of angels, long-dead relatives, helpful spirits, and even deities. This is a healthy example of the subtle body compensating for the physical body.

However, when the defenses of the Self are activated repeatedly, the physical and subtle bodies begin containing the experiences of disintegration in the muscles, organs, connective tissue, blood, lymph, dreams, fantasies, and sensations of the physical and subtle bodies, creating discomfort and dis-ease. Physical pain and illness, mental illness, nightmares, overreactivity, anxiety, and depression are some of the signals that there is a need for conscious containment and introspection. When symptoms of dis-ease become teachers instead of tyrants, they yield information and understanding.

Clinical Vignette: Physical Body

Eileen was a close friend of mine. She died of congestive heart failure in 1980 at 40 years of age. When she was 14, she contracted bulbar polio and her biggest physical accomplishment was learning to breathe outside an iron lung. She was paralyzed from the neck down and could only move her head. She still experienced physical sensations. In her twenties she had what she called a powerful spiritual experience during which she felt as if she had been given a choice to live the rest of her life as a "shut-in" or to accept her frailty and find a way to give something back to the community she lived in.

She chose to accept and give back. Since she was stuck in one place, Eileen decided to "be there" regularly for anyone who needed help. She lived on $100 a week from social security, and her father provided her with a home and food. Eventually the family ran out of money and could no longer afford home nurses. Eileen trained high school girls to care for her. These girls fed her, gave her enemas, massaged her, moved her and took care of her feet. Their lives were changed because they worked so closely with Eileen's absolute physical helplessness.

The people who cared for Eileen talked about her to other people. Eventually Eileen spoke at retreats, edited her church's newsletter, acted as a counselor to many teens and adults, wrote poetry, and painted. She told me once that people often looked away from her when she was out in her wheelchair or sometimes patted her on the head with pity. Both of those responses from others made her grit her teeth and pray to keep going. Those who looked at her and really saw her, learned to love her and to allow themselves to be loved by her.

The week before she died, she told me that she felt as if all of her physical tethers were gone except one and that when she felt that one snap she would die. She told me she was afraid to die and yet somehow ready. The day before she died, she had her helper call many of her friends to come to see her because she was fairly certain she was going to die soon and she wanted to tell them "goodbye." The following morning I had to leave her in order to go to work and she told me: "If I don't die today, I am going to feel like a real asshole." She went into a coma and had a quiet death the next night.

Eileen was a wonderful example of containment and self-reflection in spite of her physical limitations. The following poem reflects her balance.

WINTER TALK

if you love life,
taste the snow flakes
fallen silent on your face
turn upward
catch the blue
but just a trace

and hesitate
oh, hesitate . . .

> *listen soft*
> *   to the sound*
> *   cotton candied*
> *gentle down*
>
> *if you love life*
>
> *feel your crisp*
> *and carefree step*
> *count the angels recent lept*
>
> *if you love life*
>
> *open deep*
> *   to earth's sweet breath*
> *warmed within*
> *awoke from death*
>
> *and hesitate, oh, hesitate*
> *   this little while*
> *   will soon pass*
> *   in swiftness,*
> *   offering but one*
> *moment's giftness*
>
> *if you love life,*
> *   hesitate, oh, hesitate. . . .*
>
> *Eileen Kral*

Clinical Vignette: Dreaming Body

The patient was a seven-year-old victim of leukemia. He had been in and out of the hospital for two years. He was an only child, and his parents spent every moment they could with him. They were willing to do anything to keep him alive. He was quite thin and told me that he was really tired of pills, shots for pain, and blood cell transfusions. I was one of those people who brought him shots and pills. He was very weak and speaking was an effort for him.

Nurse: "I have your pills and some water. There is no shot tonight. How are you doing?"

Patient: "I'm really sick, aren't I."
Nurse: "Yes, you really are sick."
Patient: "My mom and dad are really scared about me being sick. I feel bad for them."

Nurse (internal observation): I think that this child knows he is dying. His parents are still looking for a miracle cure for him. He is really worried about them. They are afraid to let him go. That means giving up. They think the doctors will find something to help him at the last minute. It is so painful to see his thin little arms and legs with that big belly full of fluid. He is really carrying a heavy load.

Nurse (to patient): "Is there anything I can do to help?"
Patient: "I don't know what to do. I just know I need to do something for them."
Nurse: "What about making them a card with a picture?"
Patient: "I can draw them the angel I see, and then they can be like me, not scared."

Because he was so weak, it took us three evenings to finish his parent's card. He died eight hours after he gave the card to his parents. He hated the pills, shots, and transfusions—and who wouldn't. What none of us could see was that his dreaming body stood in the presence of an angel, and he was not afraid to die. What was most important to him was to share his experience of the angel with his parents so they would not be afraid either.

Memory: The Collective Unconscious: The Air

In order to maintain balance, human memory, and experiences of the collective unconscious must be receptive like the air. Air is invisible and silent; it is moved by the wind and filled with the shapes of clouds. Human memory is filled with motor, affective, perceptual, and behavioral experience that provides ego consciousness with a sense of continuity over time. The collective human memory or collective unconscious contains regularly occurring phenomena that have nothing to do with individuality. It contains impersonal components called archetypes, which have formed and structured human performance from the beginning of time. The archetypes influence human memory, acting in a compensatory way, creating the seeds of future experience. The collective unconscious contains memories of the pre infantile period and the residues of ancestral life (*CW* 7, 1977, 77).

When memory is receptive, personal memories exist as accurate records of real events and ego consciousness has a grounded relationship with archetypal images as they occur in dreams, visions, and fantasies. When a person is receptive, he or she is able to listen deeply to others and to understand things from another's point of view without losing his or her own center. When memory is receptive, ego consciousness develops wisdom and knowledge. For example, the old Indian man *remembered* the oil paints that he had never seen. When memory is rigidified or nonreceptive, a person is prone to judgments, comparisons, and a form of tunnel vision that creates labels and categories, naming experiences rather than having them. Rigidified memories or memories that are absent, distorted, or replaced by numinous fantasies are indicators of the presence of a pathological complex.

Clinical Vignette: Memory

Patient: "I have to know whether it happened or not. I can't remember a thing except feeling awful and dirty all the time. I tried to stay away from everyone, but then I remember hanging onto my mother's leg and that just doesn't make sense. In the present and in my memories I don't even like my mother. I remember that I was always afraid to go down to the basement, but I don't know why. I keep seeing images of my dad doing weird things to my brother and me, but I can't see what those things were. When I get those feelings I get really sick to my stomach and anxious. I have to find out the truth."

Therapist: "What have you done so far to try to remember?"
Patient: "Hypnosis, other therapy, painting and body work. I didn't remember anything. I feel like I was abused, but I don't know it. I just feel it in my body."
Therapist: "What makes it so important for you to remember actual pictures of events when you have strong physical memories?"
Patient: "My physical sensations aren't real. I have to have actual memories so that I know what happened."
Therapist: "I don't understand."
Patient: "I have to have actual evidence to accuse him. What if I am making it up?"
Therapist: "I don't know how to give you memories other than what you already have. Is there a part of you that doesn't trust or believe your physical memories?"
Patient: "I don't know. Maybe I have parts. Does that mean I have multiple personalities?"

Therapist (internal observations): There is a part of me that wants to help her find her memories and another part of me that is frustrated with her. I don't understand what is going on in this hour at all.

Therapist (to patient): "I have seen no evidence that you have multiple personalities. I have seen evidence that you have physical memories of abuse, that you are depressed and sometimes very anxious and have trouble thinking. Is that your experience of yourself?"
Patient: "Pretty much."
Therapist: "Pretty much?"
Patient: "Well, I think you're right, but I'm not sure."
Therapist: "What would help you know for sure?"
Patient: "I don't know."

Therapist (internal observation): I'm so frustrated. She appears to be becoming more anxious. Am I doing something to make her more anxious?

Therapist (to patient): "What is going on in your body right now?"
Patient: "My heart is fast and my mouth is dry. I am frustrated because this therapy is not working."

Therapist (internal observations): I feel anxious. I feel like a failure. I am afraid that if I ask her another question I will make her more anxious. If I don't do anything then I will not be helpful. Oh. I am making this personal instead of attuning to her.

Therapist (to patient): "What happened inside you when I said I couldn't make you remember?"
Patient: "I just sort of gave up and I felt frustrated. I had hoped I could finally get this settled in my mind, you know, whether I was abused or not. Now I just feel hopeless, like I will never know the truth and always worry about it and wonder and then think about it all the time."
Therapist: "I should have listened more closely to what you said. Help me understand what it is that is going on inside you."
Patient: "I feel tainted and evil. If I was really abused those feelings would make sense. If I wasn't abused, maybe there is something really bad wrong with me. I don't know which one is right. I think about it all the time, like I can't get it out of my head. I could get it out of my head if I really remembered what happened."

Therapist (internal observation): I really missed what she was saying.

Therapist (to patient): "What I hear you saying is that a part of you feels tainted and evil and another part that says you should not be feeling that way unless you were abused. Is that right?"
Patient: "Yes. That's exactly how it is, and if I could remember exactly, then I would know for sure whether or not my feels are real or not."

Therapist: "So what is important for you is to know for sure."
Patient: "That's right. I need to know for sure, and I don't know how to remember."

Therapist (internal observation): I feel much more relaxed, and the patient looks much more relaxed. I think I am more on track with her.

Therapist (to patient): "Let's begin by working with what you already know. You know that you have a part of you that feels evil and tainted and another part that says you are wrong for feeling evil and tainted unless you have been abused. We also know that you worry a lot. Is the worry attached to one part or both parts?"
Patient: "Not knowing for sure is what worries me."
Therapist (to patient): "Can you tell me about feeling tainted and evil?"

The patient went on to describe her feelings of being tainted and evil. When the therapist was finally able to attune to and listen to her, portions of the patient's emotions began to emerge into consciousness. This took place gradually and was quite painful for the patient because she had a great deal of difficulty containing the emerging affect. Finally, the patient was able to draw the images locked within her feelings and the abuse emerged in her drawings. The patient's unwillingness to accept her physical memories was a way for her to avoid the reality of what had happened to her and the feelings of annihilation associated with the abuse.

Clinical Vignette: The Collective Unconscious

Patient: "I came to see you because I am having dreams that wake me up in the middle of the night. I see angels, devils, Jesus, and the Buddha. In the daytime I get a sense of what people are feeling and thinking. I am afraid that I am going crazy."
Therapist: "Would it be all right with you if we begin getting to know each other before we begin discussing your dreams and waking experiences?"

The patient was a 32-year-old housewife with three children. Three years previous to coming for therapy she developed a pulmonary embolism and had what she called a "near death" experience. A blood clot stopped her heartbeat and she was pronounced dead when cardiopulmonary resuscitation failed after seven minutes. After nine minutes she began breathing again spontaneously. During the time that she had no heartbeat and no respiration, she experienced herself being drawn toward a light. She felt deeply joyous and peaceful. A voice from the light told her that she could not die yet because she had something to finish. She did not know what it was she had to finish and so she went about her life hoping that she would eventually discover what it was.

She was sensible, grounded, and well educated. She sounded as if she was a good mother and she described her husband as her "best friend." However, she described her affect as depressed and felt as if something was missing in her life. She was anxious about what she was supposed to do with her life and very anxious about her dreams and waking experiences. She had never had these kind of experiences before her "near death" experience. She was very healthy and seemed contained and introspective. Her memory was excellent, and as she described both her family of origin and growing up as well as her present life there was some evidence of a pathological complex that included anxiety about thinking, and creativity. The anxiety was not pervasive nor was it damaging to the patient or her relationships.

It took four weeks to gather a comprehensive history so that both of us knew each other well enough to develop a fresh context for her dreaming and daytime experiences.

Therapist (to patient): "Do you feel ready to begin talking about your dreams and your waking experiences?"
Patient: "I have not said anything to anyone but my husband about it, so this is really scary for me."
Therapist: "Can you stay with that scary feeling?"
Patient: "Yes. I feel shaking all over. My mouth is dry. I feel nauseated. Now I am dying again, and I am outside my body. I see the light and I feel okay. There is someone telling me something I can't understand. I don't understand the words. Then I feel this someone placing their hands on my head and then I am back here."
Therapist: "You are back here and where is your fear?"
Patient: "It is gone. The fear is gone, and now I feel like everything is going to be okay. I don't know what to make of that. I guess I would call it a quick daytime dream."
Therapist: "That sounds like a good name for it. What is happening in your body right now?"
Patient: "I feel open and relaxed and I am wondering why, and as I do I feel myself tightening up."

Therapist (internal observation): It appears as if she has two parts. One has had and is having powerful dreams and awarenesses. The other part is afraid of these experiences.

Therapist (to patient): "It sounds as if part of you is having powerful experiences and another part of you is afraid of these experiences. Is that your experience?"

Patient: "Yes, that is exactly right. I am having the experiences, and I am afraid of having them or talking about them. I didn't know it but I am at war with myself.

Therapist: "How would you like to proceed now that you know about your parts?"

Patient: "I think I had better start talking about my dream last night. I was in a strange place and there was a lady in front of me. She had snakes for hair. Her face was painted white, and she was naked on top. She had on a skirt. She was awful. I woke up from the dream feeling terrified. I know they say that everything I dream is a part of ourselves. She looked really evil. I am really scared. I don't think I am evil, but that woman is a part of me and she looked evil."

Therapist (internal observation): This is a powerful image of the goddess. This woman has not studied Greek mythology. She could not have heard of the Medusa. The collective unconscious is communicating with this woman. If I interpret the image for her, I might interrupt what the unconscious is saying to her with my own ideas. I can recommend that she read Jung and learn about the collective unconscious. I can recommend that she draw the image or dialogue with it.

Therapist (to patient): "That woman is a powerful image from the collective human memory or what Jung called the collective unconscious. This memory of human experience has existed from long before you were born and it is communicating with you. The image is what is called "numinous," which means it has powerful energy. Since you don't know anything about it, of course you are feeling scared about it."

Patient: "It is as if a part of me can still see her. Ugh! All those snakes wiggling on her head make me feel nauseous."

Therapist (internal observation): She has good ego strength and common sense. I can suggest that she speak with the image or draw it.

Therapist (to patient): "Can you speak with her and ask her who she is and what she wants?"

Patient: "In my imagination she won't talk to me, but she takes me by the hand and shows me a lake with a marsh. She leans over a place where there is clear water, and when I see her face in the water she is very beautiful. I look up at her and she still has snakes in her hair, but her reflection in the water doesn't have snakes. She reaches in the water and hands me a golden cup and then she is gone and I am holding the cup. Am I making this up?"

Therapist: "You have just done what Jung called "Active Imagination."[7] It is a dialogue with a part of the collective human memory that is like having a relationship with another person. The person changes you, and you change the person because you have spoken together. The images you meet may not look like regular people, but even though they look a little different it is important that you relate to them the same way you relate to people in your waking life. You might want to write your conversations down or draw pictures of it–whatever feels right to you."

Patient: "I think I will write it down. So this isn't crazy–it's normal. Can I go back there and see what happens next?"

Therapist: "Of course. Keep a record in words or drawings or both."

This woman performed active imagination, painted and drew her experiences over a period of five years. She also studied cross-cultural mythology and read extensively to develop an understanding of the function of her images across time. Her worldview was transformed. She returned to school part-time to obtain a law degree and began to practice environmental law. Her dialogue and study of the image of the Medusa that appeared spontaneously in her nightmares gradually changed her frame of reference so that environmental law became that the something she was "called to do."

The Behavior: The Spirit: The Fire

Behavior and spirit function like fire, defining the way energy moves. Behavior can support individuation or reinforce a pathological complex. In order for behavior to support individuation, the other aspects of ego consciousness must be functioning in relative balance with affect/soul giving energy, physical and dreaming bodies containing energy for introspection, and memory and the collective human memory being receptive to energy.

Pathological complexes can be diagnosed on a scale from one to ten: one is mild, five is moderate, and ten is severe. The greater the severity of the complex, the less human behavior is aligned with the individuation process and the more it reinforces and builds the contents of the pathological complex. When behavior is in balance the individual is maturing and takes responsibility for his or her actions. He or she learns from mistakes and is more interested in gathering energy and aligning with the Self than in gathering power and being in control of or approved by others.

When a person is arrogant, entitled, has negative expectations, is overly reactive, and is filled with self-importance his or her behavior is out of alignment with the development of ego consciousness and individuation. Persons like this often create chaos around them like a fire that is out of control.

Little children are close to Spirit, and this is why our eyes are often drawn to them. They are curious, intensely interested in things, filled with wonder, and have a deep sense of pleasure most of the time because they are connected with the Self and with nature. When we meet an elder (someone over 60) who is close to spirit, they usually have some of these same attributes and we love being around them. The "Old Indian Man" and "The Woman Who Once Walked in Balance" are examples of elders who are in the process of individuating.

Clinical Vignette: Behavior

Patient: "My children get so upset with me when I give them suggestions about how to raise my grandchildren. I simply don't understand it. I am only trying to help."
Therapist: "What is that like for you when they get upset with you?"
Patient: "I feel old and useless. I have learned so much in my life. I can't believe they don't want to listen to me."
Therapist: "And when you feel old and useless what happens inside?"
Patient: "My heart hurts and I feel grief that I am losing my children."
Therapist: "You are losing your children. Your heart hurts and you really feel grief."
Patient (*crying*): "I know I haven't lost my children. They love me. They just don't want to take my advice—and it's really all I have to give them. I am grieving because I have nothing to give them."

Therapist (*internal observation*): This woman has good ego strength and is especially strong in exploring new ideas and new experiences.

Therapist (*to patient*): "I don't believe you have nothing to give them."
Patient: "What do you mean? What could I possibly give them?"
Therapist: "I am going to ask you to explore what happens if you change a behavior with them. Would you consider listening to what I ask and then telling me what you think about my suggestion?"
Patient: "Sure."
Therapist: "What do you think might happen if you noticed the things they are doing right and complimented them and at the same time overlooked those things you think they are doing wrong?"

Patient: "That would be hard. I would have to be quiet most of the time."
Therapist: "Would it be difficult for you to be quiet with them?"
Patient: "No. I am getting quieter all the time just to avoid the arguments that start when I offer suggestions. They seem to regress to the way they were as children before my very eyes. I am too old to parent again. I just want to get along with them and enjoy being with them. I can grieve my old age in here with you and work with my dreams."
Therapist: "Yes, you can. In here is a good place to work things. What I am hearing you say about your children is that they take your suggestions as criticisms rather than as help. What would happen if you suddenly just smiled at them and became quiet and inept when you were with them?"
Patient: "I don't know. I have never been that way."
Therapist: "Would you be willing to find out?
Patient: "Yes, I would, and I will next week. We'll all be together for Mattie's birthday."

The patient smiled at her children and her grandchildren and was quiet at Mattie's birthday party. Each one of her children approached her at different times and asked if she needed anything. No one asked her opinion on anything, and everyone was nurturing and loving. She realized that her presence as a smiling, quiet elder in the family was important to her family; however, it was her presence as a parent that was important and she was not known outside of her role as "mother." She spent months grieving, and as she let go of her idea of "family" to accept the reality of family, she began to create a new life that included old friends and seeking new adventures.

SUMMARY

The Medicine Wheel provides a diagnostic tool for therapists to assess the aspects of ego consciousness. When we understand the energetic function of each aspect of ego consciousness and how each aspect balances the other aspects of ego consciousness, we can develop the ability to attune to the patient's most developed aspects of ego consciousness and begin to explore and understand the patient's experiences of those aspects of ego consciousness that are not well developed.

In our profession, symptoms are grouped together statistically and then named to help us diagnose and communicate with one another about differing forms of pathology. The Medicine Wheel creates a new template for diagnosis based on the way each of the aspects of ego consciousness function.

In order to learn to understand the wheel it is not necessary to memorize it, but to play with it, work with it, and live with it. Locate each of the four directions and think about the basic energy associated with each of them. Observe your patients and diagnose the presence, absence, and balance of each of the archetypal foundations of ego consciousness. The Medicine Wheel is a working diagnostic system that can be used within a clinical setting in order to observe which components of ego consciousness are balanced and which are not balanced. The therapist and patient can both work with the Medicine Wheel in order to understand strengths and limitations imposed by a pathological complex.

THE LAYERED VIEW OF THE PSYCHE

What is the relationship between the components of ego consciousness and the unconscious? Jung (1921) used the term *psyche* to describe all psychic processes, those that are conscious as well as those that are unconscious (*CW* 6, 1977, 463). He divided the psyche into three artificial layers: ego consciousness, the personal unconscious, and the collective unconscious (484–485). *Ego consciousness* is the experience collected around the four archetypal components and eight aspects discussed above. It is like a flower that grows up out of the earth. Its roots are invisible, deep in the soil of the unconscious; and its leaves, seeds, and beauty are dependent on the forces of nature and the nurturing it receives. *Ego consciousness* is dependent upon the unconscious and everyday life experience for continued growth and development. The *personal unconscious* is composed of those portions of ego consciousness that are close to awareness but not being utilized at the present moment, as well as the memories and experiences of the personal and familial history. It also contains portions of complexes, experiences of past behavior, dreams, meanings for events that have been outgrown or forgotten and cultural influences (485). The *collective unconscious* is composed of all of the archetypes that form human experience into patterns including the archetypal/developmental processes and the archetypal components of ego consciousness. This aspect of the unconscious is independent and impersonal. It is the largest structure in the psyche (*CW* 9_1, 1936; 1980, 42–43).

This perspective provides an entirely different frame of reference for ego consciousness than that of other forms of therapy because in it, ego consciousness is only a tiny portion of the entire personality. Jung believed that the unconscious was unlimited and that the science of psychology has only barely plumbed the possibilities for human growth and awareness.[8] He believed that transformation and integration of a pathological complex was not due to the skills of the therapist or the will of the patient. Instead, he believed that both the patient and the therapist formed a relationship with the unconscious as well as with one another and that growth in awareness was the result of working with the unconscious processes that came out of both parties involved in the relationship. This perspective has been validated repeatedly in my clinical experience and has taught me that my experience with each patient must be reflected upon and thoroughly studied from multiple viewing points. The unconscious is a difficult and demanding taskmaster for both the clinician and the patient because it is continually providing a perspective that is foreign for both persons.

In my personal experience the theoretical divisions between the layers of the psyche are not at all clear. However, they can be used as a basis for exploration of the patient's experience and interpretation. During the clinical hour, parts of the pathological complex, as well as the patient's observing ego, portions of the archetypal/developmental processes and their mediation, as well as components of the collective unconscious flow in and out of conscious awareness. It is up to the patient and the therapist to pay attention and to reflect upon these experiences in order to gradually understand them. The therapist must have the discipline and focus to be able to track some of what is happening. The patient must have the discipline to face the pathological complex, to step aside from patterns of reactivity and instead, contain and reflect upon them.

Clinical Vignette: A Layered View of the Psyche

Patient: "I don't remember much as a child except working all the time. Sometimes I would hide and read a book. That would make my father really angry and he would come after me with a strap."
Therapist: "Did he hurt you?"
Patient: "No. He just threatened me. He beat the boys but not the girls. I was terrified of him because he would get so angry."
Therapist: "What was that like for you when he got angry?"
Patient: "I just stood there frozen. I couldn't do anything."
Therapist: "You came for therapy because you want to learn to be assertive in your work. Do you think that freezing when your father got angry taught you to freeze in the workplace in case someone gets angry?"
Patient: "That makes a lot of sense. I have been responding that way for 30 years."
Therapist: "What happens in your body when you freeze?"
Patient: "I feel like I get smaller. I shrink into my belly and just watch what is going on. That reminds me of a dream I have had almost every night for the past few weeks. In the dream I see a woman with a black face. She has a tongue hanging way out of her mouth and skulls around her waist.

She is dancing with a sword and a shield. I have never seen anything like that. What could that possibly mean?"
Therapist: "That woman with the black face and tongue hanging out of her mouth is one image of what ancient cultures called the great mother. I have a picture of a Native American Kachina doll called EhHeeYe the Warrior woman and a picture of the Hindu goddess Kali who may look like the image you saw in your dream. Are these images anything like the woman you saw in your dream?"
Patient: "They both look a something like her. She is really fierce looking. I've never seen anything like them. What are they?"

Therapist (internal observations): I have only seen this woman three times. I don't know enough about her to recommend that she dialogue with the image. However, she can learn more about her dream image by doing research.

Therapist (to patient): "She is part of the shadow of all women. She is not nurturing, demure, or kind. She is not beautiful. She is a part of feminine energy that does not fit with our culture. I think you may have to do some research on this image to find out more about her and get some understanding about what she is trying to tell you in your dream."

The patient researched the image and found the Great Mother, the feminine principle that births life, supports life and takes life back into her womb for rebirth. As the patient studied and read about Kali and EhHeeYe and learned about the Great Mother she felt drawn to learn how to become a warrior and began training in Martial Arts.

The personal unconscious contained the experience of freezing when someone around her appeared angry or aggressive. The patient worked cognitively and behaviorally to change her responses. The image of the great Mother that appeared from the collective unconscious led her into the practice of Martial Arts. Her training gradually changed her physical responses allowing her to remain embodied and peaceful when someone around her was angry or aggressive.[9]

The image of the Warrior aspect of the Great Mother came from the patient's connection with the collective unconscious. The problems with freezing in the face of anger and aggression came from the patient's personal unconscious. The transformation of the pathological complex came from the patient's own willingness to consciously engage the material that arose from her own experience.

THE CYCLES OF NATURE

There is another viewing point into the pathological complex that allows both the patient and the therapist to observe, understand, and interrupt the power that the pathological complex has over ego consciousness. Elisabeth Kubler Ross introduced me to the idea that life moves in cycles that include death, change, and rebirth and that when these cycles are accepted, life can be lived more fully. Mary Loomis introduced me to the idea that nature has cycles that include life, movement, change, and death, which brings new life. In physics, chaos theory discusses these cycles and presents chaos as a process of transformation bringing forth a new structure.[10]

Figure 10 presents the cycles that create life, movement, death, and transformation in nature. The cycles can move in any direction in the circle—clockwise, counterclockwise and beginning in any direction. What is important about the cycles of nature is that change, death, and chaos must occur in order for growth to take place. Life brings movement, movement brings change, change brings death, death brings imbalance, imbalance brings chaos, and chaos brings transformation and new life. It is my belief that the cycles of nature influence the development and growth of ego consciousness. Ego consciousness is part of nature and undergoes the same cycles to develop and evolve. When a pathological complex is operating, often the movement through the cycles of nature is blocked. What would that look like in a clinical hour?

Clinical Vignette: Movement Without Change

The patient was a 30-year-old man who lived in a state of continual busyness. He grew up in a home where he was the oldest of 11 children. His father worked three jobs to support the family. His mother worked day and night taking care of the children. Early in his life, he was forced to take the role of a *parental child* (an older child who becomes responsible for taking care of younger siblings). It was his job to come home right after school and watch the younger children so that his mother could get dinner ready. He did not have time for friends, sports or fun. His mother was too busy raising children and being pregnant to show much affection. The younger children kept him so busy that he hardly had time to finish his homework before he fell into bed each night. He followed a strict schedule during the week. On the weekends, he helped his father cleaning offices. He had no time to rest, no time for reflection and no time for feelings. His family's survival was dependent upon his contribution. He put himself through college and had a successful career. When he was 28 years old, he married his college sweetheart.

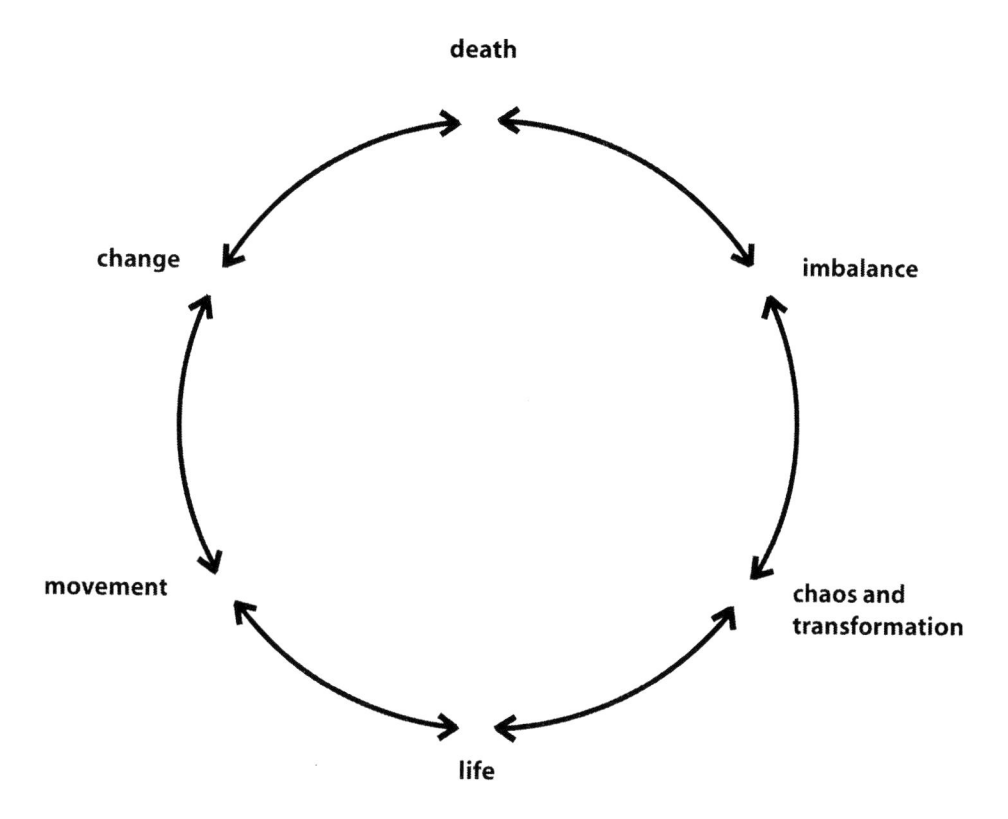

```
                        death
                    →       ←
        change  ↙                    ↘  imbalance
                ↑                    ↑
                                              
                ↓                    ↓
      movement  ↖                    ↗  chaos and
                                         transformation
                    →       ←
                         life
```

The diagram indicates that the cycles can move clockwise or counterclockwise. Blockage of one or more of the cycles pushes increasing amounts of energy into the other cycles. As energy increases in the other cycles, it finally becomes strong enough to break the blockages and restore the full movement of the cycles of nature.

FIGURE 10
The Cycles of Nature.

Gradually, his spouse became very unhappy with their relationship. She was pregnant with their first child and physically unable to work because of problems in the pregnancy. She stayed home all day and in the evenings she wanted time with him to sit and talk and share feelings and information. He was very busy at work and because his position was so important there were always last-minute emergencies that kept him working until quite late. When his wife tried to speak with him about her loneliness he got defensive and angry. He felt unappreciated because he worked so hard to contribute to their family. Eventually he and his wife entered marital therapy in order to work on their relationship. She was an only child who came from a family that was very nurturing and cooperated when decisions had to be made. When she had a problem to solve she wanted to discuss it with her husband so that they could make decisions together. She also wanted time with him to talk about feelings and was angry because she felt that the only way they connected was sexually. He wanted her to make all decisions about their home because he was too busy. He believed that wasting time talking about feelings took time away from work, which was important to the family's survival. Both blamed the other for the failing relationship.

Both of them were going through the cycles of nature because of the pregnancy and the changes that was bringing to the relationship and to their identities. She was filled with life and he was filled with movement. Neither wanted to deal with change. However, as the pregnancy progressed both of them would have to go through all of the cycles and both of them were stuck in one cycle. Together we began to explore what it was like for each of them to be embedded in their own place in the cycle and how that blocked change, death, and transformation in the relationship. Up until this point each partner had tried to change the other partner, rather than each one working with the other to move through the cycles together and let that movement strengthen their relationship. As each partner began to understand the other partner's position in the cycle, and how terrifying it was to move out of that position, the relationship began to change. Both of them were afraid that the baby might die. She wanted to talk about it and he was terrified to discuss it because he did not know how. Both were afraid of the responsibility of being a parent and of making mistakes that might hurt the child psychologically. Both were worried about what was happening to their own relationship and neither knew how to fix it. Gradually the relationship deepened as the idea of the cycles of nature became a tool to teach individual awareness and responsibility and a metaphor that supported change, death of old ideas and ways of being, and movement into the chaos of labor, delivery and having a new baby.

Identifying a rigidification in the cycles as a tool to teach a patient about a pathological complex provides another point of view for the therapist that may be useful in the clinical hour.

THE CYCLES OF NATURE: A VIEWING POINT INTO THE PATHOLOGICAL COMPLEX

When a pathological complex becomes constellated, it replaces the patient's normal awareness. As has been pointed out, the pattern of the pathological complex contains the experiences of misattuned mediation of the archetypal/developmental processes; the numinous energy of the archetypal/developmental processes; denied and split off components of ego consciousness; and the painful affective theme that holds them together. The person who is complexed is no longer present in the here and now. Instead, he or she becomes like the man whose shoe is caught in the railroad track with the nightmare train bearing down upon him and is living in an altered reality. The altered reality of the pathological complex has a profound effect on reality, relationships, and communication.

The content of the experience of the pathological complex is a rich source of information for both the patient and the therapist. The idea of the cycles of nature is an impersonal way to explore a pathological complex and can be used as a way to understand and observe how a pathological complex stops movement and transformation. The therapist and the patient can observe the individual components of the cycles of nature, ask questions about the way it functions when the complex is constellated, and create ways for the patient to change his or her behaviors to create room for the movement of the cycles in the patient's everyday life.

Life: What is the quality of the patient's life? What can he or she do to improve that quality? How does the patient stop him or herself from creating nourishing and life giving experiences?

Movement: What is the quality of the movement of the patient's life? How does he or she spend time? What happens to movement when the pathological complex is constellated? Can the patient make a conscious effort to slow down or speed up the movement of time in his or her life?

Change: How does the patient describe his or her experiences of change? How does he or she respond to change? How does he or she avoid or embrace change? What is he or she willing to do to create change?

Death: What are the patient's experiences of death and loss? How easy is it for the patient to let go of something or throw it away? What does the patient do to avoid loss? How does the patient cope with physical illness, with aging, with death of a relationship or death of a loved one?

Imbalance: How does the patient maintain the balance in his or her life in work and family, self-care and care of others, self-trust and trust of others? How would you evaluate the patient's capacity for practicality or common sense? How does the patient stay grounded? How flexible is the patient? How does he or she maintain boundaries? What is he or she willing to do to accept imbalance and learn from it?

Chaos: How is the patient's life chaotic? What does he or she do to defend against chaos? How does he or she manage chaos when it enters his or her life? What are the feelings the patient has during chaotic times? How able is the patient to know when to let go and endure the process of chaos and wait until it is time for new life? What does the patient need to do to learn to endure the process of chaos?

The circular movements of creation allow space for the development of consciousness for as long as we live. Going against creation/nature creates pathology. Our work as therapists is to create a space where choices are freed from poorly mediated archetypal developmental processes and the ongoing attachment to only a part of the cycles of nature, working with the patient to create behaviors that create space for movement, change, death, imbalance, chaos, and new life.

Clinical Vignette: Behavioral Change and the Cycles of Nature

The patient was a 50-year-old engineer who was laid off at work because of company cutbacks. His wife hated him but remained married to him because she was financially dependent on him. He was depressed and described himself as "numbing out in front of the TV" instead of dealing with his problems.

Patient: "I am just overwhelmed and feeling sorry for myself. I can't seem to get myself mobilized to do anything."
Therapist: "What is that like to feel so immobilized?"
Patient: "I just sort of shrink inside myself and then forget about things. Why can't I just get going?"

The patient spent six sessions doing parts work with the part of him that felt frozen and the part of him that criticized him. He was out of work, his wife continually found fault with him, and he felt as if he was useless. As he began to separate his parts and observe them, he began to realize that numbing out and avoiding things were the way he had learned to survive when he was in a great deal of stress.

We explored the cycles of nature together, and he realized that he was stuck in death and too frightened to challenge his wife or look for a job (change or move into imbalance). Because of his shame and stress, the functions of ego consciousness were diminished; however, his strengths were his ability to explore (do) and to think.

He spent one session exploring his options and finally asked me for help. I recommended that he change his behavior and spend one hour a day writing about his work-related ideas and interests, whether he felt like it or not. He agreed to do that and spent four clinical hours discussing his ideas and interests in engineering. These discussions did not constellate his shamed/shaming complex. As his thoughts and his ideas became clearer in the clinical hour, I asked him if he was willing to begin to change the way he was looking for a job and explore some kind of work that supported his thoughts and ideas. He agreed and began interviewing for a job that would support his interests rather than continue to try to find just any kind of work. He finally found a small company where he could work in ways that interested him and also have time to explore some of his ideas.

He did not feel strong enough to deal with his wife or change their relationship, and he took a vacation from therapy after he was settled in his new job. He decided he needed to build up his confidence at work before he was ready to change his marital relationship.

ANOTHER LOOK AT THE WOMAN WHO ONCE WALKED IN BALANCE

The Woman Who Once Walked in Balance is a description of the formation of a pathological complex, healing, and transformation. When our heroine was a young girl, the components of ego consciousness were gathering experience, her awareness was deepening, individuation was occurring, and she felt in harmony with herself and with the community around her. She was protected, empowered, and given permission to develop. Her emotions gave her energy. She found deep meaning in her life. Her physical body was strong. She was able to tolerate visionary experiences. She did not dream because compensation was fully operating making dreams unnecessary. She was able to reflect upon her experience and learn from it, and she was encouraged to do that. Her behavior was in harmony with her individuation process, and she was developing spiritually. The patterns of mediation of the archetypal/developmental processes were operating in a way that was deeply attuned to her. She was nourished by an entire community of people who were also in harmony with their individuation processes. Because she was in tune with her own individuation process, she was also in tune with the cycles of Creation and with nature.

When the villains entered her life, they projected their own pathological complexes onto the people around them. They felt exhilarated as they locked our heroine and her people into a cycle of death, imbalance, and chaos. The villains' psychic infection split the cycles of nature, and transformation could no longer occur for anyone. The behavior of the villains produced periods of prolonged disintegration for their victims, stimulating the defenses of the Self and changing forever the way of life of a people who were once psychologically healthy.

It is clear in the story that as the pathological complex began to form within our heroine, she introjected the pathological patterns of mediation of the archetypal/developmental processes, becoming just like the villains in order to survive. Gradually, the pathological complex became more and more powerful; creating a closed system that decreased her levels of awareness and halted her development. The energy of consciousness became so depleted that she was left with only a feeling tone of rage, revenge, and death until she was finally "left for dead."

Images of the Self in the form of the old wise woman and the old wise man appeared to help her gradually learn to correct her restricted and one-sided conscious attitude. The healing process began because they were present, they listened, and they directed her. This is exactly how the therapeutic process operates. The only difference is that the presence of the therapist supports the invisible presence of the Self, and it is the therapist who bears witness to the patient's healing process.

Our heroine's complex, like all complexes, is unique. The old wise woman and the old wise man seem to be able to support the healing process from multiple viewing points, those same viewing points that protect the therapist from being overwhelmed by the pathological complex and inducted into it. The stronger the pathological complex is, the more difficult it is to separate from it. The stronger the pathological complex is, the greater potential it has for infecting others. It is the work of the therapist to present multiple viewing points into the complex, to be attuned enough to assist with containment, and to support the movements of the unconscious to restore compensation. Sometimes that takes a long time, and sometimes people simply cannot separate from the complex. For whatever reason, our heroine was able to take the suggestions of the old wise woman and the old wise man and use them. Normal processes of compensation can never be restored without great effort on the part of the patient.

Figure 11 is a review and a summary of everything that has been presented so far in the book. It is a diagnostic template to use to identify the multiple viewing points into a pathological complex. Each of the viewing points is mentioned below.

VIEWING POINTS INTO THE PATHOLOGICAL COMPLEX

1. The energetic processes supporting the development of ego consciousness: integration, deintegration, reintegration, and disintegration.
2. The archetypal/developmental processes: being, doing, thinking, identity, and creativity.
3. Patterns of mediation of the archetypal/developmental processes: symbiotic, directive, containing, reflective, cooperative, educating, and empowering.

More Viewing Points Into The Pathological Complex 117

Archetypal Patterns which Create and Develop Consciousness

* Being
* Doing
* Thinking
* Identity
* Creativity

Patterns of Mediation

* Symbiotic
* Directive
* Cooperative
* Containing
* Confirming
* Educating
8* Empowering

Cycles of Nature

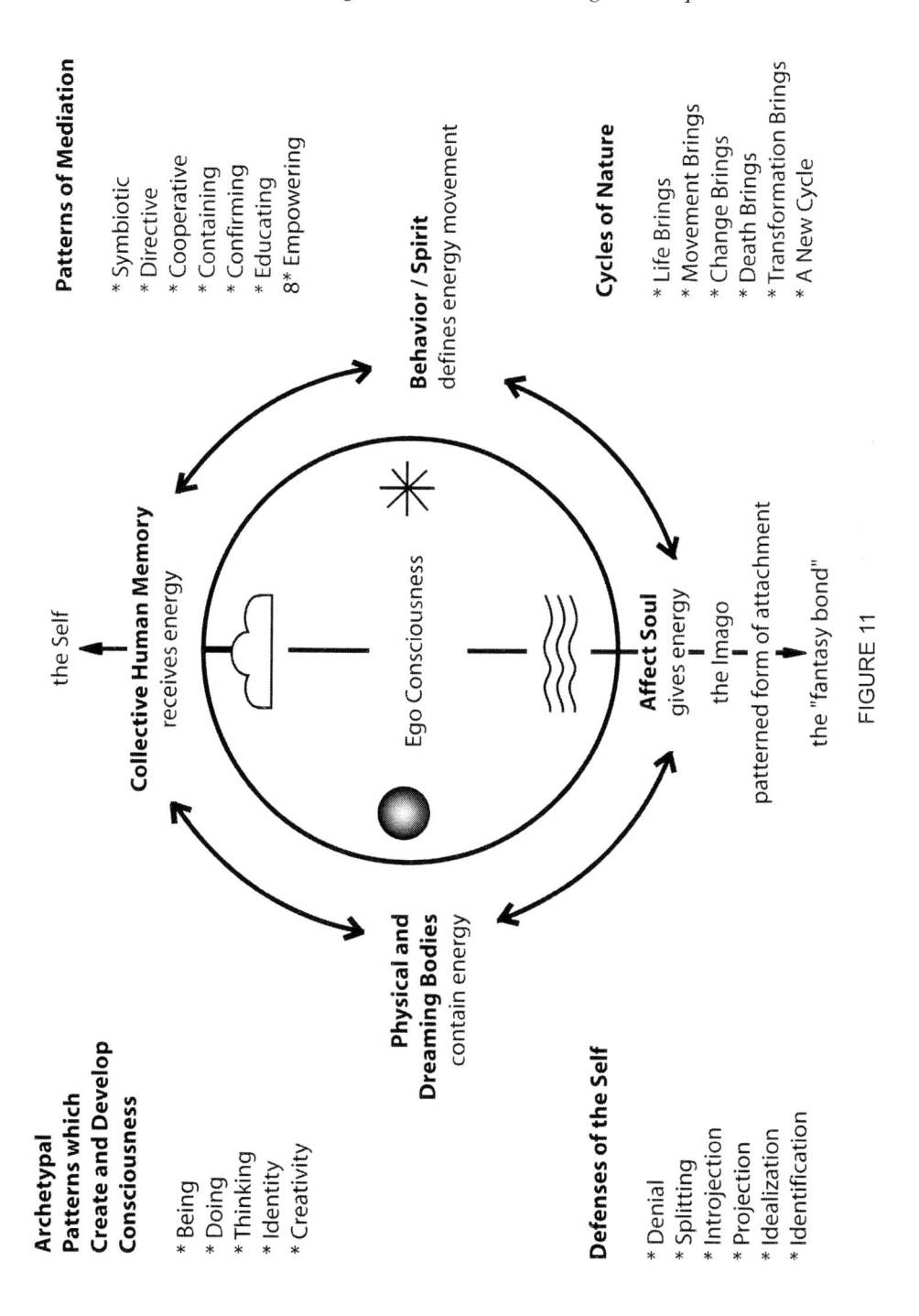

* Life Brings
* Movement Brings
* Change Brings
* Death Brings
* Transformation Brings
* A New Cycle

Defenses of the Self

* Denial
* Splitting
* Introjection
* Projection
* Idealization
* Identification

Collective Human Memory receives energy

Behavior / Spirit defines energy movement

Affect Soul gives energy

Physical and Dreaming Bodies contain energy

Ego Consciousness

the Self

the Imago

patterned form of attachment

the "fantasy bond"

FIGURE 11

4. Defenses of the Self: denial, splitting, projection, introjection, identification, and idealization.
5. Cycles of nature: life, movement, change, imbalance, death/chaos, transformation, and rebirth in a new pattern.
6. Components of ego consciousness: Affect and soul; physical body and dreaming body; memory and the collective human memory; behavior and spirit.
7. Energetic elements for the balance of ego consciousness: behavior and spirit define energy movement; affect and soul give energy; body and dreaming body contain energy for introspection; and memory and the collective unconscious receive energy.
8. Ego-Self axis in a healthy complex.
9. Ego-imago axis in a pathological complex.

The components of Figure 11 are a template for the diagnosis and treatment of pathological complexes. The template can be used by the therapist with any patient to identify parts of a pathological complex.

QUESTIONS

1. Use Figure 11 as a template for one of the patients in your practice. Identify the presence, distortion, or absence of: the eight components of ego consciousness; the archetypal/developmental processes; patterns of mediation of the archetypal/developmental processes that are distorted, absent, or present; the presence, overutilization, or underutilization of one or more of the cycles of nature; and the nature of the imago of the patient. Which components are embedded within the patient's pathological complex? Which components are available to ego consciousness?
2. Use Figure 11 to observe and explore your own life experience. Are the components of ego consciousness operating in alignment? Which archetypal/developmental process is problematic for you? What are the patterns of mediation of that archetypal/developmental process that create anguish for you?
3. What are the eight aspects of ego consciousness?
4. What is the layered view of the psyche? Are there actually layers of the psyche present within a clinical hour?
5. Name the components of the physical body of ego consciousness and how they operate energetically.
6. Name the components of the subtle body of ego consciousness and how they operate energetically.

7. Using your own clinical experience, describe four complexes, each one related to an absence of one of the components of ego consciousness.
8. Name the cycles of nature.
9. Give two examples from your own clinical experience of how blockage in the cycles of nature are linked with psychopathology.
10. Look at Figure 11. Think of one patient who has been difficult for you to understand. Work with each component of Figure 11 to identify a component of the patient's pathological complex that you were not aware of.
11. What are the seven affects and the organ systems that create imbalance in traditional Chinese Medicine?
12. What is *disintegration* and how would you describe it when you have observed it in your own clinical practice?
13. Summarize what you have learned from the chapter that will be useful to you in your clinical practice.

ENDNOTES

1. For more information and clarification on the idea of self-affectivity and complex see Tomkins (1981), and Demos, ed. (1995).
2. Another wheel that links the four elements and the four archetypal components of ego consciousness with the "four powers of grandmother earth" is found in Storm (1994, 195). The sun (fire, behavior, spirit) is in the East. Plants (water, affect) are in the south. The earth substance, e.g. mountains, dirt, gold (earth, body) is in the West. All animals, including humans, are in the North. If you add sun, plants, earth substances, and animals to Figure 8, you will discover how the ancients believed that sun, plants, earth, and animals balanced one another.
3. In 1995 I visited Beijing, China and met with Professor Pon Chao Dong for a discussion about Natural Qi Gong. During the lecture Professor Pon described the "seven emotions" that create disharmony within the organ systems of the body.
4. When the term *body work* is used, it refers to specialized therapeutic training in the use of touch, massage, therapeutic touch, physical positioning of the body, and exercises from over 20 disciplines that focus on ways to release emotions that are held in the body. Examples of body work would be Reiki, therapeutic massage, the Feldenkreiss method, the Alexander method, bioenergetics, and Rolfing.
5. This information is still taught in two oral traditions with which I am familiar, the Druid (personal communication and demonstration from Anton Rayborne, 1987) and the Native American (personal communication and demonstration from Ralph Redfox (2001). It is also present in Chinese, Japanese, and African traditions.
6. A good resource for information about chakras is *Path to the Soul* by Ashok Bedi (2001).

7. Active imagination is described in the glossary of terms at the end of the chapter. If a therapist intends to use "active imagination" in his or her practice it is necessary to learn the technique from a certified Jungian analyst by going through the process of active imagination and then being supervised by an analyst when beginning to use the technique with patients.
8. Freud (1961) describes the unconscious as being like a large room in which the various mental excitations are crowding one another like individual beings. Adjoining this room is a smaller room, ego consciousness. Between the rooms is a censor, who denies the contents of the unconscious admission to the reception room when he disapproves of them (305). One of the big differences between the theories of Freud and Jung is Jung's concept of the limitless, unknown, and unknowable scope of the unconscious, which is quite different from Freud's idea of a large room.
9. Most Martial Arts training teaches students confidence and patience. Contrary to what one would think, students are taught rules for fighting in the following sequence: avoid occasions where fighting may occur; if fighting occurs, leave the situation; if one cannot leave the situation without fighting, do as little damage as possible; if one's life is in danger and there is no other option, injure the other person severely enough to stop the danger to one's life.
10. *The Turbulent Mirror* by John Briggs et al. (1990) presents a simplified version of chaos theory for the layperson.

Chapter 4

PATTERNED FORMS OF ATTACHMENT AND PATHOLOGICAL COMPLEXES

One of the best examples I have seen of a patterned form of attachment was presented in a cartoon starring Daffy Duck. He had a new job as a door-to-door vacuum cleaner salesman. He had visions of making a lot of money and was excited and enthused. When Daffy called on his first customer, the customer slammed the door on his beak; at the second home Daffy was hit over the head; at the third home the prospective buyer slammed his foot in the door; at the fourth home he was thrown off a high porch onto the ground. Daffy kept going and at every home the owner had another way of saying "no." Finally, Daffy reached the last house on the block. He knocked on the door and a woman holding a broken vacuum cleaner answered. She looked happy to see him and before she could say a word Daffy jumped up and down screaming. "Go ahead, tell me no, hurt me. I didn't want to sell you this vacuum cleaner anyway."

PATTERNED FORMS OF ATTACHMENT

A *patterned form of attachment* is a distorted and repetitive form of relationship with significant others. It is the relational aspect of a pathological complex and is formed from repetitive experiences of painful mediation of the archetypal/developmental processes that have repeatedly activated the defenses of the Self.

Patterned forms of attachment are created by: (1) multiple genetic factors both physiological and psychological that interfere with the experience of attunement, (2) faulty mediation of the archetypal/developmental processes, (3) repetitive operation of the defenses of the Self, and (4) random experiences of trauma due to the experience of catastrophic events that occur within the cycles of nature (events that have nothing to do with the person or the family of origin).

One example of a patterned form of attachment is a patient who comes into therapy with a history of repeated abandonment in significant relationships. Each experience of abandonment has been followed by anxiety, depression, and numbing. Unconsciously, this patient believes the therapist will abandon him or her because relationships are viewed through a lens of relationship that perceives significant others as "abandoning." Consciously, the patient hopes he or she will not be abandoned; however, the patterned form of attachment has already created the unconscious expectation of an abandoning therapist, skewing the therapeutic relationship.

This chapter will focus on developing an understanding of patterned forms of attachment, how they are formed and how to work with them in the clinical setting. When a patient discusses his or her history, patterned forms of attachment emerge as repetitive and painful experiences with significant others that are also attempts to "overcome the effects of earlier traumatic family experiences" (Sable, 2000, 77). Transformation of patterned forms of attachment into healthy affectional bonds is the primary measure for therapy that has been successful.

The man who suffered from the "nightmare train dream" had a repetitive patterned form of attachment. When he experienced someone as an authority, he experienced that person as train-like, and he slipped away from the relationship by no longer defining himself or speaking his truth. Any possibility for relationship with a significant other disappeared when this man experienced the other person as train-like, and in response to his perceptions he became a helpless victim. His patterned form of attachment made it impossible for him to remain married or keep a job. Eventually, it brought him to therapy where he began discussing his problems with relationships. How could a therapist, initially perceived by this man as an authority remain outside the patterned form of attachment and help him? This chapter will attempt to answer that question.

THE FORMATION OF PATTERNED FORMS OF ATTACHMENT

Ego consciousness cannot develop without human caregivers to mediate the archetypal/developmental processes. The quality of mediation depends on multiple factors: the genetic constitution of the infant, toddler, child, adolescent, and adult; the way he or she experiences mediation; and the caretakers own experiences of mediation as well as his or her ability to perform attuned mediation.

In addition to relationships with caregivers, patterned forms of attachment can develop from relationships with siblings, grandparents, teachers, friends, and roles projected onto the affected person by the family (e.g., "the scapegoat," "the stupid one," "the one just like____," "the one with the brains") or from watching pathological mediation without actually experiencing it. For example, a patient might say, "My sister and my mother were emotionally abused by my father. I was his favorite and I hated him for what he did to them. I swore I would never be emotionally abused and now I am in an abusive relationship. How could that happen?"

The experiences of mediation gradually form ways of relating or patterns of attachment that can broadly range from secure to insecure, avoidant (Ainsworth 1984), or disorganized (Main and Solomon 1990). When mediation is experienced as good enough, ego consciousness develops; and even though life presents painful experiences the person can remain flexible, attuned and form relationships that are relatively free from distortion (Karen 1998, 149). However, repetitive experiences of disintegration can occur at any time in life, as in the case of the Woman Who Once Walked in Balance, creating rigid and patterned forms of attachment. How does that happen?

When ego consciousness experiences high levels of disintegration, the defenses of the Self (denial, splitting, introjection, identification, projection, and idealization) mobilize in order to protect ego consciousness. Denial pushes the accumulated experiences of disintegration into the unconscious. Splitting divides the experiences from consciousness. The experiences of mediation as well as the mediators themselves are introjected. When the defenses of the Self operate repetitively, these experiences are summarized into a repetitive pattern that distorts outer relationships through identification, projection, and idealization. The repeated experiences of disintegration are summarized into a pattern that eventually becomes an unconscious filter with a limited range of perceptions of reality accompanied by unconscious beliefs about what can and cannot happen in relationships.

When the patterned form of attachment is constellated, a person's posture, language, skin color, facial expression, and tone of voice will change. It is as if an invisible pair of contact lenses has suddenly appeared over the person's eyes; the wearer is totally unaware of any changes in his or her frame of reference until asked and even then may not be aware of the change.

The father of attachment theory is John Bowlby. His colleagues, Mary Ainsworth (1984) and Mary Main (1995), did extensive research on attachment and identified three broad areas of patterned forms of attachment in children: secure, ambivalent, and avoidant (Karen 1998, 161, 226). In addition, Main identified a fourth form of attachment that appeared as disorganized and disoriented (Main and Solomon 1990). The securely attached child acts as if the mother is trustworthy. The child with an ambivalent attachment seems anxious about the ability of the mother to be trustworthy, seeming overly concerned about receiving attention from her when he or she is upset, and yet fighting attempts to be soothed. An avoidantly attached child appears to need nothing from the mother and seems to have no interest in being soothed, yet internally is quite anxious. The disorganized and disoriented forms of attachment usually arise from neurological problems in the child such as ADHD or from dynamics of abuse that occur in chaotic families. All of these patterned forms of attachment persevere into adulthood (Karen 1998, 226-227; Fish and Dudas, 1999, 27-40, and Main 1990). They can also become worse in dysfunctional relationships or better in healthy relationships (Sable 2000, 75–79). The research done by Bowlby, Ainsworth, Main, and others certainly compliments Jung's theories on complex and provide one more viewing point into the highly individual and unique structures of pathological complexes, both for ourselves and for our patients.

Understanding of a patient's present and past forms of attachment is one of the most important keys for successful therapy. Patterned forms of attachment are both rigid and repetitive. They possess three characteristics: similarity of emotion or affect, generalization of experience, and repetitive behavior over time (Weiss 1991, 66–76).

Psychologist Harry Harlow also did research on patterned forms of attachment by subjecting baby monkeys to differing forms of caretaking using different kinds of mothers (Karen 1998, 124, 147, 204). In the experiments going on during the early 1940s, the baby monkeys were divided into four groups. The first group had a real mother; the second group had a soft, terry cloth mother; the third group had a wire mother; and the fourth group had a terry cloth mother that delivered random electrical shocks. The healthiest monkeys (those that were able to be relational as well as sexual with other monkeys) were those who were attached to the real mother. The babies of the terry cloth mother and the wire mother did poorly. Those with terry cloth mothers had trouble relating to other monkeys, were sometimes violent with their offspring, and had difficulty being sexual. Those with wire mothers were often violent with their offspring and unable to socialize at all. The monkeys with the randomly shocking mothers died or barely survived. Those that survived were able to eat yet they spent the rest of their time curled up in the fetal position.

Harlow also did research on attachment between monkeys with similar mothering.[1] What was most interesting for me about that research was that the monkeys with similar patterns of "mothering" accepted one another. The experiment was done using a large plastic tube that was big enough to contain five monkeys. Four monkeys, each with a different pattern of mothering, were placed in wedge-shaped cubicles that were connected with one large circular cubicle in the center of the tube. Each one of the wedges had an opening into the center cubicle. One monkey with one of the patterns of mothering mentioned above was placed in the center cubicle. Each one of the four monkeys placed in the wedges could join the monkey in the center. A monkey who had a similar pattern of mothering always joined the monkey in the center. The other monkeys remained in their wedges. The experiment was performed over and over using all of the experimental patterns of mothering mentioned above. The results were the same, indicating that some sort of bonding occurred that was related to the pattern of mothering, not to species.

I have observed many couples with complementary patterned forms of attachment. For example, a husband became extremely angry and loud as soon as he became frustrated. The wife responded by becoming frozen with shame and fear. Communication between them deteriorated to such a degree that they sought therapy as a way to negotiate their way through a divorce. As each of them explored his or her internal experience in therapy, it became clear to both of them that beneath the husband's anger was shame and fear and beneath the wife's feelings of shame and fear was her anger. These feelings perpetuated a sense of ambivalent commitment that perpetuated each of the partner's ambivalent attachment to the family of origin. As each partner's ambivalence surfaced and he or she chose to contain and reflect upon his or affect rather than react, the relationship gradually became more secure. Communication improved as both he and she stopped reacting to the partner when his or her complex was constellated.

The experimental monkeys who received negative mothering and the children with ambivalent and avoidant attachment described by Ainsworth operated with negative patterns of attachment that affected both their internal experience and their communication with others. The Woman Who Once Walked in Balance was deeply affected by a pathological complex. Before she was able to begin her healing process, she had to make a choice between life and death and staying alone or being with others. She chose life, and that meant having a relationship with her teachers and taking what they had to offer.

VIEWING POINTS INTO PATTERNED FORMS OF ATTACHMENT

Patterned forms of attachment interfere with the clinical relationship and are the basis for transference/countertransference reactions, miscommunications, and misunderstandings within the relational field. Pathological complexes and patterned forms of attachment never disappear. No one is immune to them or above them. However, patterned forms of attachment can be contained and reflected upon, and portions of them can be transformed. The most positive way to deal with them is to choose to allow them to become teachers. The teachings are given when the patterned form of attachment is constellated and instead of a person reacting, the experience is contained, reflected upon, and learned from.

A patterned form of attachment is often stronger than the patient or the therapist. However, when the patient's experience in the here-and-now of the clinical hour is gradually connected with one viewing point of the patterned form of attachment after another, the pattern begins to unfold into parts, weakening the structure and exposing them to consciousness. Ego consciousness can be overwhelmed when patterned forms of attachment are constellated, making it difficult for the person to remain grounded in the actual relationship. The development of containment, introspection, awareness, and ego consciousness becomes easier when the pattern is broken down and observed from multiple viewing points. The following material presents multiple ways of observing patterned forms of attachment.

Figure 12 describes the relationship between ego consciousness and a patterned form of attachment. Under normal circumstances, the pattern is unconscious. When a the patterned form of attachment or pathological complex is constellated, normal ego consciousness falls into the unconscious and the person begins to perceive and react from the pathological complex and the patterned form of attachment. When the complex and the patterned form of attachment accumulate more and more energy, the possibility for a relationship between ego conscious and the Self (ego/Self axis) as well as between ego consciousness and others diminishes. Pathology can be thought of as a range that depends upon how often the complex and the patterned form of attachment is constellated. When they are constellated for most of a person's waking hours, the ability to learn, communicate, relate, and work is weakened. The less often the pattern is constellated, the more energy is available to ego consciousness for development within the present moment.

PATTERNED FORMS OF ATTACHMENT AND THE COMPONENTS OF EGO CONSCIOUSNESS

When a patterned form of attachment is constellated, one or more of the functions of ego consciousness are out of balance. When these functions of ego consciousness are in balance: affect and soul give energy; the physical and dreaming bodies provide containment; receptivity allows memories to emerge and the connection with the collective unconscious to function, and behavior and spirit define the movement of life energy in harmony with the

Patterned Forms of Attachment and Pathological Complexes 127

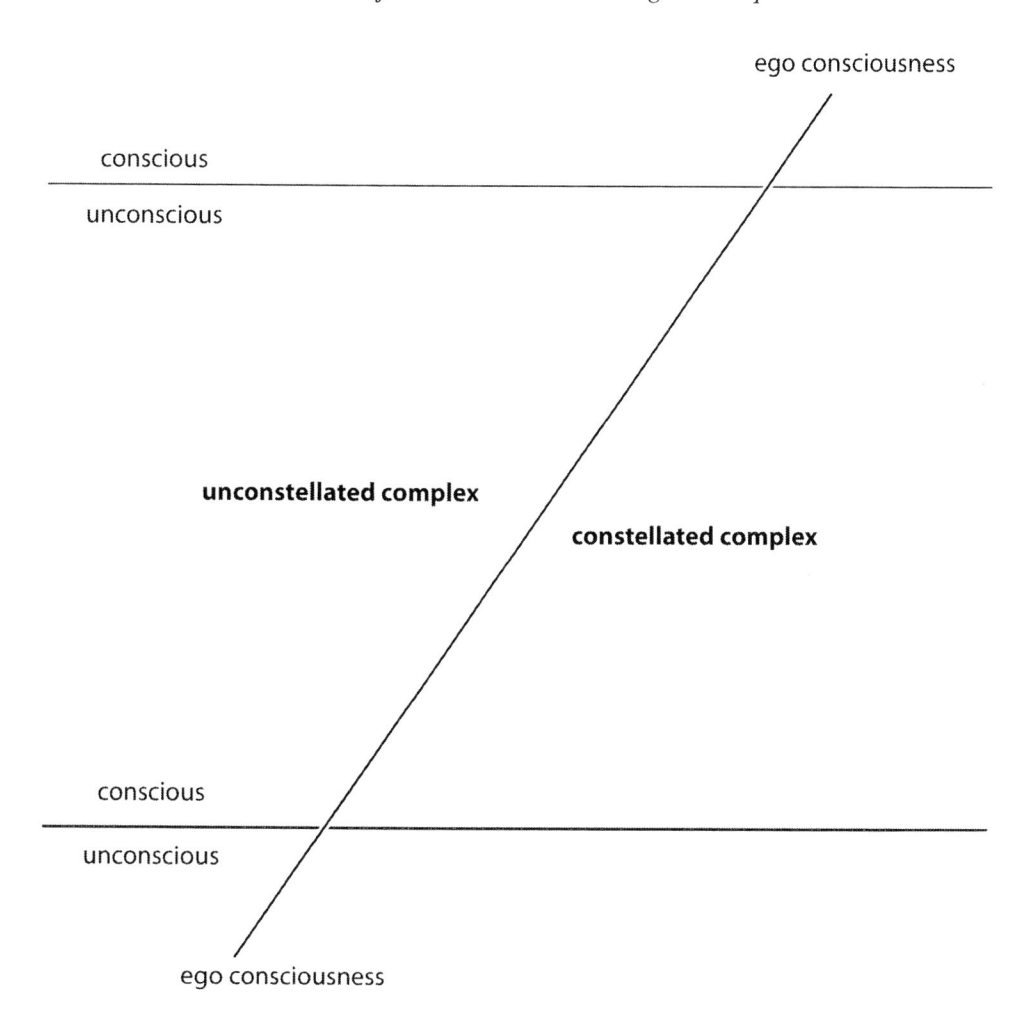

FIGURE 12
The relationship between ego consciousness and a constellated complex.

individuation process. When these functions are out of balance, a person may remember dreams and be receptive to memories and experiences of the collective unconscious but may be distressed or depressed because of an inability to express affect appropriately in relationships or to experience it internally. Loss or decrease of function in one or more of the eight aspects of ego consciousness is one way to diagnose a patterned form of attachment. For example, a patient who has posttraumatic stress disorder has very clear memories of being sexually abused and experiences very little affect.

In the beginning phases of therapy, it is important to note those functions of ego consciousness that are the strongest and attune to them. Focusing on the patient's strengths will give him or her a sense of feeling understood as well as assisting with containment as he or she begins to give the therapist a history.

When I speak of attunement, I mean coming into a harmony and an understanding of the patient's experience. Imagine that the relational field is a circle that connects both the therapist and the patient to one another. Some patients have small circles and others have circles that are quite large, depending upon the function, depth, and balance of the components of ego consciousness. Attunement is the ability of the therapist to locate and understand the size of the patient's circle and to communicate within the range of that circle and at the same time gently stretch that circle a little at a time.

In order to develop attunement, it is important to sink into a state of relaxed pleasure and hold the patient's goodness and health in the back of one's mind. One part of the mind focuses on listening to the patient and attempting to understand his or her experience as if it were one's own, and the other part of the mind is relaxed and receptive, always holding the patient's goodness and health in mind.

Affect and Soul

True emotion is experienced and passes through us like water, eventually carving our experience into an internal landscape that is both meaningful and beautiful—our soul. An affective theme lasts for minutes, hours, days, or years. It is a unique blend of the innate affects twined together into a repetitive theme that holds the patterned form of attachment together. The terror felt by the man with the "nightmare train" dream is an excellent example of how an affective theme operates. When the affective theme was constellated because someone else was perceived as a "train-like" authority, both ego consciousness and the relationship lost energy because the dreamer's perceptions and experience were locked into the patterned form of attachment. For the dreamer, the reality of the other person ceased to exist and he or she became "train-like." The affective theme kept him far from others and his affective experience was so blocked that it could not flow to carve his life into meaning.

The affective theme in a patterned form of attachment produces a history of relationships with the same repetitive themes. As therapy progresses and the patient begins to identify the parts of the patterned form of attachment, the affective theme will begin to separate into the affective parts that have formed it. For example, when the man with the "nightmare train" began to experience affect in the present moment, the experience created such a sense of disorganization within him that it was difficult for him to think or speak.

Clinical Vignette: Example of an Affective Theme

Patient: Every time I tell her what I think she puts me down. After that I feel as if my body is on fire. I hurt and I can't think. It is terribly painful and lasts for days.

Body and Dreaming Body

When the physical and dreaming bodies are weakened, the patient may describe him or herself as feeling "not present" or disembodied. There may be chronic physical problems that deplete energy. The person may not be able to contain and reflect upon his or her experience and dreams may appear as nightmares. Relaxing into the experience of having one's patterned form of attachment constellated rather than reacting is the heart of learning to develop both the physical and dreaming bodies.

It is easy to think of the physical body as a container, but most therapists are not taught to think about dreaming as a container. The following clinical vignette describes how a dream might become a container for experience.

A Clinical Vignette: Dreaming as a Container

A 44-year-old man came into therapy because he felt unsuccessful in his business and lonely at home. He grew up in a family where he was considered "the good child that no one had to worry about." Although the family was caring, there was little affection, and emotions were not expressed. The patient described a childhood nightmare in which he did everything perfectly to prepare for a race, but when the gun went off, he could not move because his feet were encased in cement. As we explored the feelings evoked by the dream we discovered an affective theme of shame mixed with terror. The patient was able to link this affective theme with an inability to reach out and ask for affection from his wife or to market his business successfully. The images in the dream gave him his own way to understand his inability to move and provided a way for him to eventually learn to change his behavior.

When the physical and/or dreaming bodies are weakened because of a patterned form of attachment, the patient's ability to contain is weakened. *Containment* is the ability to hold the material of a patterned form of attachment and observe what is going on both internally and externally, rather than reacting. The man whose feet were "stuck in cement" explored the physical sensations of being stuck and linked them with his fear and shame. As he became more able to explore his fear and shame these affects became linked with memories of being shamed when he felt very happy and his learning to shut down rather than express himself in relationships.

When large parts of the experience of the physical body are held within the patterned form of attachment, people may develop physical symptoms or experience high levels of stress a great deal of the time. When this is the case, it is important for therapist to encourage the patient to find ways to explore the muscle, joint, tendon, and organ tightness linked with his or her experience as well as developing the ability to nourish the body through diet, rest, relaxing into a state of pleasure, and daily exercise. These activities build somatic awareness. No one is too busy to find ways to nourish the body. Exploration of what the patient can do and what he or she cannot do to nourish the body leads directly into the patterned form of attachment. Getting enough sleep, eating healthier foods, gentle exercise, and meditation are ways the patient can begin to develop containment and somatic awareness.

Patients who do not dream may be able to find images from the dreaming body contained in muscular tightness, physical sensations, and medical problems. As therapy progresses, the patient will become able to discover affective themes in the form of images or simple awareness that are locked within his or her physical experiences. This is a sign that the patient is developing containment.

Memory and the Collective Unconscious

When memory is functioning well, the person is receptive to information and can begin to remember how the patterned form of attachment becomes constellated and how it operates. He or she can connect his or her life experiences and relationships with that pattern. The person may also be receptive to the images that come from the collective human memory, gradually providing a new frame of reference that allows the person's awareness to grow beyond the confines of the complex.

When large portions of the personal past are unavailable to ego consciousness, the person's patterned form of attachment can be located in significant relationships in the present and later linked with the patterns from past relationships. When the receptive functions of ego consciousness are weakened, memories of the past are distorted and unreliable. The person simply cannot remember accurately because the patterned form of attachment interferes. I call these "rigidified memories." The patient presents them as irrefutable fact–rigidified, one-dimensional sequences that include a muted range of affect and the inability to develop associations. An *association* is "a spontaneous linkage of ideas, perceptions, images, fantasies [with] certain personal . . . psychological themes, motifs, similarities, oppositions or causalities" (Samuels et al. 1986, 28). For example, a clinical encounter between a therapist and a person with "rigidified memories" might sound something like this: A 45-year old minister enters therapy because of recurring fantasies of violence. The fantasies intrude in his dreams and also his driving. He is quite upset about them because they are so different from his values, the way he lives his life and his religious beliefs.

Patient: (after five weeks of therapy) "I'm still having those fantasies about beating up cops. I wake up with them, and I still have them when I am driving." *(The fantasies are always variations on the same theme.)* "This time, a cop tries to give me a ticket when I haven't done anything wrong. I get out of my car, beat him up, and then force him to apologize to me."

Therapist: "What would that be like for you to beat that guy up and then make him apologize to you?"

Patient: "Oh, I'd never be able to do that really. It's just something I have dreams and fantasies about. I am not and never could be a violent person."

Therapist: "What would make a nonviolent person have violent fantasies?

Patient: "I really hate these fantasies. They just come up and I can't stop them. I don't understand them at all. Why would I have these kinds of fantasies when I would never do such things? "

Therapist (internal dialogue): He and I have been over this territory repeatedly. He seems unable to create associations between his fantasies and anything in his past or present experience. He wants me to give him a logical reason for his fantasies and make them disappear. He seems unable to understand or accept a part of himself that feels angry and aggressive. I feel frustrated. He sounds frustrated. Internally he must have some pretty good reasons for not being able to remember his feelings of anger and aggression.

Therapist to patient: "It sounds like you want those fantasies to stop bothering you."

Patient: "I really do. I am so frustrated, and I am driving myself crazy asking myself why they are there. What could I have done to make them happen?"

Therapist (internal observations): He is a minister; perhaps he believes that violent fantasies are sinful. He seems to be very hard on himself for having the fantasies. Since he has some affect about having the fantasies, perhaps he and I can explore his affect.

Therapist (to patient): "What is it like for you to keep having these fantasies and feel so frustrated and crazy?"
Patient: "I really hate them." (Long silence.) "I must really be a bad person to have these fantasies."
Therapist: "What happens inside when you feel like a really bad person?"
Patient: "Like everybody is looking at me because I am stinky and dirty and *bad.* I don't ever remember that happening in my life, but I feel that way when I have those fantasies."

Therapist (internal observation): The patient's face has reddened; he has pulled his body into the chair. He appears to be experiencing a high level of what might be shame.

Therapist (to patient): "What is happening inside?"
Patient: "I want to run away and hide right now. I don't want you to see me. I hate myself for feeling this way. I feel as if somebody really big is standing over me and laughing at me."
Therapist: "There is so much pain inside."
Patient: (*long silence*) "I don't know where this comes from. Why do I have it? I hate it. I want it to go away."

Therapist (internal observations): He seems strong enough to be able to stay with the feeling. His "why" may be a way for him to move away from his internal experience.

Therapist (to patient): "What is it like for you to sit with me in such pain?"
Patient: "I feel numb and dumb and blind. I am helpless, nothing. I hate myself When I feel this way. I just want it to go away."
We sit quietly together.

Therapist (internal observations): He is doing a good job of holding and being with his pain. I wonder if his fantasy material, aggression, and apology from an authority are what he needed as a child and did not receive. Am I pushing him too hard?

Therapist (to patient): "What are you feeling now?"
Patient: "I don't know, just really uncomfortable."

Therapist (internal reflection): His face looks gray and drawn. I think it is time for me to assist him in containing his experience.

Therapist (to patient): "I really believe you when you say you are uncomfortable. You look pale and shaken. What you are experiencing is the work of therapy, and this kind of work makes therapy really hard. This is the space of deep pain and not knowing, a place of crucifixion. It is a hard place to be."

Patient: "I feel so helpless and so chaotic. I don't know what to do or how to think about this. Will this just go on and on forever?"

Therapist (internal reflection): He is beginning to sound younger and more helpless. I think he may be regressing because he is overwhelmed by affect. His observing ego and our relationship is not strong enough to support a regression. I am moving too deep, too quickly. We need to contain the affect.

Therapist (to patient): "Your pain brings new life. It is important to place some of the pain outside of yourself and express it so that both of us can try to understand what it is telling us. Some ways to do that are drawing, painting, working with clay, or using the sand trays and the figures on the shelves around the room to express what you are feeling."

Patient: "I want to use those figures and put them in the sand box."

This man worked with the sand tray for about a year. Each time he completed a tray I took two pictures of it with a Polaroid camera and dated them. He received one picture and I kept one for his file.

He never did remember much about his childhood or early school years. However, he was able to link his shame with being shamed both within his family and at school because he had big ears as a child. We discovered that his fantasies of aggression followed by an apology from an authority were what he needed as a child and compensated his shame. He was so unaware of his assertiveness that the people in his church repeatedly took advantage of him, calling him at all hours with their demands.

As he repeatedly moved into and through his painful sense of shame, we learned that when he wanted to say "no" to someone, he experienced shame. In order to avoid the feeling of shame, he did whatever anyone asked him. As he sat with the shame, he became stronger and gradually grew assertive enough to say "no." The sand tray figures he used to express his feelings sometimes appeared in his dreams as images from the collective unconscious. One image in particular, the "wild man," a primitive, earthy, and strong male spirit appeared in many guises in both the sand tray and his dreaming, gradually transforming his narrow religious attitudes about men into compassion and acceptance of his own manhood and deepening of his own experience of Christ.

Behavior and Spirit

Behavior defines the movement of life energy toward or away from individuation. The Old Indian Man is a good example of how behavior and spirit work together to foster individuation. He paid attention to his dreams, his visions, and his own longing, letting them carry him into a life he could never have imagined. He could have remained a rage-filled alcoholic. He could have ignored his nightmares. He could have chosen not to study with the medicine man. He could have ignored the paints. As he made choices and behaved in ways that honored and respected his own experience, he fostered his connection with the "higher power," or spirit. His awareness developed gradually, and as it did, he was able to make better choices. His better choices fostered the development of his spirit and his options for living life fully increased.

The word *spirit* means both breath of life or the life energy that enlivens the body and disconnects from it at death. Our spirit is connected with our behavior and our will. Our spirit develops or shrivels because of our choices, our relationships, and our behavior. Even though our spirits are not visible and are unknowable, each spirit is connected with every aspect of the entire personality, both conscious and unconscious. At any one moment in time, the energy of our spirit is composed by the sum of our intentions, our choices, and our behaviors, both conscious and unconscious. When our behavior is aligned with our own individuation process, our spirit is developing and our conscious energy increasing, creating a more focused intention and opportunities for us to make better choices.

There is nothing mystical about behavior or spirit. A dear friend of mine was the administrator of a mental institution in a foreign country. The nurses and doctors complained about patients in one ward who seemed more depressed and less active. My friend went to the ward, observed the patients, and asked them to take off their shoes. The patients had not had their toenails clipped for several years. As it became more and more difficult for them to walk, they became more and more sedentary. Common sense is one of the most necessary requirements for observing a patient's behavior.

The patterned form of attachment will always surface when the patient discusses his or her relationships; however, the awareness of the impact of his or her behavior on others may remain hidden. There are several indirect ways to observe behavior: (1) in the way the patient relates to the therapist: late cancels, not showing up, being late for appointments, repeated attempts to extend the clinical hour, repeated phone calls, showing up at the wrong time and expecting to be seen, slow payment, or no payment; (2) in the way the therapist relates to the patient: containment, attunement, boredom, fatigue, not listening with a focused attention, sarcasm, unwillingness to make the effort to attune to the patient, or forcing the patient to conform to the therapist's beliefs or ideas of who or what the patient was or should become; (3) in the way the patient treats him or herself; (4) in a meeting with the patient and a significant other in the clinical hour to answer questions about how the therapeutic process is affecting the relationship.

Therapy is a contractual process, and both the patient and the therapist are accountable to the relationship. The four components of the subtle body are deeply connected with the unconscious and interact with one another. Even though this connection is almost impossible to track, it influences the relational field. In the introduction to "The Psychology of the Transference," Jung talked about the intensity of the therapeutic relationship, likening each person to a chemical substance: "When two chemical substances combine, both are altered" (*CW* 16, 1946, 1977, 171). We are as changed by our patients as they are by us.

As the therapy progresses, the components of ego consciousness embedded within the pathological complex begin to appear as "parts" of the patient that may seem foreign, overwhelming, lost, hateful, needy, overwhelming, or frightening. One woman, whose memories of childhood abuse were very clear, had great difficulty as she began experiencing affect. During the months when she felt overwhelmed and chaotic because of her emerging feelings, she and I cooperated to build a "containing structure" for her that included three clinical hours a week, two scheduled therapy phone calls a week, physical holding every day by her husband, and weekly contact with two supportive friends. Her willingness to act within this structure and use it to create containment helped her create a new life. Her behavior made all the difference.

THE IMAGO AND PATTERNED FORMS OF ATTACHMENT

The parental imago[2] "is constituted on the one hand by the personally acquired image of the parents, but on the other hand by the parent archetype which exists a priori, i.e., in the preconscious structure of the psyche" (*CW* 16, 1945, 1977, 96) and (*CW* 11, 1977, 259). What this means is that the structure of the imago is a blend of experiences of the caretakers enmeshed with the numinous energy of the archetypes. When the imago is encountered in the clinical situation, it can be thought of as a pathological structure that functions within consciousness, the preconscious, and the unconscious. The conscious portion of the imago is what the person believes about his or her history, caretakers, and experiences, which is only the tip of the iceberg. The preconscious portion of the imago often acts as an internal censor that judges parts of the patient's experience. A good example of the preconscious function of the imago is when a person discovers an internal voice, image, or physical sensation that dictates whether or not he or she can feel certain emotions, perform certain behaviors, or be, do, think, have an identity, or create certain things. The unconscious portion of the imago functions with the authority of an almighty being. This portion of the imago is communicated to a person through dreams, active imagination, fantasies, and/or spontaneous intuitions.

Clinical Example of the Imago in a Patterned Form of Attachment

A woman came into therapy because of repeated failures in her significant relationships. She felt controlled, misunderstood, and victimized by others. She was in individual and group therapy for two and a half years. Her observing ego was well developed, and she felt strong enough to do an enactment between her "mother part" and her "observing ego." She described her mother as "overprotective, controlling, and always right."

The patient became aware that she was really angry with her therapist and was afraid to talk about it. However, she finally brought it up in group therapy. The therapist explained to her that her anger was a part of her that could be expressed without destroying the therapist, the patient, or their relationship. The patient decided to enact what she called her "angry mother part" in group therapy. She placed pillows one on top of the other for her "mother part" and created a space on the floor for her "observing ego." The therapist was asked to "do therapy" with each part.

Patient (enacting the mother part and speaking to the therapist): "You are just a puny woman. You can't make my daughter do anything. I can tell her anything I want and she has to listen. If I tell her something it is for her well-being. I protect her from the "bad things" in life. You are just some jerk with a license that thinks she knows something and takes money for it. You don't care about her at all. She is MY daughter."

Therapist (to mother part): "It sounds as if you really love your daughter and care about her and it also sounds as if you don't approve of me at all. Is that right?"

Patient (enacting the mother part): "I think you are not good enough for her. She needs a therapist who is better trained and has more degrees. You are not helping her at all. I hate you."

Therapist (*internal observations*): I am so glad this possessive mother part of her is finally ready to speak her piece to me. It will be a relief to have the hostility toward me out in the open.

Therapist (*to mother part*): "I am relieved that you are finally speaking about how angry you are at me. What is that like for you to finally tell me those things?"
Patient (*enacting the mother part*): "I don't feel relief at all. I am really angry that you are interfering with MY daughter and I want you to stop it. She shouldn't be talking to you at all. This is all book nonsense. She should be at church tonight, not here with you."
Therapist (*to mother part*): "Your daughter belongs to herself and no one else."
Patient (*enacting mother part*): "She belongs to me. I am her mother. I birthed her. I sacrificed for her and I tell her what to do. She has to have me. The world is not a safe place."

As the dialogue continued, the "mother part" became less angry at the therapist and finally revealed that she was raped and became pregnant with the daughter. As the "mother part" continued to speak, she revealed her ambivalence toward her daughter, the love she had for her as well as her hatred of her pregnancy and her pain at having to raise a child alone. The mother never told the daughter that she was raped, only that her father had disappeared. When the patient checked this "memory" with her mother, she found out that it was true. (This information arose spontaneously from the collective human memory during the patient's enactment of her "mother part") The therapy progressed well as the woman began to trust her own experience and understand that her mother's pain and ambivalence toward her had undermined her ability to relate to significant others.

THE EGO/IMAGO AXIS

Figure 13 describes the ego/imago axis and the components of the patterned form of attachment. When a patterned form of attachment is interfering with learning, communication, significant relationships, and/or work, the imago has become a barrier between ego consciousness and others as well as between ego consciousness and the Self. If the patterned form of attachment keeps accumulating more and more material, the imago eventually eclipses relations between the ego consciousness and the Self and between ego consciousness and others. The result is an ego/imago axis. Pathology is directly related to the strength of the components of the ego/imago axis.

138   *C. G. Jung's Complex Dynamics and the Clinical Relationship*

Misattuned Patterns of Mediation
Symbiotic
Directive
Cooperative
Containing
Confirming
Educating
Empowering

ego consciousness

the unconscious
personal and collectives

THE EGO

THE IMAGO

subtle body

physical body

Archetypal Developmental Process
Being
Doing
Thinking
Identity
Creativity

objective reality

the self

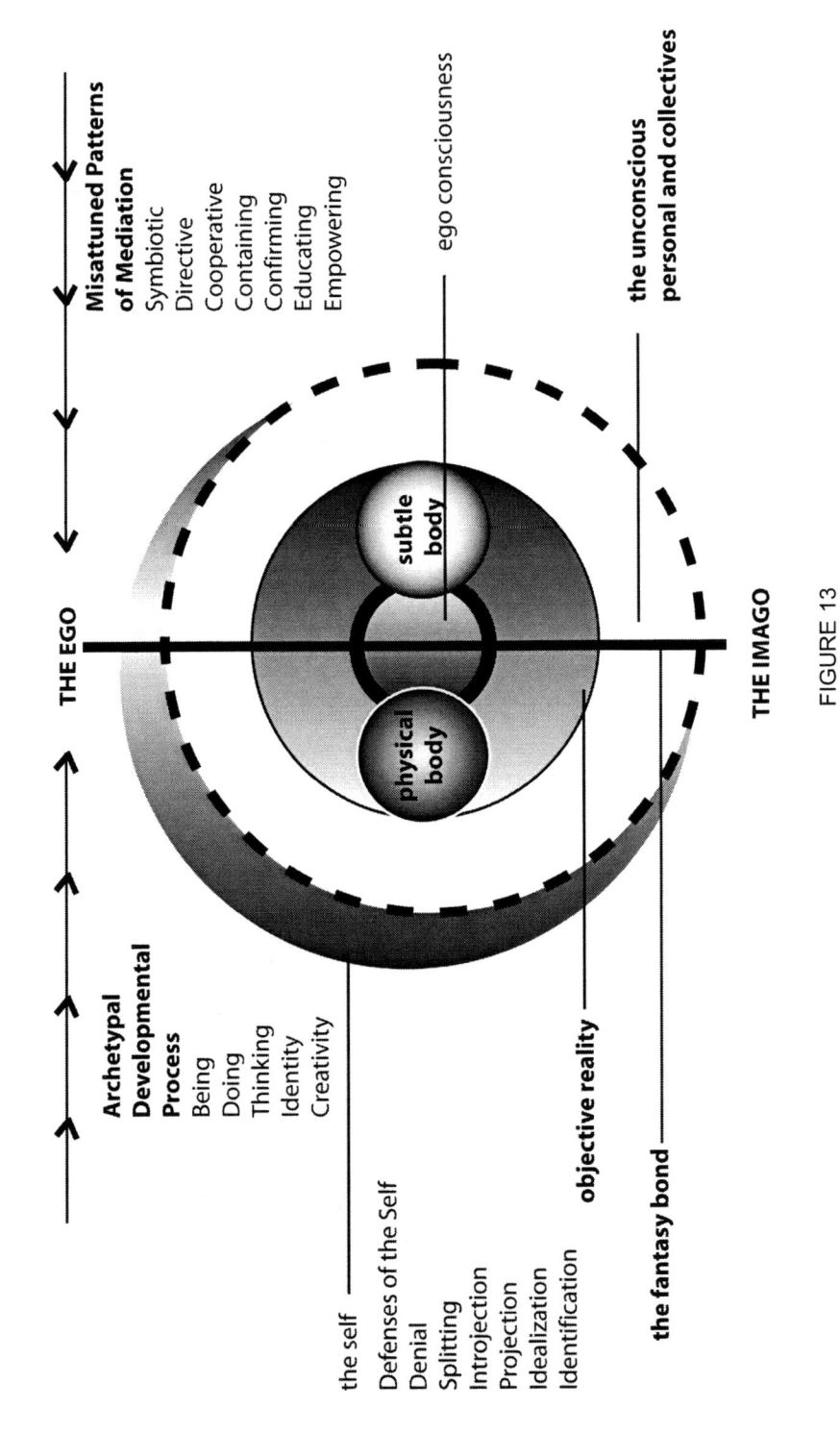

Defenses of the Self
Denial
Splitting
Introjection
Projection
Idealization
Identification

the fantasy bond

FIGURE 13
The ego / imago axis.

Daniel Stern (1985) described Representations of Interactions that have been Generalized, or RIGs, and noted that the internal experience of these structures is "felt as an I experience with an other." He called this other the "evoked companion" and noted that as ego development takes place, the evoked companion and the RIGs accompanying it "serve as a clue that alters behavior, without a reliving of the generalized event" (97). The actual experiences of mediation with real caretakers become unconscious cues that alter behavior. Stern's observations confirm Jung's description of experiences of actual caregivers as part of the imago; however, Stern does not include the introjection of numinous archetypal energy. The strength of the imago depends not only on the caretaker but also on blocked and thwarted archetypal energy enmeshed with the experiences of the caretaker. Abusive, neglectful, and poorly attuned mediation of the archetypal/developmental processes distorts and/or partially blocks the ability of ego consciousness to use these processes to develop and adapt.

Erskine, Moursund, and Trautmann (1999) have applied Stern's ideas to the clinical setting in their book *About Empathy: A Therapy of Contact-In-Relationship*. According to the authors, we introject characteristics of caregivers, teachers, and so forth, including their psychological characteristics, self-limiting decisions, and ideas; and they become "introjects." When these introjects are linked with the defenses of the Self, archetypal/developmental processes, and the mediation of these processes, they operate unconsciously, remaining primitive and undeveloped. As a transitional space is developed between the imago and the ego, and the patient begins to become aware of the operation of the imago, therapy with the imago in the form of "parts work" becomes an invaluable tool (263). This technique is described at length in *About Empathy* and has been used and clinically refined for more than 30 years by Erskine and other practitioners of what began as gestalt therapy (Perls 1973; McNeil 1976, 61–67). However, therapy with "parental introjects" as described by Erskine et al. focuses on experiences with actual caretakers and does not deal with archetypal energy.

When patients have been in therapy long enough to identify the internal voice, image, sensation, or memory that is their experience of their caregivers and observe the experiences, they are ready for parts work with the parental imago. It is important that a patient has developed enough space between the ego and the imago to observe its operation in everyday life and see how it affects both internal experience and relationships with significant others. It is also important that patients be able to contain their reactions when the patterned form of attachment is constellated. During parts work, the patient creates several spaces, one for the imago, another for anyone the patient wishes, and another for the observer of the work.

A Clinical Example of the Imago

A 32-year-old man sought therapy because he had difficulty being assertive with other people and had a difficult time trusting his feelings, thoughts, memories, and behaviors. He was in both individual and group therapy for more than two years. Gradually, he became aware that when he experienced anger, he became very anxious and that he would rather agree with others than feel the anxiety associated with disagreeing. He began to realize that people often took advantage of him at work because he never said no. The diagnosis of an ego/imago axis was made because he was unable to interrupt the pattern of behavioral reactivity of being subservient to others or to sink into his anxiety and explore it.

He began to talk about feeling like a failure in therapy because he felt so "stuck." He felt resentment toward me and also toward the other people in the group. He felt as if he kept swallowing the resentment and doing what he thought I wanted, and he thought that he was not succeeding in meeting his own goals for therapy. His discussion of his resentment was a big step for him because his usual pattern was to say "yes" and withdraw. As we discussed the part of him that felt resentful, he felt that it was somehow associated with his father and that he had another part not associated with his father who felt anxious about his resentment.

This man was dating a woman and wanted to marry her. She was the first woman he had dated that he felt close to. He realized that when he was in a relationship with someone significant, he felt so much anxiety about disagreeing with the other person that he just agreed with whatever he thought the other person wanted. As he did this repeatedly, he became resentful and angry enough to list all the things he felt his partner had done to hurt him, read his partner the list, and then sever the relationship. He was aware that he was gradually beginning to resent his new partner also, and he could not understand where his resentment was coming from. He decided to face his feelings rather than project blame. His goals during his two years of therapy had shifted from learning how to stay in relationships without becoming angry or anxious to learning how to say "no" without leaving a relationship.

He associated the word "*no*" with his father, who went into violent rages when he was displeased. His father never physically abused anyone in the family; instead, he threw things, yelled, swore, and stalked around the house. The patient's mother and all of his siblings were terribly frightened of the father and what might happen if his rage ever got out of control. During the two years of individual and group therapy, the patient began to become aware that his father lived within him as a frightening presence. The patient began to believe that if his "father part" ever got angry, that part of him would destroy everyone and everything around him.

As we began to explore this problem together, the patient found a part of him that felt like his "father," another part of him that felt like a "terrified little boy," and a third part that we called "the observer." The patient decided that in order to understand his inner experience, he would have to enact each of these parts of himself in group therapy so that he could begin to understand these parts of himself.

He made an agreement with the two therapists who facilitated the group, and each one of the group members to support him while he enacted his parts. He was especially concerned that he might hurt himself or someone else when he enacted his violent "father part." Everyone agreed that if he became violent, he would be gently held so that he could express his rage without damaging himself or someone else. He also asked for support and encouragement for the "frightened little boy part" of himself who was terrified of his father's anger. He agreed that when he felt he was finished with his work, he would summarize his experience from his "observer part." He asked his individual therapist to speak with both his "father part" and his "little boy part" and "do therapy with each of them." He agreed to tell everyone that if the "father part" of him felt like going into a rage, he would communicate that from his "observing part" so that the group could support him as he expressed his rage as loud and as long as it felt right to do so. As this patient began to enact his roles, he took huge pillows that were placed around the room and made several into a throne for the "father part." He used a small pillow in front of the throne for the "terrified little boy part." He placed a third pillow to the side of the throne and used this place for his "observer part."

Patient (enacting his father part and glaring at the group): "I am the god. You are just a bunch of silly people who use big words and don't know anything. I am going to strike you dead with my lightning."
Therapist: "Would that make you feel better, if you struck me with lightning?"
Patient (enacting his father part): "I hate you. You tell my son lies. He has to do what I say when I say it. I am going to get him out of this place. Women are good for only one thing and talking is not it."
Therapist: "It must be hard for you to come here every week when you hate me so much."
Patient (enacting his father part): "Oh I really lay into that kid of mine after we go home. All the while he's pretending to tell you the truth, I am telling him the real truth, that stupid little liar. He isn't anxious; he's just a little scared wimp. He just needs to stand up to people and be a man instead of a wimp. He lies all the time. He's just a prissy little yes man."
Therapist: "It must have been hard for you to have a son who didn't live up to your expectations. Is that how it was with you and your dad?"

Patient (enacting his father part): "My dad beat the living shit out of me whenever he felt like it, and I took it like a man. I'd just yell back at him and say, 'Go ahead hit me some more.' When I was 16 I joined the army and pulled myself up by my bootstraps. I never went home again. I knew if I did, I would kill the old bugger."

Therapist: "You have really had a hard life. You really did pull yourself up by your bootstraps didn't you?"

Patient (enacting his father part): "Yeah, I really did. I swore I would never be like my father. He was one of the meanest men in town. Most people liked me. I worked hard and was a good provider."

Therapist: "Were you happy?"

Patient (enacting his father part): "Not really. I was so tired all the time from working that I just wanted to come home to peace and quiet. Instead, I came home to a whiney wife and six bratty kids."

Therapist: "How did you become god the father?"

Patient (enacting his father part): "I am god because I can scare the shit out of anybody I want, any time I want. You wanna get scared?"

Therapist: "I am not afraid of you. I am sorry that you were never happy."

Patient (enacting his father part): "I always had to work. We were always moving. I was always the guy who could handle everything. I was always so tired I just needed time alone and somebody to appreciate me. Alice [patient's mother] acted so helpless all the time. I just wanted to shake her. Sometimes I did. She expected me to come home after a long day and help her with the kids. She didn't work. I paid her bills and never saved anything for myself."

Therapist: "You have really worked hard and all the time did nothing for yourself. You must have felt tired and lonely all the time. Did you?

Patient (enacting his father part): "I felt nothing. I am the god and not a little sniveling wimp like my son."

Therapist: "You don't have feelings? I thought you told me you got really tired and just wanted time alone and someone to appreciate you."

Patient (enacting his father part): "Some affection, some appreciation, just somebody to tell me I was doing a good job. None of my kids appreciated me, and this one was a lazy, no good liar. All of them were so lazy, never picking up after themselves, lying that they had to go to school on Saturdays to have fun doing sports. One of them changed his grades on his report card. Not one of them could stand up to me like I did to my dad. They were little wimps and liars. You're a liar too, lady. You think people can have good relationships. All you people do is use one another, you included. You make money on all this bullshit and my son is a wimpy, little liar."

Therapist: "Your father beat you and you became bitter and resentful. Your life has been lonely and painful. You got no appreciation. Your family

treated you like you were a monster when you were just tired. Your life has been lonely and hard."
Patient (as himself): (tearing up) "I am full of feelings right now. I want to move to the observer place."
Therapist: "Would you mind if I spoke with your 'father' to ask him to come back?"
Patient: "That's okay."
Therapist: "Father, would you be willing to come back again and talk a little more with me?"
Patient (as father part): "I have no choice. I come with him."
Patient (from his "observing part"): "I am overwhelmed. I never realized that I don't trust others or myself because he was always calling all of us kids liars. There is so much going on in me I don't have words for it."
Therapist: "This was an experience filled with different feelings and new awareness. Would you like to draw or paint or do a sand tray about this father work you have just done?"

The patient painted his experience, and then summarized his experience at the end of group therapy during the checkout time.

This patient thought that his inability to be assertive was due to his father's rages. Instead, he discovered, as Dorothy did in the *Wizard of Oz,* that the fire-breathing, numinous man he believed was so powerful was really a small, resentful man who blamed people and hid himself behind a screen of anger. The real damage was the unconscious message from the patient's father and god the father that he was not strong and not masculine, that he was a liar who could not trust himself or trust others. It took this patient four months to integrate his experience of the enactment of his "father part" and begin to identify what he had taken in from his father that truly was a part of him and what he had taken in that belonged to his father that was the result of his painful relationship with his father.

CREATING A TRANSITIONAL SPACE BETWEEN THE PATTERNED FORM OF ATTACHMENT AND EGO CONSCIOUSNESS

Figure 14 describes the transitional space, a place created by mutual cooperation and dialogue between the therapist and the patient. When the patterned form of attachment operates most of the time, normal processes of compensation between the ego and the unconscious are impeded or do not exist. Creation of a space between the imago and the ego allows material, neither imago nor ego, to emerge from the unconscious and be observed, expressed, and contained.

ego consciousness
words

parts work...body work
dreams...painting...active imagination
sand play...drawing...poetry...body imaging

the transitional space

unconscious
wordless

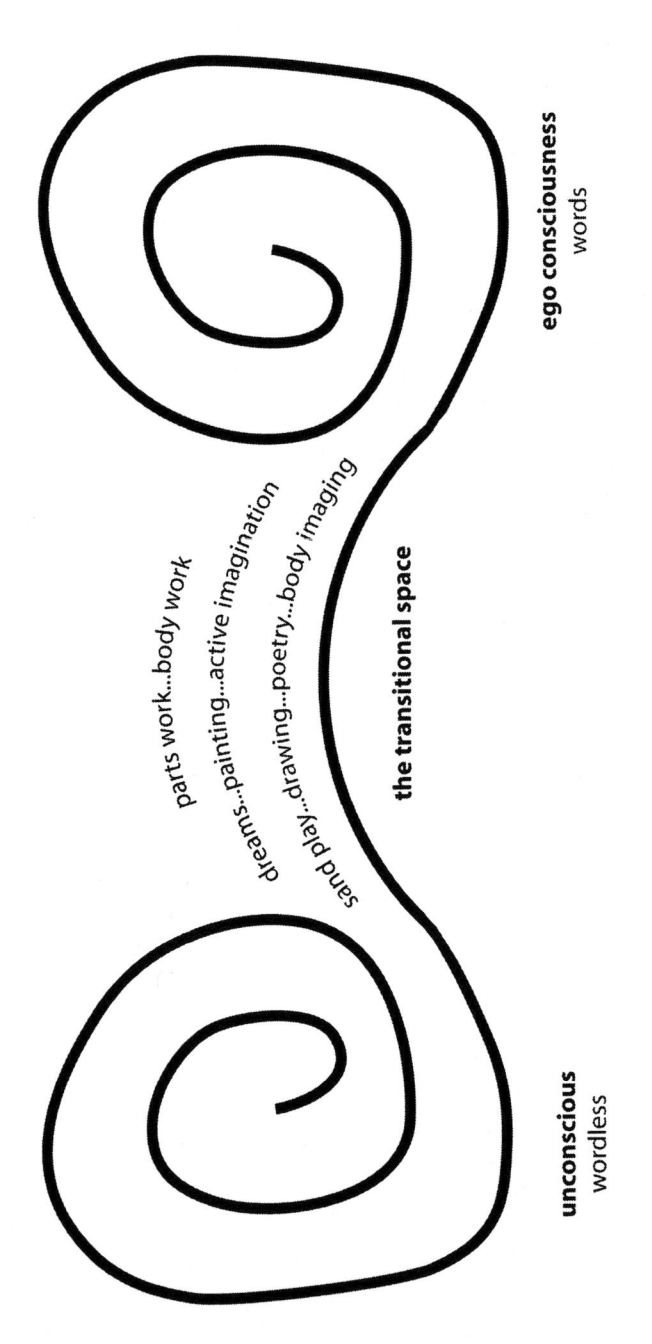

FIGURE 14
The transitional space.

The material locked within the patterned form of attachment is unconscious and has never been languaged. The transitional space does not need language. It is a space where primitive layers of the unconscious more connected with play than verbalization can emerge. One of the simple ways for a therapist to evoke the patient's unconscious is by creating an image of what the therapist hears the patient saying. For example, the patient says, "I work so hard I just can't seem to stop." The therapist responds by saying, "It sounds as if something is driving you to keep working. Does that feel right?" The patient responds, "Yes, I feel as if something is behind me pushing me to go on even when I am tired." Or, the patient can refuse the image and say, "No, it doesn't feel that way." The therapist can ask the patient to create an image of how it does feel. Most patients respond to this kind of invitation. The images lay the groundwork for dividing the patterned form of attachment into parts. Neither the therapist nor the patient can work with the entire pattern, it is usually too old and too overwhelming. However, when the patterned form of attachment is broken down into parts, the patient can begin to encounter it little by little, eventually making enough of the pattern conscious so that it can be interrupted.

In the case of the man with the train nightmare, his dream was composed of four images: the train; the tiny, terrified, imprisoned child; the lost shoe; and the relief of the "slipping away" child. These images, or parts of them, operated in relationships when authority was projected onto the significant other who was experienced as train-like. These images, as well as the their connection with the patient's relationships, gave us a space outside the patterned form of attachment that we could mutually explore.

Clinical Example of Creating a Space Between the Ego/Imago Axis

A 50-year-old woman entered therapy. She was a recovering alcoholic and had been sober for 18 years. She had had extensive therapy and was very aware of the operation of her pathological complex. Her marriage was solid, and though the couple was no longer sexual due to her husband's health, they were good friends and got along well together. She had two grown children who were independent and successful, with children of their own. Communication among all of the members of the family was good.

She sought therapy because she had become quite anxious at work and was afraid that she might begin to drink to manage her anxiety. She attended regular AA meetings but felt that she also needed therapy so that she could learn how to manage her anxiety. She worked for a large legal firm and was responsible for the work of 20 secretaries. It was her responsibility to see that the reports requested by each attorney were completed on time without mistakes. The atmosphere in the office was chaotic because the attorneys often worked until the last minute, turning their rough drafts in with deadlines that were almost impossible to meet. Secretaries were expected to remain all night if necessary to complete documents and to work on holidays when it was necessary. The attorneys also operated with this same work ethic. The pay was very high; however, the rate of turnover among the secretaries was also very high because of erratic work hours and the pressure to perform without mistakes. Training new people took time and created more work for the people already trained. Upper management had the same work ethic for younger lawyers and openly supported the status quo, refusing to budget for more secretaries.

The patient worked more than 60 hours a week, and in addition to her regular responsibilities, she often finished work for those secretaries who could not stay all night. She felt pressured to remain in her job because of the high salary and excellent benefits. She and her husband both needed her salary and medical benefits for their retirement in ten years.

The patient believed that discussing her history and family of origin was a waste of time. She did not want to take any medication because of her history of addiction. She wanted to find ways to manage the overwhelming anxiety and stress from work so that she could remain there. She responded well to changing her breathing patterns and developing ways to relax muscles and organs. She was nurturing herself at work by taking short breaks to eat, drink water, and rest.

Therapist (internal experience): This woman has developed a solid observing ego. She is quite aware of her internal states; she has loving relationships and a good support system. She is able to tell me what she wants and what she does not want in therapy. She has used the tools I have given her. Perhaps it is time to attempt to develop a transitional space using images.

Therapist (to patient): "When I think of you at work, I imagine a woman carrying an enormous backpack on her shoulders. She is followed by an enormous hooded figure cracking a whip to make her go faster. As she hurries along, she spends time cleaning up after the people around her, hurriedly placing their garbage in her backpack. No matter how she feels, that thing that whips her forces her to keep moving."

Patient: "That's just how it feels. I can't see behind me, but I know there is something there yelling at me to go faster and faster."

Therapist: "What is it yelling?"

Patient: "I can't hear it, I can just feel it yelling at me and I can feel myself going faster and faster." The patient begins to cry. "This is just what it is like all the time. You understand how it is for me."[3]

Whether the image the therapist presents is right or wrong is not the important element in this technique. What is most important is for the therapist to ask the patient to correct the image in terms of his or her own experience. When the therapist creates an image, it is presented as an attempt to develop a deeper understanding of the patient's experience. When the patient corrects the image given by the therapist, he or she teaches the therapist more about his or her experience, and the sense of attunement in the relationship is deepened.

As we explored the image of the patient's patterned form of attachment, the image changed. It was composed of several parts: a terrified woman carrying heavy stones in a backpack followed by a hooded death figure whipping her and continually threatening her to go faster or die. Issues about life and death are connected with mis-mediation of the archetypal/developmental process of being. As she began to present different images of her anxiety and stress at work, the patient realized that she continually experienced high levels of anxiety regarding the safety of her existence, such as being fired and dying penniless, being hit by another car while driving to work, getting a life-threatening illness. As she presented image after image, I remarked that she was always alone with no one to help her. It had never even occurred to her to ask for help or to slow down to think of strategies that might lessen her workload.

A new image came to her that carried unspeakable terror and a sense of helplessness. She could not see the figure behind her but could hear the sound of a whip cracking. This sound was ongoing and frightened her so much that she felt continually driven to perform or die, even disregarding her own physical and mental health. She was aware that her continual busyness was her way of running from this image of her terror. As she began to draw the image and express it in sand play, the terror began to lessen and she learned to go slowly, one step at a time, relishing each step on her way toward her death. This image was the real beginning of our relationship and our work together. Her therapeutic process went on once a week for two years, and she was able to ask for help and integrate her experiences in therapy with her own twelve-step process.

It was not until the final stages of therapy that she connected the images of her patterned form of attachment with her family of origin. She was the oldest of seven children and could remember being a toddler who felt responsible to help her mother and siblings survive. Her father was an angry, unpredictable, and abusive alcoholic. She realized that she had learned to be overly vigilant and a perfectionistic caretaker in order to protect her mother and the other children from her father. Her terror was associated with the idea that her father might kill her mother; the stones were her siblings whom she carried; and her hypervigilance, her nurturing of others, and perfectionism were the tools she developed to keep her mother and siblings alive.

She connected her own alcoholism with numbing her anxiety. As she recovered from her alcoholism day by day, she learned that her husband was someone she could trust and rely on. Their relationship was durable and secure. The chaos in the workplace had constellated her patterned form of attachment and the anxiety associated with it. She learned to ask her husband for help when she felt driven and overwhelmed.

ARCHETYPAL ENERGY AND THE IMAGO

Archetypes, the invisible structuring forms that mold human experience into patterns, are a significant part of patterned forms of attachment. Even when patterned forms of attachment are identified and made consciousness through awareness of the experiences of mediation of the archetypal/developmental process, the patterned form of attachment will shift but not transform. It is only when the archetypal/developmental underpinnings of the patterned form of attachment are freed that transformation of the pattern can take place.

The archetypal aspects of the imago can be observed in patterned forms of attachment that appear as repetitive dramas that seem to be bigger than life, for example, repetitive dramas of death, love, war, vengeance, good and evil, predator and prey. These dramas have a theme that includes regression to one or more or the archetypal/developmental processes and contains aspects of caretakers that possess a power that seems larger than life. These parts of the imago are held together and balanced by opposition (*CW* 14, 1976, 169–170). For example, in the clinical vignette discussed above, when the patient enacted what he believed to be his "numinous" father, the unconscious, unappreciated, tired, and irritable human being father emerged, who was just the opposite of what the patient believed his father to be. Enactments of the imago should not be performed when the patient has not developed an "observing ego" or the skills needed to contain his or her reactions when the patterned form of attachment is constellated because when the opposites appear, they will be unobserved and/or uncontained. In addition to the structures mentioned above, there are four other archetypal structures that become enmeshed within an ego/imago axis, adding dramatic intensity to the patterned form of attachment. These archetypal structures were discovered by Jung and provide four more viewing points into the ego/imago axis. Each one will be discussed below at length.

The Persona

The *persona* is an archetype that operates as a role we wear to create a bridge between ego consciousness and the outer world (Jacobi 1959). It is concerned with adaptation to the outer world and the development of consciousness. A rigidified persona has a rigidified and repetitive pattern that can be readily identified: mother, father, child, fireman, doctor, lawyer, and artist. The persona carries numinous energy because it is a pattern of roles formed by an archetype. The persona becomes filled by the roles we observe within our family, friends, and teachers, in books, and on television as well as those assigned to us by our culture; life experience; and psychological, genetic, and physical characteristics.

When the patient has a rigidified persona, he or she operates within certain rules and laws that have to do with a particular role. For example, a woman is identified with her role as a mother. She mothers her children from what she thinks good mothers do, rather than paying attention to her children's needs. Her children grow up and have children of their own. She feels entitled to run their lives because she is identified with her role as mother. She has never developed a life of her own, and if her children and grandchildren reject her efforts, she is devastated.

A rigidified persona prevents heart-to-heart communication with others and creates dramas that are insensitive and destructive to human communication and relationships. The persona is a dramatic role and has a costume that displays that role—for example, wealthy, powerful, homeless, guru, predator, prey, gang-banger, prostitute, lawyer, doctor, geek. The persona is rigidified when a person relates to others only through a particular role because he or she is unable to step out of it.

In the story of The Woman Who Once Walked in Balance she learned to change her persona when she went to the city by becoming a child, an elder, a cripple, a man, and a woman. She was deeply identified with her role as a victim and had to learn to wear other roles in order to let go of her rigidified persona.

When caretakers operate out of their own patterned forms of attachment, they also operate from rigidified roles. As a child develops, he or she gradually introjects some of these roles as deeply held beliefs, for example, "I'm dumb" (my father is smart); I'm ugly" (my sister is beautiful); "I'm a father (or mother)"; "I am a person who cannot be, do, think, have an identity or be creative"; "I have to grow up and be a concert violinist just like my dad."

A rigidified persona can easily be identified when a patterned form of attachment is constellated because normal ego consciousness is lost, and relations with the unconscious and significant others are blocked because the patient has identified with a rigidified role—for example, the victim, the abandoned one, the perpetrator, the hero/heroine, the guru, the disciple, the caregiver, the good child, the bad child, the healer, and the needy or wounded one. A complementary role may be projected onto significant others in the patient's life, including the therapist. For example, when a patient wears the role of the "abandoned one," the therapist or a significant other being discussed may become the "one who abandons." Exploring the patient's experience of being the "abandoned one" deepens into a stream of associations that leads to one of the many parts of the patterned form of attachment. The patient's associations can be used to create images and develop the transitional space.

A woman with four children was married to an alcoholic who drank late at night after she and the children went to bed. She felt terribly alone, uncared for, and burdened by the responsibility of caring for four children alone. Her husband denied drinking, even though she found several bottles he had hidden away in the garage. He accused her of being controlling, of interfering with his relationship with the children, and of always being angry. The children, unaware of his late-night drinking, sided with the father and also accused her of being overly critical and controlling. Because she worked full-time, she was tired and needed help with cooking, cleaning, and laundry. Her husband did nothing to help, and neither did the children when she asked them for help. She felt as if she were going crazy.

As we worked together to develop an image of her situation, she could not create an image of the family. Instead, she developed images of her different roles within the family. They were the "bitch queen from hell," the abandoned, lonely wife; and the terrified woman who felt as if she was crazy. As we explored each of these images, she began to become aware of how each role operated and how often she felt pushed into playing that role.

She had grown up in a traditional Asian family. Her father was a doctor. She met her husband in college, and after she completed her master's degree in computer engineering and he finished his doctorate in bio-medical engineering, they married. He came from a WASP family.

She was able to link her image of "being crazy" with experiences growing up watching her father beat her mother. Her mother refused to discuss it. She wondered if her mother had done something wrong to deserve the beatings. She observed her mother vigilantly and was never able to discover her mother's mistake. Yet she was unable to believe that any father/doctor would deliberately harm another person. She thought perhaps she was only imagining the beatings; maybe they weren't really happening. She was able to identify the image of "the bitch queen from hell" with her overly responsible, mothering style and her anger about not receiving help or respect from her husband or her children. The most difficult image for her to identify with was the abandoned, lonely wife. Expressing the grief and loneliness in her marriage created a great deal of shame for her that was quite painful and difficult to contain. Her father/doctor taught her that women were worthless and deserved to be beaten. She realized that she had never respected her mother as a person or her role as wife and mother because her father had never respected her mother. She assumed that because her husband did not beat her, she was not like her mother. As her denial began to fail, she began to realize how painful her mother's life had been and how she was playing some of same the roles her mother had. As we sat with and began the process of imaging her rigidified personae, she experienced them as choking the life out of her. The rules and laws, shoulds and oughts that fortified the rigidified persona began to emerge in opposition to the components of her ego consciousness. She decided to develop a new persona by returning to work part-time, while balancing her duties as a mother and continuing therapy to set herself free from her codependence.

The Shadow

Jung was very aware of the reality of evil in human life and often discussed how ignorant and unconscious we human beings are and that we hurt each other from our *shadow* because of our own lack of awareness (*CW* 11, 1938, 1977, 76; *CW* 16, 1946, 1977, 262). The best way to describe the shadow is to use an image. A person stands in the sunshine and has a shadow at his or her feet. The person standing in the brightness of the sun is an image of ego consciousness and awareness. The shadow that forms beneath the feet contains everything that ego consciousness is unaware of. When an ego/imago axis is operating, a person is cut off from his or her unconscious. The greater the disconnection, the darker the shadow is because it is so far from ego consciousness. What is lost to awareness is evil and beauty, as well as the possibility for development and the hope for morality.[4] The operation of the shadow can easily be observed in human relationships.

The shadow is difficult to find both within oneself and within the patient. It is helpful for me to remember that the bad, the ugly, and the beauty of what I could never have imagined always accompany whatever I am. The shadow is what each of us carries with us: the hidden and undeveloped parts of our personality, our misuse of power to overcome the inferiority that we project onto others, the beauty we cannot see within ourselves, the evil that is contained in every good action, all of the parts of ourselves that we do not wish to know (*CW* 16, 1977, 218–219).

For example, a young mother and father with one child came to therapy to work on communication skills. They felt caught between his parents and her parents who both gave them a great deal of advice on how to parent their child. Her mother and father provided day care for the child. The issue the couple discussed was the formula that the child was fed. The husband's mother believed that the child was allergic to the formula he was getting. She thought it was making him sick because he constantly had a runny nose, ear infections and chest congestion (signs of allergy). The wife's parents supported the use of the formula because they had used it with their own children. I asked the couple to do research on the formula, gave them the titles of several books on allergies to read and we worked on developing communication skills.

They were frightened, confused and felt quite defensive about their parenting style because both of them worked full-time. They wanted the argument about formula to disappear. They told me that they researched the problem and that the formula had been changed. They completed therapy in four sessions after their communication skills improved.

After two years, the couple returned to therapy after the birth of their second child. They wanted to work on communication because they had no time for each other. Both worked full-time and with two children life seemed to busy for their own relationship. When I asked about the children, I discovered that both of them had surgery to insert tubes in their ears because of constant sore throats and chest congestion (signs of allergy). The oldest child was already hearing impaired, and the second was going to have her first surgery at seven months of age. The couple admitted they had decided not to discuss the formula with her parents because they were afraid they would lose the free daycare. The shadow of ignorance was alive and well in the fear of communication with the grandparents. In order to avoid shaming the couple, I asked each one to name the parts that had gone into not making an informed decision about the formula. As we explored the parts we discovered that the couple was so dependent upon the grandparents that in many ways they remained children themselves, which interfered with their communication. Neither could face the idea that their unwillingness to discuss the children's formula with the grandparents might have contributed to the surgeries and hearing impairment. They called to cancel just before their second session and did not want to discuss the termination.

The couple left therapy because I exposed them to a shadowy area that they simply were not able or ready to face. This case exposes my own shadow as a therapist.[5] How long do I attune to someone when the shadow is operating? When am I ethically bound to speak the truth to the patient about his or her shadow? How do I separate my own beliefs about what is ethical from what the patient believes? These questions and the answers to these questions are embedded within each clinical encounter and must be reflected upon and acted upon sooner or later, depending on the impact of the patient's behavior on others and on the therapist.

The Anima and the Animus

The unconscious compensates and balances consciousness. The anima and the animus act as bridges between consciousness and the inner world. The archetype of the persona acts as a bridge between ego consciousness and the outer world, fostering adaptation and the development of awareness. The personae or the many roles we wear get filled out as we grow and adapt to the demands of the environment. Jung described the *anima* and the *animus* as functions that, like the persona, act as bridges. The persona acts as a bridge between ego consciousness and the outer world. The anima and the animus act as bridges between ego consciousness and the unconscious (*CW* 7, 1916, 1977, 299). Instead of forming from individual characteristics and potential roles in the outer world, they appear in dreams, visions, and projections that often appear to compensate the persona.

Jungian analyst Peter Mudd (1998) has thoroughly reviewed the development of Jung's theories about the anima/animus and noted that Jung's theories gradually moved from the idea of the function of the anima and the animus to personifications that became more and more specific to the gender they represented. Mudd points out that like the persona, the anima and animus are bridges between ego consciousness and the unconscious that "serve the processes of adaptation, individuation, and evaluation" (10). Neither the anima (the name for a man's bridge) nor the animus (the name for a woman's bridge) is a personified form of the opposite sex even though it may appear as an image of the opposite sex.

The contents of the anima/animus are influenced by the archetypal developmental processes and the mediation of these processes as well as by the genetic heritage, the persona, the culture, and the shadow. In order for the anima or the animus to properly function as a bridge to the unconscious, they must gradually be separated out from the shadow, the imago, cultural influences, and the fantasy bond.

Jung believed that both men and women had difficulty locating and relating to the anima and the animus as internal, psychic factors and first experienced them as a projection located in a significant other. The encounter is emotionally charged and constellates the persona, the shadow, and the patterned form of attachment, imbuing it with a numinous quality. The experience is different for everyone, yet it is captured by "falling in love" and the longing for the beloved that accompanies it.

As numinous figures, the anima and the animus cannot be integrated; they must be related to in a dialogue with the unconscious. Jung called this dialogue "active imagination" (*CW* 6, 1977, 433), and his extensive research in alchemy describes this process at length.

When a patterned form of attachment is constellated, neither the anima nor the animus will be able to function as a bridge to the unconscious.

Instead, the archetypal energy of the anima or animus accompanied by the archetypal/developmental energy inflates the imago, reinforcing the pathological complex.

Clinical Example: One Man's Experience of the Anima

A man came into therapy because he was experiencing such high levels of anxiety that he had difficulty functioning at work. He felt overwhelmed and depressed most of the time. His symptoms began when he lost a legal battle worth millions of dollars and a large part of his fortune. As the therapy began to progress, he began to have repeated nightmares about terrorists and gangsters imprisoning a beautiful woman. When he tried to contact the police, they began shooting at him. He found the dreams interesting and associated them with watching television.

He was the oldest of three children; his brother was one year younger, and his sister was born five years later. He described his mother as cold, withdrawn, sarcastic, and unavailable and his father as a harsh, angry, critical workaholic. Both he and his brother believed that his parents preferred his sister.

He had few memories of childhood. All of them contained images of being alone, bearing injuries stoically, and being more intelligent than most of the people around him. He impregnated a woman he met in college and married her, completing his law degree after the birth of his first child. He believed that both he and his wife resented the fact that they "had to get married"; however, they never spoke of it.

He was the only one in his family of origin to obtain an advanced degree, and he believed that the other members of his family envied him. He was a wealthy, respected, and powerful man, who described himself as being committed to being a good father to his family, and he spoke highly of each of his six children. He appeared to be quite split off from any affect other than his debilitating anxiety, which he attributed to a bad investment that cost him millions of dollars. He believed that his money provided him with a sense of safety and was deeply shaken by his financial losses.

At the time he came into therapy, he had ongoing, long-term sexual relationships with three women, including his wife. Each relationship nourished him in a different way, and he was aware that he found relief from his painful anxiety through physical, verbal, and sexual contact. When one of the women asked him to spend more time with her, he would become so anxious that he would make promises he could not keep and then totally withdraw from her. The woman would respond to his withdrawal by pursuing him, and the relationship would resume until the next cycle of demands.

What was interesting about his relationships was that one or two of the women always had a flaw, while one remained flawless. The women remained the same; however, the perception of flaws and flawlessness changed often.

His patterned form of attachment was avoidant. He was a workaholic and was too busy with his family and other women to have time for friends and fun. As we began to settle into the therapy, it appeared that his anxiety was a symptom of undifferentiated affect. He had received little containment as a child, and when he experienced any raw affect at all, it turned into overwhelming anxiety. Medication and alternative medicines were not helpful. Conversation during the clinical hour was limited to discussions of stress at work and difficulties in his relationships. I felt helpless each time we met. I sometimes had trouble with my own feelings that accompanied my countertransference responses to his dismissing style of communication. Sometimes I mentioned it when he dismissed me and questioned him about his internal experience when he said so and so or such and such. He had no response and was genuinely unaware of his avoidance.

He was not at all interested in the woman held prisoner in his dreams; however, he could identify with the men in his dreams, who often attacked him with guns if he saw the woman. He could admit he was afraid that the police would kill him. As he began to work with these images, he began to understand that he was terrified of death and change and of losing his family; while at the same time another part of him placed his life and his finances in situations that kept him in a continual state of anxiety.

I began inviting him into the transitional space by repeating what he said, using images. I invited him to change the images, and then I offered more images to mirror what I understood about his experience. As we did this, he began to realize that imaging his experience helped him contain his anxiety. When he was working, he began to doodle, drawing images of what was going on and avoiding placing himself in risky situations. Doodling was a wonderful way to allow images to emerge from the unconscious without anxiety.

Gradually, his dreams and images of the anima changed from a woman held prisoner into women who were primitive, earthy, and not beautiful according to his standards. They frightened him. He began to pay close attention to their appearance and draw pictures of them. The pictures were linked with images of blood, death, and nature. He began to paint them. They were like no woman he had ever seen. Over time, he began to dialogue with these images and they confronted his stoic, heroic attitude with his mortality and his negligence in caring for his life.

He became aware that the two women he had relationships with metabolized his feelings for him so that he didn't have to experience them himself;

and because his wife did not do this for him without his having to ask, he resented her.

For two years our regular twice-weekly therapy sessions and his dialogue with the unconscious helped this man begin to be able to contain his own anxiety. He was able to withdraw from each of his extramarital partners in a respectful and honest way and experience his own pain instead of allowing someone else to manage it for him. He became aware of his avoidant, patterned form of attachment and accepted it as something he felt he could not change. He chose to remain with his family.

One night he awoke in panic. He had difficulty breathing and felt as if he was going to be annihilated. His wife awoke and held him without saying a word. This experience was very powerful for him, and for the first time in his life he felt totally loved and accepted. He began painting the colors of his feelings as they began to emerge.

As he developed and deepened his relationship with his wife, the anima began appearing in his dreams in ways that confronted his past behavior. It was as if she was feeding him his shadow bit by bit; and as she did, he began to experience how he had used people and hurt them. He grieved for his past and suffered with the understanding that he could not repair what he had done. Eventually, he understood that he had to accept and live with what he had done because he could not change the past.

When he felt ready to finish his work with me, his anxiety had disappeared. He had taken in a partner and delegated more than half of his workload to him. He felt happy with his life. He was in therapy for almost six years.

Clinical Example: One Woman's Experience of the Animus

A woman entered therapy with complaints of depression, suicidal thoughts, fantasies of hitting and hurting her children, nightmares, and the feeling of being overwhelmed by the needs of her family. She was aware of feeling resentful because of the constant demands the family made on her, and then she felt guilty for having resentful feelings. She decided to come in for therapy because of her fantasies of hitting and hurting her children.

After the first clinical hour, she had a dream. In the dream she was looking up at an enormous vampire seated far above her behind an enormous desk. The vampire was laughing at her as she cringed in front of him.

As we explored her history together, we discovered that she was identified with the rigidified persona of being "the excellent wife and mother." When we explored "excellent wife and mother," we discovered that she operated the way her mother had–anticipating her husband's and her children's needs, keeping the household operating smoothly, getting the children to their activities, and supporting her husband in his business, all with minimal conflict. She was terrified of what might happen if she hit or yelled at her children. She was terrified to stop anticipating her family's needs or to take time for herself.

After about a year of working together, she had the same nightmare several times. She was standing in a courtroom looking up at an enormous desk. Behind the desk sat an enormous devil in the form of a vampire who was going to suck her blood and make her a vampire too. She awoke from these dreams so frightened that she could not go back to sleep. She was afraid the dreams were a punishment for her resentment and anger. It occurred to her that vampires drain the blood, or life force from their victims. They do that in the dark (the unconscious) and they cannot live in the light (ego consciousness). I wondered if the vampire might be an image that showed her what was sucking the life out of her.

Dream images appear in the transitional space and have a teleological function–to gradually restore normal processes of compensation. That means that when dream images are consistently explored and the dreamer attempts to understand them, they gradually shift a distorted conscious viewpoint to one that is more congruent with the individuation process. Her patterned form of attachment was still quite unconscious, and the dream image led us into the transitional space with material from her own unconscious.

I explained the transitional space to her as a way to explore her problems without words, using other options such as physical movement, drawing, painting, working with clay, sand play, or, eventually, a dialogue with the vampire called "active imagination" when she felt ready to speak with him. For more than six months she painted and drew the image, and as she did so, the image changed to something a little more approachable.

Eventually, she began her dialogue with the vampire during the clinical hour by drawing it and then speaking aloud to the image in the picture and telling me what the vampire said to her.

Patient: "Who are you and what do you want from me?"
Vampire: "I am the king of your soul. You had better bow down to me and worship me."

Patient (*internally*): I am making this up. This is so stupid, talking to a drawing of a vampire. Why would he want me to bow down and worship him?

(*Externally*): "Why do you think I should bow down and worship you?"
Vampire: "I am the one in charge. I am the one to obey. You are mine. Bow down."

Patient (to the therapist): "Right! I belong to everybody, even in my imagination. This ticks me off." To the vampire: "Who put you in charge? Who says I have to bow down and obey you?"

Vampire: "This has been ordered from the beginning of time as you know it."

Patient (to the therapist): "This is sort of silly and scary at the same time." To the vampire: "I don't think I ordered you to be in charge of me from the beginning of time. I have only been around for 38 years. If someone else ordered you to do this, I would like to know who they are?"

Patient (to the therapist): "This is really weird. The image of the vampire changed to a deck of cards that fell down at my feet. What do you think that means?"

Therapist: "I don't know. What kind of cards are they? What do they look like? How are they arranged?"

The cards turned out to be tarot cards. The patient drew them and spent a great deal of time learning about the images; she painted them and dialogued with each image.

She believed that this same image might have terrified both her grandmother and her mother. When she asked her mother about the vampire, her mother shared with her that she had repeated dreams about a man she thought was a god sitting high above her on a throne. She believed that this figure could see her all the time and that if she did not do everything she could for her family, she would go to hell and burn forever when she died.

The patient's vampire was an inflated, negative image of the animus that compensated her rigidified persona as a victim. This inflated image was embedded in the patterned form of attachment by a caretaker who was similar. The patient's patterned form of attachment made her overly cooperative with anyone's rules and laws about how she should behave think, remember, and be. Her center of authority was located in the imago inflated by an animus that was the final authority on anything. Her constant neglect of herself in favor of nourishing her family supported her pattern of attachment, the ego/imago axis, and a shadow that sucked the life out of her.

THE FANTASY BOND AND THE PATTERNED FORM OF ATTACHMENT

Robert Firestone (1987) created the term *fantasy bond*. He believed that infants and children create an "imaginary protector" who saves them from pain and suffering by providing comfort, understanding, and a rudimentary form of justice. In later life this image is projected onto significant others (1987, 73–124). A fantasy bond is operating when a person is dependent on another person or on a set of values, principles, or rules that create the illusion that the person is protected, understood, cared for, and secure.[6]

Fantasies," says psychoanalyst Ethel Person (1995), "are among the most powerful catalysts that infuse and organize our lives, dictating romantic, familial, and professional goals; fueling behavior; engendering plans for the future. In turn, our experiences, and the myths and stories of the culture in which we live, shape our fantasies" (1). Fantasy provides a seamless transition from one state of awareness to another, from the unconscious to consciousness and back again. Fantasies can be observed when a person discusses their assumptions about the way people, places, and things are. Although the "fantasy bond" can include religious beliefs or membership in a group that makes its members superior to others, it does not include actual spiritual or psychic experiences.

Firestone believed that the "fantasy bond" is a built-in response to an infant's feelings of absolute helplessness, including the sense of immanent annihilation when his or her needs are not met (1987, 183–185), and is a core defense against experiencing this sense of annihilation (241–254). When the fantasy bond is operating in an adult, it is based on what Firestone thought of as an illusion of fusion with the other person, idea, value, or belief and offers protection and safety from feelings of disintegration that are locked within a patterned form of attachment. It is always accompanied by regression to earlier phases of development, and when constellated, it denies any reality that exists outside the bond.[7] When a patterned form of attachment is formed through repeated experiences of disintegration that activate the defenses of the Self (denial, splitting, introjection, projection, identification, and idealization), the fantasy bond is the way the "other" is perceived.

When a fantasy bond is operating in a relationship, the party or parties involved are unconsciously regressed as well as dependent on the recipient of the fantasy to maintain the illusion of safety (Firestone 1987, 183–190). In reality, no relationship can survive the projection of the fantasy bond. When reality intrudes in the relationship, there is usually a struggle, sometimes individual and often mutual, to force the other person to conform to the partner's fantasy so that he or she can maintain a sense of safety.

Clinical Vignette: The Struggle for Power

Wife: "He's always angry. I just can't stand it. When he's angry, I can't think and I shut down."

Therapist to husband: "Could you tell her what you heard her say about what she feels when she experiences you as angry?"

Husband: "I will not. She's lying. I am not angry all the time. She just makes it sound that way."

Therapist (internal observation): They appear to be increasing the negative affective intensity between them. I think it's time to slow them down and help them observe what is going on by educating them.

Therapist (to the couple): "This is a powerful moment for the three of us because the problem in communication that brought you both to therapy is right here in the room with us. I am going to ask each of you a question, and when you respond, I want you to use the word I and not discuss your partner at all."

Therapist (to wife): "What are you feeling inside right now?'

Wife: "I feel shut down, and I hate that feeling."

Therapist (to husband): "What are you feeling inside right now?"

Husband: "I am feeling really angry, and I wasn't angry at all until just now. I felt great."

Therapist: "I am happy that the problem is here in the room with us so that we can begin to observe and understand it. Each of you has your own point of view and each of you has your own feelings. What is necessary for your relationship to work is to respect your own point of view and learn to accept and respect the fact that your partner may experience things differently. Do you think you can learn to do that?"

(The therapist has spoken to the couple as a unit, and neither partner responds to the question. The therapist will wait for several minutes as a way to assist the patients to develop containment and self-reflection.)

Therapist, making a confirming statement to the wife: "You experience your husband as angry a lot of the time, and when he is angry you shut down. Is that right?"

Wife: "Yes, I shut down."

Therapist, making a confirming statement to husband: "That is your wife's internal feeling when she experiences you as being angry. I respect her feeling, and I believe you when you say that you are not always angry."

Husband: "Yes. I 'm not always angry. She is lying about that just to embarrass me."

Therapist, making a confirming statement to husband: "Your experience of your wife is that when she says that you are angry all the time she is lying and trying to embarrass you and you feel ashamed. Is that right?"

Husband: "Yes, that's right."

Therapist's educating statement to couple: "The painful pattern of communication is right here with us in this room. It is created by misunderstandings and hurts. Neither one of you is deliberately hurting the other, yet somehow each of you experiences the other as intentionally hurtful. I know that right now neither of you believes that and you don't have to. I want you to listen to me anyway. Your hurts are based on assumptions (the "fantasy bond") that each of you makes about your spouse's reality."

Therapist to wife: "There are many things you could do when he gets angry. For some reason you freeze and feel helpless is that right?"

Wife: "That is right. I never thought of even having options, I have frozen all my life."

Therapist to husband: "Getting angry was the way you survived in your family, right?"

Husband: "Yes, that's true."

Therapist to couple: "This is what I think is going on between the two of you. When you (husband) get angry and she shuts down instead of giving you what you want, you as if she doesn't love you. Is that right?"

Husband: "Yes, it is."

Therapist to wife: "When he (husband) gets angry you feel terrified and shut down. You think that if he really loved you he wouldn't ever get angry. Does that help sound right?"

Wife: "I do feel that way. His anger terrifies me."

Husband: "Right. And after I get angry I feel really bad about myself, and that makes me more angry."

Therapist: "Good. Every week each one of you will have half of the hour to explore your own pattern of reactivity. The other will have the next half hour. It is important that while one person is working, the other person listens well enough to understand what the other person is experiencing. At this time you are both in a relational nightmare,[8] not because you don't love each other, but because of habits from an entire lifetime. It will take time, patience, and honesty for each of you to learn to understand each other and change some of your reactions.

Therapist to husband: "Does what I am suggesting sound like something you are willing to do?"

Husband: "It sounds really hard."

Therapist: "It really is hard."

Husband: "Well, it's so bad between us now and that is so hard that I guess I can do the other hard stuff in here."

Therapist to wife: "Does what I am suggesting sound like something you are willing to do?"

Wife: "I think my husband is right. It is so bad between us right now that I guess I can do the other hard stuff in here."

In order for therapy to be successful for this couple, she will have to find new ways to respond to his anger and he will have to learn to manage his anger and find other ways to ask for what he needs. She will have to let go of her fantasy of being with a strong, patient man who understands her. He will have to let go of his fantasy of a strong, patient woman who anticipates his needs and remains unaffected by his anger. Each partner will have to contain, reflect upon, and take responsibility for the reactivity contained within the patterned form of attachment. This is difficult because the affective intensity that prompts relational reactivity is very difficult to endure and contain, especially because the assumptions contained within the fantasy bond can no longer be used as a defense.

For some people the experience of losing the fantasy bond is so painful that when the bond is broken they find a new relationship as soon as possible, never really understanding quite what has happened. Others come to therapy when they begin to realize that relationships have changed but patterns in relationships have remained the same. I have often wondered what makes one person able to endure the therapeutic process and another person unable to tolerate it. Part of the answer is that the one who is able to endure has usually had some kind of experience with a "higher power" that has enlivened and strengthened that person's core sense of self.

The basic forms of attachment outlined by Bowlby, Ainsworth, and Main are good predictors of how an adult will function in significant relationships. Those who have a secure attachment will do well unless they marry someone with a pathological form of attachment that changes that secure pattern. Those who are disorganized, ambivalent, or avoidant will have great difficulty maintaining relationships unless they are lucky enough to marry someone with a secure form of attachment or find help. Our culture unconsciously supports the fantasy bond through the pervasive ideal of falling in love that is so prominent in our music, novels, soap operas, and advertising.

"Falling in love" can only be described because the experience is both so numinous and so unconscious. It is as if the archetypes pull us into relationships, mating, having children, and raising them. Falling in love is a direct experience of archetypal energy that attracts us to an "other," temporarily overriding the pathological complex and the patterned form of attachment. Falling in love is not limited to heterosexual mating and child rearing; it is just as powerful in same-sex relationships. Archetypal numinosity flows into the fantasy bond, heightening perceptions, sensual experience, and awareness, bringing a feeling of well being to both the body and the psyche.

However, since most of us are afflicted with pathological complexes and patterned forms of attachment, we (our bodies and our psyches) are not able to maintain the high levels of energy that accompany being "in love," and gradually the numinosity begins to fade along with the heightened perceptions and sense of well-being. The fantasy bond gradually becomes vulnerable enough to be broken upon the rocks of reality. When a person has learned to accept the death of the fantasy bond and, with his or her partner, learns to understand and accept the reality of that "other" while remaining loyal, committed, and empathic, that person has attended the best of the most private of schools. The lessons are detachment, empathy, containment, respect, and understanding of the operation of the relational field. The reward is love.[9]

PATTERNED FORMS OF ATTACHMENT AND REGRESSION

There is a discussion in Chapter 1 about how the archetypal/developmental processes appear in the clinical setting when they are fostering individuation and when they are rigidified because of the existence of a pathological complex or patterned form of attachment. Because the defenses of the Self deny and split off repeated experiences of disintegration, portions of the affected archetypal/developmental processes remain primitive and undeveloped because they are unable to be used by ego consciousness for adaptation and individuation. They remain locked within the unconscious, guarded by the imago. When the patterned form of attachment is constellated, it includes a regression to those unused, primitive archetypal/developmental processes. In the case discussed above, both the husband and the wife assumed that the other should take care of his or her emotional discomfort. The assumption that "my emotional discomfort should be taken care of" was located in the fantasy bond. The function of ego consciousness that was weak in both partners was containment. The archetypal/developmental process that remained primitive in the relationship was thinking. The therapeutic process involved treating the partners as individuals who could learn to contain their experience, reflect on it, and then think about what the individual needed when he or she was emotionally uncomfortable. The couple responded well to the therapy because each one had strong and flexible aspects of ego consciousness and a commitment to making the relationship work.

Jung cautioned the people he trained to avoid supporting regressive work with patients who had little ego strength. He believed that some people might become so overwhelmed by the experience of regression linked with the eruption of material from the collective unconscious that they would not be able to function in everyday life (*CW* 14, 1976, 530–531). Jung's admonition remains valid to this day.

A good example of an unrecognized regression occurred during group supervision. A therapist in training presented one of her patients for discussion. The patient was a 38-year-old male who worked nights as a janitor. He came into therapy because he was unhappy with his job and suffered from depression. He had no friends and was very reclusive. The fact that he remained in therapy at all was a tribute to the therapist's skills at attunement. The patient was also a gifted photographer. During one of his many visits to the library, he was helped by a librarian who found him some photography books that were out of print. He began fantasizing about the encounter and often sought her out. In his fantasies, the librarian gave him special attention, was attracted to him, and wanted to date him. At the time he came into therapy, he had begun taking pictures of her when she was not aware of it.

Instead of exploring his fantasy bond and paying attention to the fact that the patient had begun stalking the librarian, the therapist bonded with the patient and encouraged him to pursue his photography (creativity) and bring his photographs to therapy. She received permission from him to use his photographs in group supervision to demonstrate his individuation process. The photographs pointed to potentials for the patient's development and compensated his strictured lifestyle.

As the therapist listened to feedback from the group, she realized how primitive the patient's ego consciousness was and how immersed he was in the fantasy bond. His strength—creativity—was a way for him to observe the world and the people in it without relating to them. He was not doing anything to improve his life or develop real relationships. The therapist was intuitively correct in exploring his creativity with him because it created attunement and the possibility for the patient and the therapist to have a relationship. However, the group was quite concerned about the patient's stalking behavior and the therapist's denial of that behavior and her focus on his photography. The therapist was open to the feedback from the group and began making the necessary changes so that the therapy could progress. The patient began changing his behavior. Her willingness to learn from the group had a positive effect on the therapy as well as on the willingness of group members to be more open about their own cases.

The regression that is part of a patterned form of attachment has a teleological function that attempts to restore normal compensation. That is because enactment of the regression meets with resistance; the environment provides negative feedback that the behavior is inappropriate in some way (*CW* 5, 1911–1912/1952 and 1974, 419–420).

For most patients, regression is normal and part of the healing process. It is important for the patient to understand that a regressed "part" is not the whole of his or her experience and that it is a normal, painful, and an important part of the healing process. The regressed part, accompanied by the painful experiences of disintegration, can gradually be moved into and expressed in the transitional space, where the patient can learn to understand and care for this part with the support of the therapist.

Sometimes patients whose regressed parts are beginning to emerge may need to be seen two or three times a week because the experience is so painful. The patient is literally plunged into chaos because he or she is experiencing intense, painful affect, the destruction of deeply held beliefs about both internal and external reality, the annihilation of self-importance, the disconnection from the illusion that life is fair, and the loss of the sense of being in control of life events.

The patient may begin to feel crazy, confused, as if he or she was "coming apart," unable to cope, overwhelmed, and/or frightened. That is because the regressive experience that is becoming conscious is quite alien to the conscious worldview. The raw and painful affect must be expressed and also contained. The relational field, the therapeutic container, that holds this kind of regressive experience must have secure boundaries and be firm enough to hold the intensity of the affect that emerges as the patterned form of attachment begins to dissolve. This kind of intensity in therapy limits the amount of time a therapist can be away from his or her practice, because the presence of the therapist is literally part of the container.

The therapist cannot make the regression go away or change the raw pain associated with the emergence of early experiences of annihilation at the core of the pattern. Being present, believing, and encouraging the patient while assisting him or her in moving the painful, wordless material into the transitional space is difficult clinical work. In addition, the patient may unconsciously attempt to manipulate the therapist in an attempt to replicate the familiar, painful patterns of mediation he or she has previously endured and replicate the familiar patterned form of attachment through acts of self-hatred, hatred of the therapist, or by treating significant others the way he or she was treated.

The clinical vignettes that follow are an attempt to clarify how a regression might appear within the clinical hour. Each is based on one rigidified archetypal/developmental process that is part of a patterned form of attachment.

Clinical Example: Being

Patient: "My mother didn't want me. I don't want me either. I just want to shrivel up and disappear. I can't stand this pain. I feel like I am on fire, my skin hurts."

Therapist (internal experience): I am really scared he might hurt himself. We have a no suicide contract. What if he hurts himself? I want my fear to stop. I want to tell him he is wanted. If I do that, I will muck up his work. He needs me to be with him. I need to slow down and breathe so I can be with him.

Therapist to patient: "You are in a great deal of pain."
Patient: "I have no words, I just hurt."

Therapist (internal experience): The pain in the room is palpable, and I feel so helpless.

Therapist to patient: "There are no words. You hurt."
Patient: Silence
Therapist: Attentive silence of being with the patient.

Thirty minutes later:

Patient: "I feel it passing."
Therapist: "What has passed?"
Patient: "I don't have words. I can draw it." The patient draws his "black hole" and there is a small yellow circle in the center.

Therapist (internal experience): I feel so relieved. He and I have walked around this patterned form of attachment for two years. He understands it and he knows how to draw it. This is the first time he has used any color except black, gray, and blood red. His patterned form of attachment is composed of an annihilating caregiver and a helpless child. When the pattern is constellated, he becomes angry, overcontrolling and overly busy. He either avoids the people closest to him or tries to get them to go away. I really wanted to go away; it was hard to stay present.

Patient (crying): "I feel you somehow. You aren't running away from me. I feel so ugly, so deformed, and I feel you looking at me and just being there. I am so grateful—I have no more words."

Clinical Example: Doing

Patient: "I feel helpless. I just can't move. I am stuck everywhere I look, work, home, everywhere."

Therapist (internal observation): She's on antidepressants and has done a lot of exploring to find a different kind of job. She has internalized a critical, discouraging voice that keeps her on a leash. When she attempts to explore options or step outside of rigidly defined boundaries, she becomes so anxious that she shuts down and becomes helpless.

Therapist to patient: "Is that old critical, discouraging voice pounding you to pieces?"

Patient: "It really is. I can't believe how strong it is. I give up way too soon."

Therapist (internal observation): She sounds as if she's still being pounded.

Therapist to patient: "Is that old 'pounder' being hard on you right now?"
Patient: "Yes, and I am so sick of it. I'm sick of being hard on myself and feeling helpless and being pounded. I hate work. I know I can make more money. I am just so scared that if I do something different I'll ruin our lives. We need every penny for college expenses."
Therapist: "I can understand how scared you are, especially with two kids in college. I also think it's important to sink into the scare so that we can begin to understand it."
Patient: "I've always liked the bioengineering side of my job and developing new products but I am so stuck managing communications between the other engineers. They don't have anyone else who can do that. I'm afraid to ask them to let me go back to developing new products. What if I ask them and they think I'm not a team player? What if they say 'no'? What if I upset the apple cart and they fire me? I'm so well paid now, what if I mess that up for my family?"

Therapist (internal experience): She didn't hear me. She is really into "what iffing." I am beginning to feel anxious, frustrated, stuck, and like a failure as a therapist. We have been over this same ground so many times. I just want to tell her what to do. I am frustrated. I wasn't feeling that way at all before I saw her. I need to breathe and confirm her experience.

Therapist (to patient): "You seem to really be in a bind. All those 'what ifs' sound scarey."
Patient: "I wish you would just tell me what to do. I am so sick of being stuck."
Therapist: "I wish I could fix it."
Patient: "I just wish I could trust myself and get over the what-ifs."
Therapist: "I wish I could trust you for you."
Patient: "I think I just have to get off the pity-pot and keep exploring no matter what the 'pounder' says."

Therapist (internal experience): Her patterned form of attachment is for her to be criticized and then become filled with so much anxiety that she becomes helpless and unable to do anything. Exploring her options, no matter how she feels, is her path to freedom. At this point in therapy she is still unable to sink into her anxiety. However, if she continues exploring in spite of her anxiety she will have disobeyed the imago (the pounder) and she will earn more trust in herself. I have to keep encouraging and confirming her without being directive and she will begin to trust her own experience.

Clinical Example: Thinking

This vignette is about the couple described above. The husband got angry to get what he wanted and the wife froze when he got angry. In this session, the wife spent the first half of the hour exploring her experience of freezing when someone around her became angry. She was beginning to contain and reflect on what "freezing" was like for her and how she "froze" as a child when she felt manipulated into taking sides with one parent when both of them fought. She was terrified of their anger and believed that if she ever expressed her own anger her parents would divorce each other and her family would cease to exist.

Husband: "I feel like I'm going to blow up. I am sick of this. She doesn't freeze. She just lies all the time so she can ignore me and do what she wants."

Therapist (internal observations): He hasn't been listening to her. He has been in here feeling angry and not heard. I should have begun with his experience of the patterned form of attachment.

Therapist to wife: "You have done good work tonight. Your husband has not been able to hear you because the marital nightmare is right here in the room with us. I am going to listen to him now, the way I did to you, and I want you listen to me as he and I work together. Will you listen?"
Wife: "Yes."
Therapist (to husband): "What is that like for you to feel as if you are going to blow up, to feel as if you can't stand it?"
Husband: "I don't know. I just know I am really angry at her."
Therapist: "Tell me a little more about the anger. What happens in your body when you are so angry?"
Husband: "I get tight all over, especially in my belly. I feel hot, and then I yell to get some of it out. Why doesn't she just do what I ask her? I hate feeling angry and yelling. Afterward I feel awful and just want to be left alone."
Therapist: "You are doing good work today. Your feelings are really right here in the room and right here in your body. Is that right?"
Husband: "Yes, I really feel the tightness in my belly and I want to fold in."

Therapist: "Can you remember when you first felt that tightness in your belly and wanted to fold in?"

Husband: "When I was in high school playing football and crushing the opposition. I loved it. It was the first time in my life I didn't feel like a geek."

Therapist: "I never knew you felt like a geek before high school. What was that like for you?"

Husband: "I was shy. I had a face full of zits. I just wanted to hide. Once I grabbed this little girl and held her by the neck. I felt up her dress for a long time. I told her if she told what I did, I'd come back and kill her. Her father came over to talk to my dad. I lied and said she was making it up. I got away with it. Inside I felt like I was just one big ugly piece of acne walking around in the world. I didn't want to do that 'little girl' thing ever again. Instead, I played ball and felt like a champion every time I ran somebody down on the field and made them go down. I wasn't a geek then, I got cheered."

Therapist (internal experience): I think his feelings of aggression are linked with feeling deeply shamed. The aggression protected him from feeling shame. He seems to have connected his anger with the pleasure of crushing any opposition. When he experiences his wife as frozen he feels shamed and then becomes angrier. If I comment on his aggression, I think I may shame him. Perhaps he and I could explore his shame and let him learn that it is all right to become vulnerable with his wife.

Therapist (to wife): "Did you know about the 'little girl'?"

Wife: "Yes, he told me about her before we got married. He was afraid I wouldn't want to marry him. His honesty made me love him more."

Therapist (to wife): "You loved his honesty and felt compassion for what he did."

Wife: "Yes, I did. But I can't take the anger. I just freeze up."

Therapist (to wife): "You and I can work on helping you learn to do other things when he gets angry. Right now I want you to listen to him very carefully as he and I speak with one another."

Therapist (to husband): "It sounds as if you have learned to crush the opposition and that has worked for you."

Husband: "It really has, and it sure has made me successful."

Therapist: "Do you ever wonder what happened to that little girl?"

Husband: "Yeah, I wonder sometimes. I had nightmares for a long time afterward and felt really bad about myself. I even looked for her to help her out, but I couldn't find her. What of it?"

Therapist: "What happens inside you when you remember that event?"

(The patient reddens and physically pulls back.)

Therapist: "Be gentle with yourself. It looks as if you are feeling something very painful. Your wife loved you for your honesty."
Husband: "I feel like crawling in a hole."
Therapist: "Is that how you feel after you get angry?"
Husband: "Yes, it is. I always try to be alone."

Therapist (internal observations): His wife is listening to him and very present to his shame and vulnerability.

Therapist (to husband): "Look at your wife. What do you see in her eyes?"
Husband (crying): "I see caring."
Therapist: "There is caring in each of you for the other. The cycle of anger and freezing between you interrupts that feeling of caring. I want you to stay out of that cycle at home and bring it in here so that we can begin to interrupt the reactions and uncover more of the caring."

Therapist (internal observations): Both of them have interrupted and observed the cycle of miscommunication, each in their own way.

Therapist: "Both of you have made the first step toward thinking before reacting. The relational problem is your shame (to husband) and your freezing (to wife)."
Wife to husband: "Does my freezing shame you?"
Husband: "I really feel small after I yell at you."

Silence while the couple look at one another in a connected kind of way.

Therapist (internal observations): Each one has observed internal responses and thought about them.

Clinical Example: Identity

Patient: "I feel so ashamed. I keep having dreams of being sexual with you. I really want to be as close as I can to you."
Therapist: "It must be difficult for you to share that with me."
Patient: "I feel really ashamed and stupid. You wouldn't want me that way anyway."

Therapist (internal dialogue): I am in a double bind. If I say no, she'll believe that I am rejecting her. If she is gay, I don't want to interfere with her process of coming out. If her desire is because of a need to be closer to me in a symbolic way, I have to explore it with her. It is really important that both of us feel safe enough to explore her experience without compromising the therapy.

Therapist (to patient): "I feel caught in a terrible dilemma. You are very dear to my heart. If I chose to be sexual with you, I would really damage both you and me."
Patient: "Well, I have never had sex with a woman. I've never even thought about it until the dreams started. I feel ashamed of wanting to have sex with you in my dreams. I feel like dung sitting here talking to you about this."
Therapist: "Feeling like dung sounds really painful. Can you say more about that?"
Patient: "You're not upset with me? You don't think I am disgusting?"
Therapist: "Look at me. What do you see?"
Patient: "I see you looking at me the same way you always do, like you care about me."
Therapist: "You are absolutely right about that, and I can care about you without being sexual with you. Your feelings and your dreams are really important to our work. The unconscious speaks in symbolic language. It is important for us to respect your experience so that we can begin to understand what the unconscious is telling us. Can you say more about what you are feeling and thinking?"
Patient: "I've always felt like dung. My father told me I was too stupid to go to college like my brothers. He thought college was a waste of money for women and I should get married and have kids just like my mom. I love my husband and kids, but after I'm done taking care of them, I just fall into bed. I hate my life. You do work you love. You have a life. Why can't I have a life?"
Therapist: "Why can't you have a life?"
Patient: "I have to take care of my husband and my kids. There's no time for me. There's never any time for me."
Therapist: "How could you make time for you? What would you do with your time?"
Patient: "I want to paint. I loved to paint when I was a kid. I want to go to a school and learn about painting and every other art kind of thing I can find out about. I want a workroom just for myself that nobody can go into. But I can't leave my husband and kids to take care of themselves. They don't know how to do anything."

The rest of the hour is spent exploring her ambivalence; part of her wants to be an artist, and the other part is identified with the role of wife and mother. After several months of therapy, the patient interpreted her dreams of being sexual with me as a way to make a deep connection with a woman she loved and respected who was married, had children, and did work she loved. She began to create an identity as a wife, mother, and artist.

Clinical Example: Creativity

The patient was an only child and her mother was her primary caretaker. Her father was the director of a large company and worked long hours. The patient learned to anticipate her mother's needs before they were expressed and meet those needs in order to help her mother maintain some kind of balance. She believed that she became so deeply connected with her mother as a child that she lost herself. As a child she also had visions of beings that surrounded, taught and guarded her. She was terrified of these visions and reluctantly mentioned them long after she began therapy. She grew up and became a successful professional woman and married a man that her family and friends loved. He became physically and emotionally abusive. She began therapy when she chose to leave the marriage and began to live by herself and as she put it "stand on her own two feet." Her parents and her friends could not believe that her husband abused her, and they blamed her for ending the relationship. The entire therapeutic process was a gradual separation from her unconscious identification with her mother. The therapeutic process depended on the patient's own dream material, her visions, and her creativity.

Shortly after treatment began, she began to experience flashbacks at work when she perceived someone in authority being aggressive with her. During a flashback she felt as if she physically shut down and stood beside herself. This experience was very difficult for her to manage because she felt as if she was "going crazy" and might even be inventing the entire experience. She spent a great deal of time in therapy crying and reliving the abuse. Gradually she learned to manage the flashbacks with deep breathing and medication.

After a year in therapy, her mother had a full-blown schizophrenic episode. She began hearing voices and losing weight. She was unable to leave home. The rest of the family (father, uncles, aunts and cousins) insisted that nothing was wrong with the mother and that she would be fine if the patient moved back home to care for her.

Saying "no" repeatedly enabled her to separate from her role as her mother's caretaker and allow the family to finally refer the mother to a psychiatrist for the treatment she needed. As the patient separated emotionally from her family she began to identify a part of her that was very "angry at everything and everyone" and another part of her that felt a painful sense of longing for a mother who could "see" and care for her. As she worked with her parts, she learned to contain and observe her experience, sitting with the longing for a mother and the rage at never having been able to be a child because she was forced to be a caretaker.

She struggled with being alone, being assertive, and being related and connected to her family while remaining emotionally separate. The focus in therapy was her dreams. The biggest gift she found in our relationship was confirmation that her own internal experiences and that her dreams and her visions meant something. The fact that she could go to work, maintain relationships with friends, and do ordinary everyday things helped her understand that normal people could have dreams and visions without being "crazy." The archetypal/developmental process of creativity emerged in the therapy in a unique way.

Patient: "This sounds so weird, but I think that people are made up of energy and that the body is one form of energy. Do you think I am crazy?"
Therapist: "No I don't think you are crazy. I think you are right."
Patient: "I can feel the energy in my body. My body and my energy are together; they change from day to day, and I can feel that shifting."
Therapist: "How do you feel that shifting?"
Patient: "I can close my eyes and look at my body and then sort of feel/see the energy. When I am awake, I feel different places that are tight in my body and it feels as if the energy is blocked there."
Therapist: "Is there a way for you to express that experience?"
Patient: "I think I could close my eyes and scan my body, and then use colored pencils to draw what I see and put that all on paper."

She drew the changes in her physical energy for over two years. At the same time she began to study yoga as a way to become more aware of her physical experience. As she continued drawing her energy in a creative process that felt more and more "right" to her, she felt less and less crazy. The therapy lasted an unusually long time–more than four years. I think it took that long for her to establish an attachment that felt secure enough so that she could accept confirming mediation from me.

SUMMARY

There are many avenues for research on patterned forms of attachment. Are there genetic patterns that are common to certain patterned forms of attachment? Are there common patterned forms of attachment linked with different kinds of neurosis and psychosis? Are different patterned forms of attachment liked with the archetypal developmental processes? Are there common patterned forms of attachment in families with a caregiver who is a substance abuser? Is there a difference in patterned forms of attachment in families that have one caregiver as opposed to two caregivers? Are patterned forms of attachment passed on from generation to generation, as Emma Furst's research on the similarity of complexes between family members suggests (*CW* 4, 1979, 303-306)?

Patterned forms of attachment foster transference/countertransference dynamics within the relational field. Managing these dynamics is both challenging and demanding for therapists. The best way to understand them is through personal therapy, ongoing supervision, continuing education, and having a study group with colleagues.

The patterned form of attachment will gradually appear in the clinical hour as the patient discusses his or her feelings, relationships with significant others, or in his or her treatment of the therapist as well as the images of people that appear in dreams and fantasies. It is very important for the clinician to pay close attention to the patient's relational material and explore it slowly. Patterned forms of attachment are unique and highly individual. They are the way the person learned to adapt to the environment and survive.

Patterned forms of attachment can be diagnosed by listening to the repeated patterns that occur in relationships with significant others. Dysfunctional patterns of mediation of the archetypal/developmental processes are part of patterned forms of attachment and can be identified by listening for them. In *symbiotic* forms of mediation, the patient will spend a great deal of energy anticipating the needs of others or will expect others to anticipate and meet his or her needs without having to ask. In *directive* forms of mediation, the patient will experience him or herself as being directed and controlled by others or have difficulties in being overly directive with others. In *cooperative* forms of mediation, the person will have difficulty taking responsibility for him or herself and/or be overly responsible. In *confirming* forms of mediation, patients will have difficulty trusting their own experience or respecting the experiences of other people who may have a different point of view. In *containing* forms of mediation, the patient will lose the ability to contain and reflect on his or her experience, or be unable to remain contained when another person is expressing affect, or be overly contained. In *educating* forms of mediation, the patient may have difficulty listening to others and be unable to learn from someone who has a different point of view. In *empowering* forms of mediation, the patient may experience him or herself as the powerless victim of an authority or enjoy creating a sense of powerlessness in others.

QUESTIONS

1. What is a patterned form of attachment?
2. How might it operate?
3. Think about your own life and identify the patterns of attachment that have affected your personal history in terms of similarity of affect, generalization of experiences, and repetition.
4. How do the defenses of the Self create patterned forms of attachment?
5. What makes patterned forms of attachment regressive in nature?
6. How are the components of ego consciousness affected by patterned forms of attachment?
7. What is the imago? Give an operating definition.
8. What is containment?
9. Give an example of how to create a transitional space in a clinical hour.
10. What is "parts work"?
11. What is a *fantasy bond*?
12. What is a persona?
13. What is the shadow?
14. What is the anima/animus and what do they compensate?
15. What are the parts that compose a patterned form of attachment?
16. Give an example of how a patterned form of attachment might appear in a clinical hour.
17. Give three examples of a patterned form of attachment from your own clinical experience.
18. How do the archetypal developmental processes influence patterned forms of attachment?

ENDNOTES

1. I am not sure if this particular research was ever published. I have heard about it from a colleague but have been unable to find it in the literature.
2. My thanks to M. Esther Harding M. D. (1965) for her scholarly work on the imago in, *The Parental Image: Its Injury and Reconstruction*, which helped me formulate my own ideas about the imago.
3. Allowing an image of a patterned form of attachment to form is an attempt at attunement and empathy. When the image is shared with the patient, it is presented as a mirroring statement and as a question. In this case, the therapist might say, "It sounds as if you are a woman carrying a heavy backpack, stooping down to pick up the pieces others have left on the ground while somebody behind you carrying a whip is forcing you to move faster and faster." Does that fit your experience? It does not matter whether the image that is shared is correct or incorrect.

It is an attempt to mirror and validate the patient's experience, to attune to the patient, and to allow the patient to step into the transitional space.
4. Social scientist and research professor Jane Loevinger (1976) has done extensive research linking ego development with the formation of morality and conscience. Her hypothesis is that when higher levels of ego development exist, they are accompanied by higher ethical standards not linked with cultural norms.
5. A wonderful book called *Power in the Helping Professions* by Adolf Guggenbuhl-Craig (1971) discusses the shadow side of psychotherapy and the misuse of power by therapists with patients.
6. A dependent form of patterned attachment can appear as one person being dependent on another person, group, set of values, or religious beliefs. However, dependence may also appear in ongoing conflicts, violence, power struggles, or series of dramatic events that foster chaos to preserve the relationship.
7. The fantasy bond is very difficult to approach in the relational field because it is unconscious and cannot be verbalized. It carries the final defenses against the cumulative experiences of annihilation (RIGs) accompanied by a numinous imago that contains both personal experiences of the evoked companion and the numinous energy of blocked archetypal processes. However, patients come to therapy because of problems with the fantasy bond. It is helpful to think of it as the weakest point in the patterned form of attachment that contains all of the "parts" of that patterned form of attachment. It is useful to think of assisting the patient to move "parts" of the fantasy bond into the transitional space, diminishing the affective charge and making it easier for the patient to contain his or her experience. Jung often talked about complexes behaving like "partial personalities" (*CW* 8, 1934, 1981, 96–97). However, he developed his theories 80 years ago. At this time it is more correct to speak of pathological complexes, patterned forms of attachment, and the fantasy bond as composed of "parts." Jung's description of complexes as partial personalities is more congruent with the ideas developed by Fritz Perls in his Gestalt Therapy (1971) and is quite different from Dissociative Identity Disorder. This disorder produces at least two or more conscious and separate identities that are distinct from one another and are quite different from pathological complexes as parts of personalities.
8. Kathleen Powell, imago marital therapist and clinical supervisor, created the terms "nightmare" and "placing your need to react to your partner beside you" as images that help couples learn to contain painful relational experiences as well as the difficulties that occur in couples therapy (personal communication, 1997).
9. Jung developed his theories in the early 1900s and was a man of his time. His "The Psychology of the Transference" (*CW* 16, 1946/1977) described patterns and processes that occurred in the relationship between the analyst and the patient. However, in his biography of Jung, Ronald Hayman (2001) makes it clear that in many ways Jung did not know how to relate well to others.

Chapter 5

PATHOLOGICAL COMPLEXES AND DIAGNOSIS

Diagnosis is the art of discriminating or separating things from one another, and when used in psychology, it usually means that one "set" of symptoms is statistically separated from another "set" of symptoms. Each set is labeled as a category, and each category is broken down into smaller sets, finally creating a diagnosis based on specific sets of symptoms. The *Diagnostic and Statistical Manual of Mental Disorders*[1] is an international system of classification of patterns of physical/mental disorders used by professionals around the world to communicate and expand areas of psychological research. A pattern is conceptualized clinically as

> [a] significant behavioral or psychological syndrome or pattern that occurs in an individual and that is associated with present distress (e.g., a painful symptom or disability) causing impairment in one or more important areas of functioning) or with a significantly increased risk of suffering death, pain, disability, or an important loss of freedom. In addition this . . . pattern must not be merely an expectable and culturally sanctioned response to a particular event, for example, the death of a loved one. Whatever its original cause, it must currently be considered a manifestation of a behavioral, psychological, or biological dysfunction in the individual. (DSM-V 2000, xxx-xxxi)

Many patients do not fit one diagnosis because their symptoms cross the boundaries that separate one set of symptoms from another. Others do not fit because the sets of symptoms do not include enough information. We can only make a diagnosis based on symptoms that we can identify. Because we know so little about the bio-psycho-social system, there are symptoms that have not yet been identified and are not a part of a diagnosis.

The DSM-IV is the best attempt at this time to create a diagnostic system that allows professionals around the world to communicate and do research.

The manual makes it very clear that a diagnosis does not categorize individuals; rather it categorizes a group of symptoms and requests that the reader recognize the uniqueness of each patient. When the categories of symptoms presented in DSM-IV are linked with Jung's complex theory and viewed from the multiple points of view presented in this book, they complement the diagnosis from the DSM-IV and assist the therapist in creating diagnostic impressions that are based on the individual experience of the patient. The case studies presented in this chapter demonstrate how this works.

USING COMPLEX THEORY AS AN EXPANSION OF DSM-IV

Figure 15 is a map of the viewing points into a pathological complex: the components of ego consciousness, the energetic function of each component, the archetypal/developmental processes, the patterns of mediation of the archetypal/developmental processes, the cycles of nature, the ego/Self axis, the ego/imago axis, the fantasy bond, and the defenses of the Self. When the components listed in Figure 15 are combined with the diagnosis and the patient's history, the pathological complex can be broken down into components that disclose the patient's individual strengths and weaknesses. This provides ways for the patient and therapist to work together in developing goals for therapy, exploring the patient's experience as well as educating and empowering the patient during the therapeutic process.

Figure 15 is meant to be a diagnostic template to provide multiple viewing points into a pathological complex. Each point of view is unique and is dynamic, interdependent, and interrelated with every other point of view. The components of Figure 15 act together like an ecological system to maintain the structural integrity of the pathological complex. Awareness in one point imbalances the entire structure of the complex. Jung talked about the teleological function of complexes (*CW* 7, 1977, 59). Imagine a tree in the forest that cannot get enough light. It keeps bending and reaching, changing the direction of its growth in order to find the sun. In a pathological complex, possibilities for growth and individuation have been blocked and locked away from consciousness, remaining primitive and undeveloped. However, like the tree, they seek the illumination of consciousness.

As the patient and the therapist move from one viewing point to another, exploring the patient's experience and bringing that experience into awareness, the pathological complex becomes unbalanced and the energy that holds it together is gradually recanalized or transformed to support individuation (*CW* 8, 1981, 41). This process is the heart of therapy.

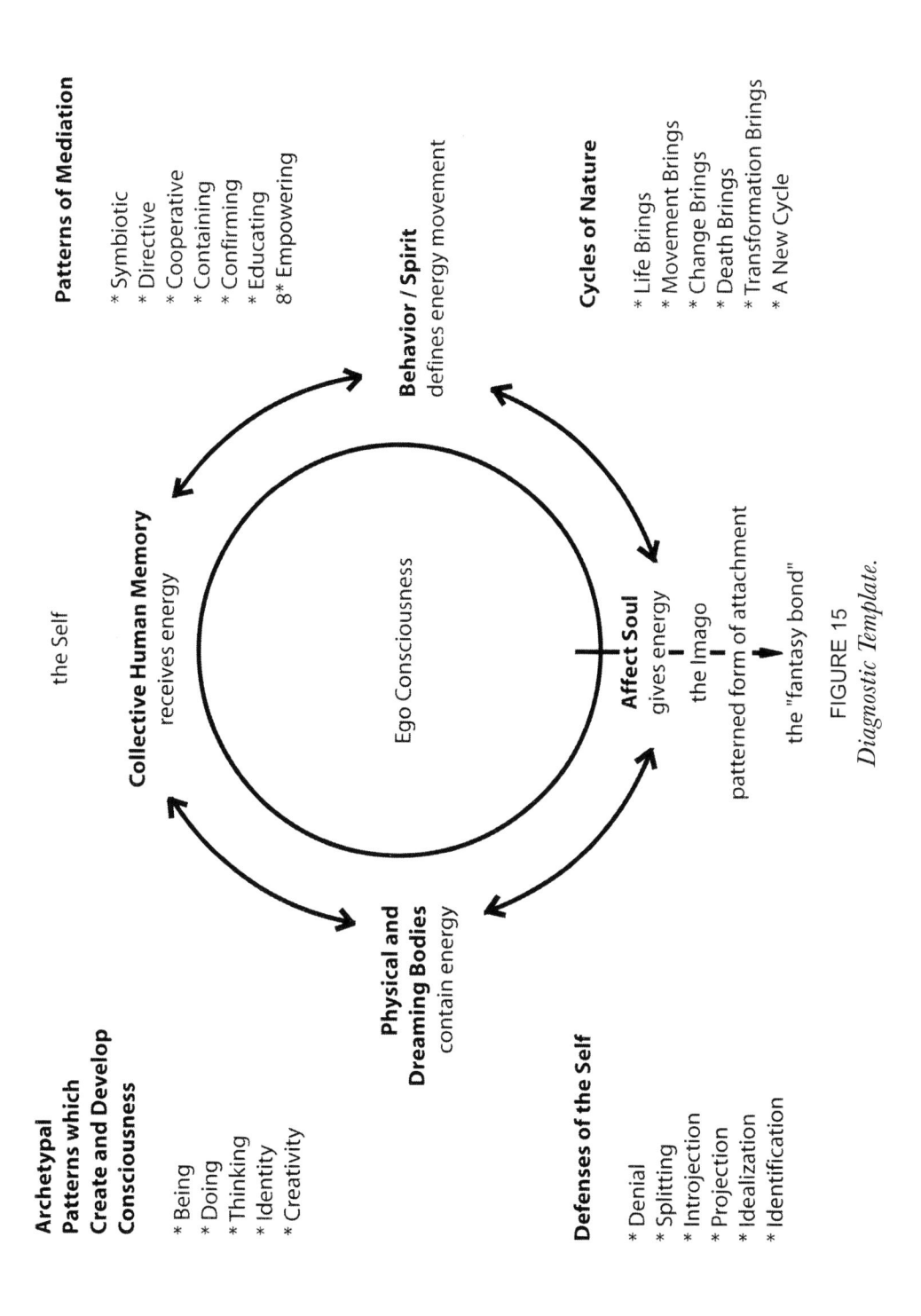

Pathological Complexes and Diagnosis   179

Archetypal Patterns which Create and Develop Consciousness

* Being
* Doing
* Thinking
* Identity
* Creativity

the Self

Collective Human Memory
receives energy

Patterns of Mediation

* Symbiotic
* Directive
* Cooperative
* Containing
* Confirming
* Educating
8* Empowering

Behavior / Spirit
defines energy movement

Ego Consciousness

Cycles of Nature

* Life Brings
* Movement Brings
* Change Brings
* Death Brings
* Transformation Brings
* A New Cycle

Affect Soul
gives energy

the Imago

patterned form of attachment

the "fantasy bond"

Physical and Dreaming Bodies
contain energy

Defenses of the Self

* Denial
* Splitting
* Introjection
* Projection
* Idealization
* Identification

FIGURE 15
Diagnostic Template.

The integration of the multiple viewing points presented in Figure 15 with the DSM-IV is illustrated in the following fictional clinical vignette. The patient is a woman diagnosed with Bipolar II disorder (Recurrent Major Depressive Episodes with Hypomanic Episodes).[2]

Clinical Vignette

Grace's psychiatrist referred her for therapy. She was on medication to treat major depression. She had a long history of chronic depression and stress from overwork, as well as discrete episodes meeting DSM-IV criteria for major depression. Her family history included several close relatives with Bipolar I disorder, epilepsy, and Alzheimer's disease. She entered therapy because of chronic exhaustion, inability to maintain close relationships, irritability, and distractibility. She was married and divorced twice and a successful professional. Her closest friends lived far away, and she saw them five or six times a year. After entering treatment, Grace mentioned that she was stressed because she was making payments to the IRS for not paying her taxes. She had a hard time discussing her financial difficulties, finally admitting that she frequently went on shopping sprees and spent all of her money.

She was referred to her primary care physician for a full medical evaluation. Her doctor reported that all laboratory tests were within normal range. However, she consulted him frequently for minor complaints and always seemed anxious about her health. She was referred back to her psychiatrist for reevaluation and her diagnosis was changed to Bipolar II. Her medication was changed to one that was more appropriate for her and her general mood and irritability began to improve.

As we explored difficulty in relationships, it became clear that even in her earliest life Grace was easily overwhelmed by what was going on around her. In order to shut the world out, she learned to read quite early and read continually. She was quite angry with her father for having seizures and called him stupid and brain damaged. Her mother was the sole provider for the family and was often absent from home. Grace was left alone with her father until she was old enough to attend school. Her mother had saved enough money to send her to a private school, which became a safe haven for a bright little girl who was willing to work hard to excel. She received scholarships to attend a university and completed graduate school.

As Grace discussed her history, it became apparent that she focused on excelling in her work. She respected her mother because she was the breadwinner—strong and intelligent even though she was uneducated. She hated her father because he was "helpless and stupid." He neglected her and ignored the honors she received at school. She blamed any failures in her life on her father and on the fact that she was easily overwhelmed. She believed that she had married strong, educated, bright, professional men who would take care of her (the fantasy bond). She admitted that when she felt really irritable, overwhelmed, or stressed she became angry and verbally abusive with others. She felt that those closest to her should understand and accept her behavior because of her past. She was aware that her anger had a negative impact on her relationships. Her response to the loss of significant relationships was to work harder and longer. Her work schedule gave her no time to develop close relationships. Many of her days off were spent in bed recovering from overwork. She was reluctant to come to therapy. However, she also realized quite early in the process that her anger, overwork, irritability, exhaustion, and excessive spending had contributed to the end of both of her marriages.

Grace's intelligence and her professional abilities were her greatest strengths. She was physically strong, had a good memory, and was able to work hard. She was able to use all of the archetypal/developmental processes in her professional life. In therapy she appeared cooperative, and she responded well to educating forms of mediation. She appeared to idealize the therapist in a positive way because her physician, whom she respected, spoke highly of the therapist. In the beginning of therapy she spent a great deal of time clarifying her therapeutic goals and explaining how she wanted to reach these goals. She did not include the therapist in her plans. This was an indication that the defenses of the Self and a rigidified, patterned form of attachment were operating in the relational field. It appeared that Grace could only feel safe in a relationship if she defined the parameters.

Grace: "First, I want to find out everything you know about therapy. Second, I want you to be really sensitive and kind to me. I really have a hard time with people who come out of left field and overwhelm me. Third, I want to work on my anger first, so I want you to recommend a couple of books for me to read."

Therapist: "I am not sure that is the right way for us to begin our work together."

Grace: "Why not? I spent hours thinking about this."

Therapist: "Therapy is a space where we have to think together, and I don't know you well enough yet to think with you."

Grace: "Oh. What do you need to know?"

When Grace laid down the guidelines for therapy she indicated that a strong fantasy bond and patterned form of attachment were already functioning in the clinical relationship. When the therapist responded to her by highlighting the fact that they really did not know each other, Grace was able to stop and reflect on what the therapist said. Her willingness to respond and think about the therapist's question indicated that it might be possible for a relationship to develop.

The change in medication because of her new diagnosis of Bipolar II was useful in stabilizing Grace's mood so that she could tolerate therapy. Figure 15 provided a useful format for me to begin understanding her experience and how it was related to the structures that made up her pathological complex. Because of her difficulties with spending, we moved into the experience of containment and self-observation. Grace slowly began to understand how to take care of her mood disorder as if it were diabetes or chronic fatigue. She had not experienced a mother who took care of her and did not know how to nourish or soothe herself.

The diagnosis of Bipolar II expanded by Figure 15 allowed us to focus on the body as a container for self-reflection. As Grace learned to contain her spending and reflect upon it she became aware of how spending helped her fill the painful spaces of the experience of neglect. The extended diagnosis created the primary framework for treatment, the relationship itself. The therapist had to remain focused on attunement, pushing the edges of Grace's awareness gently and at the same time being careful not to stimulate so much affect that the patterned form of attachment would overwhelm her. The primary forms of mediation that were used by the therapist were cooperation (necessary for the development of an adult-to-adult relationship) and education (because Grace has requested it) so that the therapist and the patient could become colleagues who worked together to discover the operations of the pathological complex.

DIAGNOSIS USING CLINICAL EXAMPLES

The rest of this chapter is designed to link diagnoses from DSM-IV with individual patients, using Figure 15 as a template. The vignettes will deal with patients who have mood, anxiety, or somatoform disorders. Each fictional case will give the presenting problem, the DSM-IV diagnosis, a brief history, and a description of the pathological complex. The viewing points described in Figure 15 will be used to separate the complex into parts: ego functions, archetypal/developmental processes, patterns of mediation of the archetypal/developmental processes, cycles of nature, defenses of the Self, the imago, the patterned form of attachment, and the fantasy bond. At the end of each vignette, a patient/therapist dialogue will illustrate one therapeutic process based on a predominant factor of the individual's pathological complex linked with one of the components of Figure 15. This will be followed by a brief overview of the treatment process.

CASE #1: Jacob and Shirley

The Presenting Problem

A couple entered therapy because they argued all the time, creating what they believed to be a terrible environment for their four-year-old child. Each partner agreed to explore his or her own negative complex and take responsibility for it, while at the same time developing enough of an understanding of the partner's negative complex to stop taking it personally. Problems in the relationship reportedly did not begin until the pregnancy and birth of the couple's daughter. However, each of the partners commented that the roots of the problems were present prior to the birth of their child. Each blamed the other for creating these problems. Both partners in this marriage were highly respected professionals in their own fields.

He complained that she was disorganized, messy, helpless, needy, controlling, and that she spent too much of their money on the house and her hobby, raising, breeding, and training dogs for obedience trials. She argued that he was cold, withholding, critical, verbally abusive, and uncaring and that he had abandoned her during her pregnancy and birthing process by being emotionally unavailable. They barely spoke to one another and had not been sexual since she discovered that she was pregnant. Each of the partners was committed to salvaging the relationship and starting over. However, neither could forgive the other for painful events in the past. Each felt unattractive, isolated, and helpless. Both of them were committed to their daughter and admitted that in spite of their difficulties there were as many positive things in the relationship as negative.

Each individual's pathological complex is presented below using a multiaxial diagnosis from the DSM-IV, followed by a brief description of each part of Figure 15 in order to make each pathological complex more accessible for observation.

JACOB

DSM-IV DIAGNOSIS

Axis I: 300.4 Dysthymia; V61.10 Relational problems

Axis II: 301.82 Avoidant personality disorder

Axis III: V71.09 No diagnosis

Axis IV: Problems with primary support group

Axis V: GAF = 68

History

Jacob was a 38-year-old man with doctorates in psychology, adult education, and finance. He grew up in a family where his father, a successful neurosurgeon, was rarely home. He was the oldest child, the first grandchild, and a boy. Both his mother and his grandparents preferred him.

Jacob had a sister who was three years younger. She was quietly defiant and embarrassed the family by wearing the wrong clothes, choosing the wrong friends, and getting good grades without working hard. The family considered her overly emotional. In addition, she told people exactly what she thought and often refused to do what she was told. Despite excelling scholastically and in sports, she was passionate about drawing, painting, and sculpting and not really interested in academia. Both her mother and father discouraged her intense interest in the arts, insisting that she take the "gifted" classes in science and mathematics. She moved away from home after completing college and rarely returned.

Jacob was very fond of his sister. He could not understand why his parents were so harsh with her and treated him so well. His parents forced his sister to be compliant by withholding or destroying things that they knew were important to her unless she cooperated. He remembered feeling anxious that his parents might discover something he loved and take it away from him, so he was very careful not to express his likes, dislikes, wants, or needs. He could not remember being cuddled or touched. Jacob described the family atmosphere as very cold and as having strict standards of behavior based on how the family appeared in public. This even included what activities the family engaged in, what clubs they belonged to, and the church they attended.

Jacob had few memories of childhood other than feeling alone and having a difficult time socializing. His parents and grandparents expected him to be exceptional in every way, academically as well as athletically. His mother gave up her career as an attorney in order to stay home and raise the children. Jacob believed that he had to excel at any cost in order to prove to his mother that she had made the right decision, especially since his younger sister was such a disappointment to her. Jacob trusted his intelligence and his ability to organize anything. He pursued three doctoral degrees and was so busy going to school that he did not have time to socialize. He felt freakish and incompetent around people unless he was in charge of the relationship. He studied a great deal and had no close friends. He longed for a group of people who could understand him and with whom he could share ideas. He believed that if he could be accepted by a group of people who shared his hopes and dreams and work together to contribute to the common good, he would no longer feel freakish and isolated.

The Pathological Complex

Jacob's negative complex was not stimulated in the workplace. He was the director of a large company and was quite successful professionally. He worked long hours, managed his company well, and even though he received feedback that some of his employees considered him harsh and judgmental, they did not leave the company because they were well paid.

When Jacob returned home in the evening after work, he wanted to come into an environment that was warm and loving. For Jacob that meant an impeccably neat, well-organized environment with a gourmet dinner, classical music, fine wine, and a welcoming wife and daughter to greet him; instead he was greeted by a cranky wife, a whiney child, a cold dinner, and a home that was noisy, messy, and disorganized. Jacob believed that if his wife really loved him, she would be prepared for his homecoming. He described himself as feeling "trashed"–unimportant and unwanted.

This experience was followed by a sense of anger linked with anxiety and shame that overwhelmed him. He withdrew into TV programs or computer games and avoided contact with his wife and child. When Shirley confronted him, he defended himself by becoming sarcastic and judgmental. Jacob described his internal experience as one of being shut down, overwhelmed, and unable to make contact with his wife.

Ego Functions

Jacob's present memory was excellent, his behavior was well thought out, and he was very contained. He did not express any affect through his tone of voice or his body language. He remembered events from his childhood, however the memories were detached from any affect. He appeared to think about feelings rather than experience them. He did not remember his dreams and did not believe in a collective human memory. Jacob felt very uncomfortable with any expression of affect other than interest, approval or enjoyment.

He attended a Christian church regularly and enjoyed the church format of philosophical and theological discussions. He did not believe he had a spirit, nor did he find much meaning in his life. He loved theological debates and when the discussions were interesting to him he felt connected with the people involved. He believed that religious study fostered good conduct and therefore was beneficial. He was physically healthy and ran at least five miles four times a week.

Jacob appeared to have separated from his affective experience early in life in order to survive in his family. His memory, behavior, and physical body were overworked. His connections with his affect, his soul (meaning in life), his dreaming body, his spirit, and the collective human memory were not operating consciously.

Archetyal/Developmental Processes

Jacob's strengths were doing, thinking, and creativity in his work. He was excellent at thinking his way through problems. He had a tendency to overwork, doing too much and enjoying too little. When someone around him expressed strong emotions, his pathological complex was constellated and his thinking shut down. His sense of identity was externally located and was connected with feedback he received from others about the way they perceived him. He described himself as "a fool with a pathological need for approval." When his pathological complex was stimulated and he did not receive approval, he became overwhelmed and withdrew into a place he described as a deep, dark hole of helplessness where nothing could touch him. Jacob was not very interested in being sexual with his wife and said he felt more comfortable taking care of his own needs in the shower. As we explored this further, it became clearer that he was anxious about failing to perform adequately. He and his wife had never discussed their sexual relationship.

Jacob described himself as the kind of person who was always working on projects that he continued to perfect. For him, the essence of his creativity was shaping his work until others were perfectly satisfied with it. Jacob's thinking was well developed. However, when the pathological complex was operating, all of the archetypal/developmental processes were constricted.

Patterns of Mediation Embedded Within the Pathological Complex

Jacob was most comfortable with styles of mediation that were directive, educating, and symbiotic. When Jacob felt he was in control of things, he was fine. He expected his wife to do things for him (gourmet dinner, fine wine, organized home), and when she was unable to meet his expectations, he felt unloved (a symbiotic form of mediation).

When Jacob experienced affect, he simply shut down. When his wife expressed her negative feelings, he withdrew. He described himself as working very hard to develop a cooperative style of relationship, and he did well as long as affective expression was not involved. Since Jacob did not experience containing, confirming, or empowering patterns of mediation in his family of origin, he did not know how to use these patterns in his relationships. He had great difficulty communicating when his complex was constellated. During his wife's pregnancy and for the first two years of his daughter's life, he attempted to help his wife and to take care of his daughter. However, his wife criticized his efforts, and Jacob felt displaced and unwanted. He responded by shutting down and withdrawing.

Cycles of Nature

Jacob grew up as a privileged child from an affluent family. There was an unchanging quality about this kind of life because changes were well organized in advance and easily made. Things were always in proper order and the way they "should be." Appearance and what other people might think about the family was very important to family life. His primary caretaker was a nanny who had adopted the family values. He remembered no particularly traumatic events. However, as we explored his history together, Jacob remembered being guilty and ashamed about the way his parents treated his younger sister who rebelled against the family values. His sister was never physically abused, but her activities were "frowned upon" by the family and she was forced to modify her behavior when the family was in public. Jacob knew that he had difficulty with change and needed a great deal of approval and recognition in order to tolerate any kind of change. When change was forced on him, he worked through it by creating lists and getting things reorganized as quickly as possible. Jacob had never experienced death, chaos, and transformation.

Description of the Defenses of the Self

Jacob's strength was that he had an ability to observe his own internal experience and behavior. He was also able to apply what he learned to his own experience. However, when his wife or his daughter expressed negative affect, he shut down and withdrew. At that time all of the defenses of the Self were activated. Jacob was aware that he pushed people away when he was judgmental, sarcastic, and withdrawn, but he did not know how to stop these reactions. Jacob believed that if his wife would appreciate him, he would be able to interrupt his pattern of withdrawal. He was unaware that he was asking others to become responsible for his reactivity or that he hoped his wife would save him from himself. Jacob was aware that parts of himself were opposed to one another. For example, he knew that he wanted his wife's approval and appreciation (one part), yet he could not interrupt his pattern of sarcasm and withdrawal (another part).

The Imago

In order to understand Jacob better, he and I created a descriptive image of his imago. As we have discussed, the imago exists in the transitional space between ego consciousness and the unconscious. It is composed by conscious, unconscious, and preconscious images from experiences with caregivers and undeveloped archetypal energy. When Jacob described his pathological complex, he spoke of himself as being so overwhelmed that he had to withdraw. If we imagine the imago as an invisible companion when the complex was constellated, it could appear as an enormous and disapproving caregiver who put Jacob in a dark cellar alone as punishment for experiencing or expressing affect. The sarcastic comments, criticisms, and judgments kept others away from the cellar until the affect associated with the pathological complex dissipates.

Patterned Form of Attachment

Jacob was a very "good boy" who wanted the people around him to like him. The way he survived was to avoid contact with other human beings because it was painful. Jacob's patterned form of attachment was *anxious/avoidant.*

The Fantasy Bond

Jacob was attracted to his wife because she was vibrantly alive, successful, creative, intelligent, strong, and independent. He was especially attracted to her warmth and genuineness, which made him feel wanted, loved, and cared for. She created a safe place for him and provided a sense of wholeness and belonging for him that kept him from experiencing overwhelming affect. She was the one who loved him unconditionally and made him whole. The fantasy bond compensated for Jacob's unconscious view of himself as socially inept, inadequate, afraid of being shamed, and unwilling to change his pattern of withdrawal unless he was certain of being accepted. He was preoccupied with the many ways his wife could demonstrate her love for him. His fantasy bond also compensated the lack of acceptance, warmth, companionship, and nurturing that Jacob had experienced from his caretakers.

Dialogue in Marital Therapy

Jacob: "Why do I shut down like this?"

Therapist (internal dialogue): His question is a way for him to avoid his experience by thinking about it rather than being with it. I don't know why he shuts down. He is the one who has to learn to stay with his experience and explore it.

Therapist (to Jacob): "Why is a question with no answer. Shutting down is your experience. What is happening inside for you right now?"
Jacob: "I feel like a freak. I don't have words. I want to hide."
Therapist: "Good work. What is the color, the shape of freak?"
Jacob: "Black obliteration. Hide. Going away."

Therapist (internal dialogue): He is in it. Can he stay in contact with me if I am directive with him? Is it safe for him to encourage him to connect with Shirley?

Therapist (to Shirley): "Jacob is in complex. Would you be willing to gaze at him the way you did with your daughter?"
Shirley: "Yes."
Therapist (to Jacob): "Jacob, look at Shirley. Keep looking at her and stay connected with her through your eyes. Let your body relax and tell Shirley with your eyes how hard it is for you to stay connected."

Long period of silence.

Shirley: "I can see how hard it is for him. I understand."
Jacob: "I don't have words. I feel shaken."
Therapist (to Jacob): "This is part of the core of your complex. Jacob you really worked to remain present."
Therapist (to Shirley): "Jacob was in his place of curling up and withdrawing. Shirley, you helped him stay connected."
Therapist (to both Jacob and Shirley): "I think you two just had a sacred moment. Don't talk about it. Allow yourselves to be with it. It will take some time to absorb it."

Overview of Jacob's Treatment

In therapy, the initial focus was on Jacob's behavior and his ability to think, because these areas of ego consciousness were his strengths. He was motivated to work in therapy because he wanted to have a good relationship with his wife and his daughter. Attunement and encouragement along with cooperative, confirming, and educating forms of mediation were important tools in helping Jacob begin to understand himself, especially his inability to contain his affect and halt his pattern of withdrawal. Teaching him to move his affect into the transitional space was probably the most important aspect of his therapy. Jacob liked to work with the sand trays.

Usually there are two sandboxes, one filled with wet sand, the other dry. A person can work directly with the sand to build things or use whatever objects the therapist has collected to express experiences that are not available to language. The patient can use one or both trays, building with the sand or placing objects in the tray that best express his or her experience. The therapist remains present but does not comment or interpret the trays. In Jacob's case, he worked with the sand trays while his wife expressed her emotions. After the tray is completed and the patient has discussed the experience of creating the tray, the therapist takes two Polaroid pictures of the completed tray, keeping one for the file and giving one to the patient.

It was important to Jacob that both the therapist and his wife listen to his experience of sand play and that she understand that he was working toward being able to remain present in the relationship. Jacob gradually learned to express and listen to expressions of painful affect without withdrawing.

SHIRLEY

DSM-IV DIAGNOSIS

Axis I: 300.02 Generalized anxiety disorder
      309.81 Posttraumatic stress disorder (chronic)
      V61.10 Partner relational disorder

Axis II: V71.09 No diagnosis

Axis III: V71.09 No diagnosis

Axis IV: Problems with primary support group

Axis V: GAF = 68

History

Shirley entered therapy to repair her marriage, which she regarded as a complete failure. She and Jacob had been married for ten years. She felt abandoned, neglected, and emotionally abused, especially since her pregnancy and the birth of her daughter, now age four. She gave up her full-time job to become a mother and worked part-time after her daughter was six months old. She designed her own schedule and worked from 7 P.M. to 5 A.M. (ten hours) once a week.

Shirley was first attracted to Jacob because he was well educated, intelligent, contained, and gentle. They dated for four years and were married for six years before the birth of their daughter. Shirley described the early years of their marriage as wonderful. She and Jacob spent all of their time together, shared the household chores, traveled, and enjoyed life. They bought a home together, and Shirley built a barn to house her German Shepherds and her horse. When Shirley became pregnant, the relationship changed. She wanted Jacob to spend a great deal of time nurturing her and helping her with things around the house. When he did not, she became angry and upset. In response to her anger, Jacob withdrew emotionally, which made Shirley even angrier. She experienced Jacob's abandonment as emotional abuse.

When her daughter was born, Shirley's whole life changed. She gave up her promising career and only worked ten hours a week. She was absolutely devoted to her daughter, who was still being breast-fed at the time the couple entered therapy. Shirley did lengthy study on parenting and had adopted several parenting techniques, including nursing the child for as long as she could; the "family bed" where Jacob, Shirley, and the daughter slept together; and a "gazing technique," where Shirley held the daughter four or five times so that they could gaze at one another to deepen their sense of intimacy.

Shirley loved animals, and during her pregnancy she decided to keep her dogs and continue training them and competing in obedience trials. Before the baby was born, she had the entire inside of the home and the barn rebuilt using her own designs. Their home was close to the city and yet was a beautiful farmette bordering acres of a wooded forest preserve.

Jacob's parents promised to finance the entire remodeling project in honor of the birth of their first grandchild. However, after purchase of the home and the remodeling, the parents refused to pay for anything because Jacob and Shirley did not visit them often enough. In addition to paying for the remodeling, Jacob and Shirley were already paying off Shirley's school loans, and the additional debt created real financial hardship. Money and the control of money gradually became the focus for the problems that already existed in the relationship.

Shirley gained weight and felt tired or sick most of the time. She was enraged with Jacob because he didn't offer enough help, and in addition she felt trapped, frustrated, unappreciated, unsuccessful, and a failure as a mother. Her daughter was four, and she was not potty trained or ready for preschool. The only time Shirley felt happy was when she was playing with her daughter, riding her horse, or competing with her dogs. Her ten-hour workday once a week exhausted her, and her schedule was so busy that she had no time at all for friends. She was unable to keep up with many of the household tasks such as cleaning, cooking, and weeding, and she felt that these activities were much less important than her daughter, her dogs, her horse, and working part-time.

Shirley's father left her mother before Shirley was born. She never saw or heard from him. After he left, her mother and her four older siblings moved back to her mother's parental home where Shirley was born. Her earliest memories were happy and she was told that her birth was a joyful experience for the entire family. Shirley was "the baby" and brought great delight to the entire family. Her siblings were three, six, seven, and ten years older than Shirley. Her grandparents lived in a beautiful home on 20 acres of land and raised horses.

Shirley's mother often spoke of feeling lonely, and when Shirley was four years old, her mother married a local rancher, a widower who raised cattle. After the marriage, Shirley's mother changed. She became totally dependent on her husband and did whatever he said. She and the children moved in with Shirley's stepfather right after the wedding. Since there was not enough space for the children, they had to share rooms, which they had not done at their grandparents' home. The older children wanted to live with their grandparents. The stepfather angrily told the children that they were going to work on his ranch and live with him.

He controlled the family's life, where they lived, how much money they received, and everything that went on within the household, including the daily menu. The new environment was quite different from the warm and loosely structured atmosphere of the grandparents' home. The stepfather expected all of the children to help with the work of running a cattle ranch. By the time Shirley was six, she was driving a tractor, mucking out stalls and feeding cattle. When any of the children stopped working, played, read a book, or talked back, that child was beaten by the stepfather and then kept out of school for a week to work on the ranch. Shirley's mother did nothing to protect the children, and the stepfather was especially brutal with Shirley because she was not quite old enough to be competent in her work around the ranch.

When Shirley was six years old, her grandparents died in an automobile accident. Her mother inherited everything and gave it to the stepfather. In addition, the stepfather had started sexually abusing Shirley's nine-year-old sister. He forced Shirley to watch and told her that she was so ugly no man would ever want her. Shirley told her mother about the abuse, but when her mother confronted the stepfather, both he and the older sister lied about it. Shirley was beaten so badly that she couldn't get out of bed for several days. Her stepfather told her if she ever said anything like that again he would break her legs. All of the money was poured into the ranch, and even though the grandparents promised the children that they would pay for their college education, the money was gone. Even finishing high school was discouraged. Her older siblings left home as soon as they could, and Shirley felt even more abandoned.

However, Shirley was a gifted student and was determined to finish high school and attend college. If the stepfather found her studying, he tore up her books. She was not allowed to stay after school for any extracurricular activities, and when she received awards, she was not allowed to attend the ceremonies if they were after school. At home her academic success was ignored or ridiculed. Shirley understood that if she could go to college she would get away from her stepfather. She won a partial scholarship to a state college, found a job, and left home three days after she graduated from high school. She continued on in school with partial scholarships and school loans and received a master's degree in psychology and then continued on to medical school. She completed her residency in pathology and became a physician in charge of research in a large hospital laboratory. By the time she completed her education and her residency, Shirley was more than two hundred thousand dollars in debt.

At the time she entered therapy, Shirley was still in contact with her mother and her stepfather who lived in another state and with her sister who had been sexually abused. Her other siblings refused to have anything to do with the family. Shirley had never asked them why.

Shirley described her experience of growing up as feeling bad and ugly, and as being constantly vigilant so that she would not be physically abused or shamed. At the time she came into therapy, Shirley still had recurring nightmares of the sexual abuse, and she admitted that she did enjoy being sexual with Jacob. She had never discussed these things with Jacob. Sometimes Shirley woke up in the middle of the night after one of her "abuse" dreams and could not go to back to sleep. When she became anxious, she felt a sense of shakiness that made her want to jump out of her skin. When Jacob was judgmental or critical she felt "bad" and ugly, and internally she became more and more resentful of Jacob.

The Pathological Complex

As Shirley and I explored her complex together, we discovered that she felt a great deal of unexpressed anger toward men in general and Jacob in particular. She was no longer angry with her stepfather and visited her mother and him regularly. She was not at all worried about allowing her parents to babysit with her daughter.

She expressed her hostile feelings by making generalizations about all men: they didn't respect women's ideas and opinions, they used women sexually, they were unappreciative of women's talents, and they abandoned women and children by being too busy to assist in parenting. When we explored these ideas, she was able to talk about how abusive Jacob was and how victimized she felt because he did not help her around the house and withheld money from her just to make things harder for her. She experienced Jacob's withdrawal as an attack, and she felt anxious, invaded, and overwhelmed because she believed that he did it purposely, as a way to hurt her. She described Jacob as a man just like her stepfather. Instead of beating her, he was critical, judgmental, unaware of how much help she needed, and always unavailable. When she was really angry, she described herself as moving into a sort of stubborn rage, just working harder to get things done. Jacob believed that the upkeep of her dogs, the obedience trials, and maintenance of the horse was much more than they could afford. Shirley believed that if Jacob really loved her, he would support her and help with the care of the animals.

Shirley wanted to hurt Jacob, so she ignored him and did whatever she wished even if she knew he would not approve. She expressed her anger indirectly by going shopping and spending money on things for the home or new projects for her dogs and horse. When she spent money that she knew Jacob would not approve of, she felt a sense of terror linked with her rage and was afraid that if she fully expressed what she felt, she would somehow be destroyed. She kept her attention on her anger, which gave her energy to work and take care of her daughter and her projects. Keeping order in the house, cleaning, and cooking were things that were not important at all to Shirley.

Ego Functions

Shirley was able to express anger, fear, sadness, and happiness and was in touch with most of her affect. However, even though she described herself as "bad" and "ugly" she was unaware of and unable to express shame. She appeared to turn shame into anger and use the anger as energy for work. She had difficulty remembering what happened during or between therapy sessions. However, she had a good memory when it came to things she was interested in and never forgot Jacob's criticisms, his judgments, or his withdrawal. In this sense her memory appeared to operate rigidly—she remembered more wrongs than rights. She was physically strong, yet she was constantly tired and often sick with colds or flu. Her behavior was based on her mood or her ability to convert her anger into work. She did not believe in any religion; however, she found deep meaning in her relationship with her daughter and with nature. She began many projects at home and had difficulty completing them, usually due to lack of time or money. She was not assertive or direct with Jacob about what she was planning to do in terms of her feelings, experience, or interests.

Shirley had a difficult time containing and reflecting on her experience. Instead, she moved away from her internal experience into activities that interested her. She remembered her dreams, and they were filled with images from the collective unconscious. This was her greatest strength. Her dreaming existed outside the pathological complex. No one in her family of origin talked about dreams, and she had never shared them with anyone. During the early phases of therapy, she mentioned a dream that moved her deeply. There were paints and papers in the office, and she painted the images from her dreams often during Jacob's time in therapy. She did a series of paintings of pictographs that appeared to be quite ancient. Later, she found some of the pictographs in a book about images of ancient goddesses. She felt empowered by the images and believed that she was being led back in time when women's knowledge was highly valued and considered sacred.

As Shirley studied her dreams, she discovered that the ancient goddesses brought life, were connected with all of nature and took all life back into the womb at death to transform it into new life. Slowly Shirley began to understand that her own life, her baby's life, and Jacob's life were sacred.

Archetypal/Developmental Processes

Shirley was strong in doing, thinking, and creativity. Her sense of being was fragile because of her experience with abuse and was linked with an unconscious shame for simply being alive. When her pathological complex was constellated, the affective theme of rage mixed with the terror of directly expressing rage interfered with her ability to think. Her sense of identity was unconsciously compromised. Identity begins to form from similarities with the same-sex parent and siblings. Unconsciously, if Shirley identified with her mother she would become like her, abandoning and passive. If she identified with her older sister she would be abused. Instead, Shirley became a genderless, nonsexual woman.[3] During the time most children begin to develop a sense of identity the child takes in many of the qualities of the parent of the same gender. Sexual preference is only one part of identity and is based upon physical predisposition and/or preference (Beebe 1985).[4] The parent of the opposite sex also influences identity in terms of influencing the formation of roles in life that enhance or diminish identity. In addition, cultural factors as well as the mediation of the archetypal/developmental process by caregivers, teachers, and friends enhance or diminish identity. The images from the collective human memory that appeared in her dreams seemed to be compensating her lack of understanding about her own identity as a woman.

Patterns of Mediation

The patterns of mediation that Shirley was most comfortable with were educating, confirming, and symbiotic. During her childhood, symbiotic, directive, containing, confirming, and empowering forms of mediation were quite dysfunctional, and cooperative forms of mediation did not exist.

The hyper-vigilance she developed as a result of being abused helped her meet other people's needs before they were expressed, creating a rigidified pattern of symbiotic mediation in relationships. She learned to focus her attention on other people's experience and confirm it in order to avoid introspection. She used symbiotic and confirming forms of mediation with Jacob during the beginnings of their relationship and then diverted them to her daughter during her pregnancy and afterward. Being symbiotic exhausted her. She wanted Jacob to reciprocate, anticipating her needs without having to ask. Directive forms of communication stimulated her negative complex. Her behavior indicated that she had not experienced cooperative forms of mediation.

Cycles of Nature

Shirley seemed comfortable with constant chaos. Her symbiotic form of relating to Jacob and then to her child kept her too busy to reflect upon her own needs or to contain her experience and learn from it. She avoided death, chaos, transformation, and living life fully by moving away from her internal experience into constant activity.

Defenses of the Self

All of the defenses of the Self were operating. Shirley was identified with the woman victim of a male tyrant. She projected the male tyrant onto Jacob and negatively idealized him. He became the tyrant her stepfather had been. It was very difficult for Shirley to believe that Jacob withdrew because of his own experiences of pain from his own family of origin.

The Imago

The imago was made up of an abusive stepfather, an abandoning mother, a victimized child, and an affective theme of rage combined with the powerful, numinous archetypal energy of compressed being and identity. The ego/imago axis prevented her from containing her experience and learning from it. The pictographs that she painted from her dreams were compensatory images that were connected with a protective, instinctual feminine energy that nourished and protected her young. Shirley became aware that she was projecting the image of her stepfather onto Jacob. She felt abandoned by him (as she had been by her mother) during her pregnancy and the first two years of her daughter's life. She experienced her husband's withdrawal as being as abusive as what she received from her tyrannical stepfather.

Patterned Form of Attachment

Shirley had a disorganized pattern of attachment. The pattern was fueled by her unconscious, stubborn rage. Her rage helped her survive, leave her family, and become successful. Jacob was the first person, outside of her family of origin that Shirley became attached to. When Jacob began to withdraw, Shirley was precipitated into the original state of disorganization that existed in her early life. Jacob became like her stepfather when he abandoned her.

The Fantasy Bond

Shirley married Jacob because he was intelligent, contained, and gentle. He would keep her so safe that she would never be abused again. He was stable, organized, and loyal–everything her stepfather and her mother were not. He was proud of her success and offered Shirley a sense of stability she had never known. The fantasy bond compensated her disorganized patterned form of attachment and gave Shirley a sense of living happily ever after.

As she began to experience Jacob's abandonment and as her mother and stepfather lent her money when she needed it, Jacob gradually replaced the abusive parent in her patterned form of attachment. The pattern remained the same, only the people changed.

Couple's Dialogue in Therapy

Shirley: "He's always making these sarcastic remarks to me. He never helps me. He is so detailed and controlling that I just want to scream at him. The house would be cleaner if he would just help me a little. Can't you get him to help me?"

Therapist (internal experience): I feel angry with Jacob myself and want to make him help her. My need to be the "therapist heroic" is surfacing. It has to be contained. I need to be quiet a minute before I respond to Shirley.

Therapist (to Shirley): "Let's be quiet together for a minute. Let yourself really sink into your experience."

Short silence.

Shirley: "I feel anxious and jumpy. I don't like the feeling. I want to get up and do something else."
Therapist: "Good work, Shirley. Would it help if you got up and moved around?"
Shirley: "No. Now I just feel angry. I feel angry at you for making me feel this."
Therapist: "Tell me about the part of you that is angry at me."
Shirley: "That part of me hates you. I want to shake you and tell you to go to hell."
Therapist: "Is there more?"
Shirley: "You're so superior, and you won't do a thing to help me. I hate you for that and I really hate feeling this way. I don't want this."

Therapist (internal experience): She looks as if she is becoming more and more disorganized. Am I pushing her too hard? Can she begin to contain it?

Therapist (to Shirley): "Does the hate have a color, a shape, a sound?"
Shirley: "It is all black, swirling with red. It is moving around me. It is coming into my nose, making it hard for me to breathe."

Therapist (internal experience): I have to be directive with her now to facilitate an experience that helps her move through the affect so the complex is not reinforced.

Therapist (to Shirley): "I am going to help you now. Let the black cloud with the red swirl around you. It cannot come in with your breath. Breathe deeply and tighten your whole body, everything in your body—your face, hands, shoulders, back, legs, even your toes. Hold tight and then relax and exhale. The cloud cannot come in when you tighten and relax. If you notice as you begin relaxing, you will see that there is an energy body around the outside of your body. The cloud cannot get through that. Breathe deep, tighten, and then relax as you exhale. Pay attention to your breath. Bring your breath into the ribs in the back of your body to deepen the breath. Tighten and then exhale and relax.

Therapist Internal experience: She is doing well. She has a short trigger into a disorganized state and real difficulty containing.

A short time passes. Shirley and the therapist breathe and tighten together.

Shirley: "I feel better. I am sorry I got so angry with you. I felt really panicky. Are you O.K.?"
Therapist: "I am happy you got through it. What made you feel better?"
Shirley: "I felt that body around my body and the black stuff couldn't get in because of the tightening and relaxing. You helped me."
Therapist: "Yes I did. Can you feel the connection between us?"
Shirley (Short silence.): "Yes I can. I feel you there. I want to paint now. If I keep feeling connected it will be too much."
Therapist (to Jacob): "How was that for you?"
Jacob: "I was able to stay present."

Overview of the Treatment

Shirley's strengths were her creativity, her comfort and skill in remaining within the transitional space, and her connection with images from the collective unconscious. The therapeutic work consisted of attunement and the use of directive, confirming, educating, and empowering forms of mediation. Shirley was encouraged to develop a cooperative relationship with Jacob by believing in his good intentions and consciously taking the tyrant's face off of him. Valuing and confirming Shirley's painting helped her validate and confirm Jacob's experiences of sand play. Jacob's strength was his thinking. He was able to contain his withdrawal and learn to remain present when Shirley had strong feelings.

Enmeshed Complexes

Both Jacob and Shirley functioned symbiotically. Both avoided feeling ashamed of being and having an identity. In the beginning of the relationship Shirley's symbiotic mediation provided warmth of affect, anticipated Jacob's needs, and took care of them before he asked. Jacob provided order, problem solving, and a day-to-day structure that was based upon his needs. They earned a comfortable living together until they remodeled the home and the barn and Shirley began to work part-time. The pregnancy and birth of their daughter disrupted the couple's unconscious symbiotic connection, bringing death to the symbiotic connection and disrupting the fantasy bond. Before the baby was born, Shirley nourished Jacob. After the baby was born she wanted Jacob to nourish her. He did not know how. When Jacob no longer felt nourished, he withdrew, constellating Shirley's fear and rage. The symbiotic bond was broken and both Jacob and Shirley struggled to restore it by demanding the other to provide nourishment. In one sense money is a metaphor for nourishment because it can be converted into anything. Spending money and how money was spent became the metaphor for their new relationship. When Jacob and Shirley argued about money, each could blame the other for not caring and arguments about money became a struggle to force the other person back into their role in the fantasy bond in an attempt to preserve it.

There were parts of both Jacob and Shirley that were not involved in the symbiotic patterned form of attachment. These parts centered on their professional achievements. Focusing on these achievements was useful during the beginning phases of therapy. It was an area that was safe to explore because it existed outside of the couple's enmeshed pathological complex.

The relational structure was unbalanced by the therapy changing it from a dysfunctional dyad to a triad that encouraged separation, containment, and self-observation.

VIEWING POINTS INTO AN ENMESHED COMPLEX

Ego Functions

Jacob's strengths were memory, physical body, and behavior. Shirley's strengths were affect, dreaming body, and receptivity to the collective human memory. The safe place in the relationship was discussion of work. The painful places in the relationship centered on the expression of affect and avoidant behavior.

Archetypal/Developmental Processes

Jacob was very good at doing, thinking, and creativity. However, when affect was vehemently expressed or he was asked to share his feelings, Jacob's thinking shut down. Shirley was very good at doing, thinking, and creativity. However, when she experienced herself being victimized her thinking shut down. Being and identity were distorted for both Jacob and Shirley.

Patterns of Mediation

The relationship was built on a rigidified, symbiotic form of mediation, which created the unconscious enmeshment that made it so difficult for the couple to communicate. The forms of mediation that were developed as the therapy progressed were cooperative, educating, empowering, and confirming of the other's experience.

Cycles of Nature

Jacob and Shirley's relationship experienced a death when Shirley got pregnant. Neither Jacob nor Shirley were able to deal with imbalance and transformation. Shirley became rigidly disorganized. Jacob only experienced movement that was rigidly organized. Movement, change, and transformation could not occur for either Jacob or Shirley because Jacob's rigidified orderliness was at war with Shirley's constant state of chaos, preventing normal change and movement.

Defenses of the Self

All of the defenses of the Self existed in the relationship. Therapy was a way for both Jacob and Shirley to learn to develop containment and to develop an observing ego.

The Imago

Jacob's imago began to emerge in the analysis as a frightening, sarcastic, judgmental, and angry personality, companioned by a needy, shamed young boy who did not know what he needed. Shirley's imago began to emerge in the therapy as an angry, rigid, directive, condemning, persecuting personality, accompanied by a terrified and shamed little girl. Both Jacob and Shirley had a well-developed ego/imago axis. The emergence of the transitional space in therapy was an indirect way of creating space between the ego and the imago in order to begin to restore normal processes of compensation.

The Patterned Form of Attachment

The patterned form of attachment contained a victim and a villain. Both Jacob and Shirley identified with the victim and projected the villain onto the other partner.

The Fantasy Bond

Jacob's fantasy was that Shirley would provide him with unconditional love, acceptance, and total understanding and would know what he needed without his asking. Shirley's fantasy was that Jacob would protect her, never abandon her, be kind to her, and give her whatever she wanted.

Dialogue: Therapeutic Example of an Enmeshed Complex

Therapist: "Which one of you would like to work first?"

Jacob and Shirley glance uncomfortably at one another, finally Shirley says, "I'll go."

Shirley: "I want to spend some time talking to you about how angry I am at Jacob, and then I want to share a dream and paint."

Therapist nods at Shirley and says to Jacob: "How are you going to stay separate from Shirley's feelings and still remain present?"

Jacob: "I am going to listen to Shirley and express my feelings using sand play."

Therapist Internal experience: Shirley has a hard time directly expressing her anger, and Jacob has a hard time remaining present. The problem will be with us in the room.

Therapist (to Shirley): "This sounds good. Would you be willing to begin, Shirley?"

Shirley: "I am so angry at Jacob I hate being in the same room with him. He is critical, controlling, and abusive. He gives me my dole of money, and I hate that—and not only that, he is accusing me of stealing money from his money market account. I am so angry I feel like I am going to boil over with rage."

Therapist: "What happens inside when you feel so angry that you could boil over?"

Shirley: "I want to lash out, then I get confused, and then I just know Jacob will be so logical and articulate and tell me how wrong and stupid I am."

Therapist: "And then?"
Shirley: "I don't know. I finally just hate him quietly. I think I want a divorce and then I think how much that will hurt the baby, and then I want to try and I still hate him all at the same time."
Therapist: "Does your anger have parts?"
Shirley: "Yes, I never thought of it that way but it does."

The therapist and Shirley discuss the parts of her anger for about ten minutes. Shirley decides to draw an image of each part of her anger as the therapist sits quietly, being with Shirley as she draws. The therapist does not comment or interpret the drawings. She asks Shirley to name each of the parts she has drawn. This process takes about 15 minutes and creates a shared language that will be used repeatedly and developed as Shirley expresses her anger in therapy.

Therapist: "Shirley, it is time for Jacob to work. There hasn't been time for you to explore your dream. Would you be willing to paint the images and say a little bit about them when we check out?"
Shirley: "That would be fine with me."
Therapist: "Will you listen to Jacob's work while you paint?"
Shirley: "Yes, I will."
Therapist: "Jacob can you say a little bit about your experience of what you have been doing?"
Jacob: "I want to talk about my sand tray." (The therapist smiles and nods at Jacob.) "There is a war going on here. On this hill are the aggressors. They are armored and they are coming down the hill to destroy that little Martian over there. I put a stream between the aggressors and the Martian and then put trees and rocks around the stream. Over in the corner there is a lake. It has trees and stones around it and the stream comes from the lake. The rest of the place is all desert, just sand, no water, no trees, no rocks, just nothing."

Therapist (internal experience): This is the first time he has put a something that is strange and alone into the tray. Usually it's all destruction.

Therapist (to Jacob): "What is your experience of this tray?"
Jacob: "It's a war and the Martian is all alone in the chaos. The Martian is not going to be killed. He is a peacemaker and will solve the war. I think there's more but I don't know how to talk about the more."

Therapist (internal experience): His thinking appears to be shut down. I can only offer him options to choose from, otherwise I am being symbiotic and directive with him rather than cooperative and containing.

Therapist (to Jacob): "There are lots of options, Jacob: another tray, clay, drawing, painting, physical movement. What would feel best to you?"
Jacob: "Another tray, a wet one."

Jacob begins a second tray using water to build mountains and hills. He begins to place war figures into the tray. Then he places rocks around the war figures and trees around the rocks. He places four stones in the tray, one in each corner of the tray. He puts the lake and stream in the tray and then places the Martian in the stream saying, "The water will carry him."

During this time the therapist remains present with Jacob saying nothing as he works. After he completes the second tray the therapist remains quiet. Jacob says, "I am finished now." The therapist takes two Polaroid pictures of each tray, one for Jacob and one for the file.

Therapist: "How was that experience, Jacob?"
Jacob: "I stayed present when Shirley got angry with me. I don't have words for the trays, but I felt present and I feel okay now."

Sixty-five minutes have passed, and it is time for both Jacob and Shirley to check out in order to close the session.

Therapist: "It's time for each of you to check out. Would each of you be willing to summarize your own experience and say a few words about what you learned about your own complex and then say something about what you learned about your partner's complex?"
Shirley: "In my dream a lady came to help me and it felt so good. This is her picture. She has snakes for hair, and this is how she helps the people around her. She touches them with her hair and then the people understand each other. I think she understands how much I need to be understood. I learned that Jacob has a Martian inside of him that is really alone and attacked, and tonight he stayed present when I expressed my anger."
Jacob: "I feel very confused, like something happened and I don't know what. I didn't know that Shirley had parts to her anger, and somehow it helps to know that there are parts to it because that makes it smaller."
Therapist: "Both of you are doing good work in here. How are you getting along at home?"
Jacob: "About the same. We have different ideas about the money and the budget. I don't think we can talk about them without real problems."
Shirley: "Yes, things are about the same. We avoid each other. I don't know if we'll ever be able to talk about the budget, but financially we are okay and the budget can wait."
Therapist: "Be gentle and patient with yourselves and focus on what is good about your partner. You are doing fine work."

TREATMENT OF AN ENMESHED COMPLEX: SUMMARY

Shirley, Jacob and the therapist developed the parameters for this course of therapy. These parameters were:

1. Creation of a safe space within a 75-minute hour where both had permission to express themselves, speak from their own point of view, and work within the transitional space in a one-on-one relationship with the therapist.
2. Development of containment and cooperation within the relational field.
3. Therapist attunement, and modeling of communication techniques. Facilitation of therapeutic techniques such as parts work, utilizing the transitional space, development of new communication techniques, role play, self-disclosure using examples of difficulties in the therapist's own relationships as an educational tool and the use of metaphors, and humor.
4. Creation of boundaries through regularity of place, time, and fee; the structure of the session (the patient identifies what he or she will work on during the session, does the work, discusses his or her experience of the work in a way that explores his or her complex, attempts to learn something about his or her partner's complex, and checks out at the end of the session with several sentences about the experience of the session). Both partners agree to keep all discussions and misunderstandings that arise within the session with no discussions on those topics outside the session.
5. Partners agree to say one positive thing per day to the other person.
6. Develop cooperation by reading about effective parenting and working together to practice effective parenting skills.

Both Jacob and Shirley found ways to become psychologically separate and remain comfortable with one another. The birth of their child created the death of their symbiotic patterned form of attachment. Each had to find a new frame of reference within him or herself in order to learn how to develop a more mature form of relationship. Words were not useful for them because each used words defensively. However, as each developed an observing ego and the ability to contain experience rather than react, the couple discovered that mutual holding was a way for them to communicate without words in order to communicate caring.

The therapy progressed over three and a half years. The relationship survived and matured.

CASE #2: BABY RICHARD

DSM-IV DIAGNOSIS

Axis I: 293.83 Mood disorder due to pneumocystic pneumonia and cystic fibrosis with depressive features.

Axis II. V71.09 No diagnosis

Axis III. 277.00 Cystic fibrosis
         136.3 Pneumonia, pneumocystic

Axis IV: Loss of primary support group

Axis V: 0

History

In the 1960s when I did my clinical nursing rotation in pediatrics at a large children's hospital, I met a patient there who changed my focus from critical care nursing to the study of psychology. Richard was six months old and weighed seven pounds when I first met him in infant intensive care. It was my second day in pediatrics, and I knew nothing about babies. My duties that day were to provide medications, perform treatments, and check vital signs on four babies. The charge nurse told me to be very careful with Richard because he had a metal tube inserted in the front of his throat (called a tracheotomy tube) to keep his airway open. He received treatments every four hours to loosen the thick phlegm that accumulated in his lungs. Medicine was inserted through the tube and went directly into the lungs. It took awhile for the medicine to work to thin the thick phlegm in Richard's lungs. When the medicine worked and secretions were thinned, a catheter was inserted directly into Richard's lungs through the tube and the phlegm suctioned out. Richard hated the procedure and often he coughed so hard that he expelled the inner part of his tracheotomy tube and sent it flying across the room. The expelled tube was dirty and had to be sterilized. A new and sterile part of the tracheotomy tube could be installed. However, everyone feared that Richard would expel the entire tube one day and lose his airway.

Whenever any nurse did anything with a baby, we took time, sat down, and held and rocked the baby. As soon as I picked Richard up, he began making faces at me that indicated he was screaming. The tube wouldn't allow him to make a sound. He screwed up his little face, held his breath and got red. In less than ten seconds, the inner part of his tracheotomy tube went flying across the floor as he looked at me with absolute hate in his eyes. I picked up the inner part of the tube, began the sterilization process and held Richard. He did not stop his silent screaming, and I felt terrified. I inserted a new tube and dropped the medicine into it. I continued to hold Richard and wait for the medicine to dilute the phlegm. Then I suctioned his lungs. When I was finally able to leave the room, I felt shaken and sick to my stomach.

During my first two weeks of pediatrics, Richard was my patient every day, and for a week our relationship did not change at all. On the eighth day, Richard did not scream when he saw me or respond at all. I went to the head nurse and told her that he was awake, listless, and not responding. My impression was that he had made up his mind to die. She believed me and said, "Richard is the youngest of eleven children, and his family lives four hundred miles away and cannot visit. He was flown here when he was eight weeks old because he had cystic fibrosis and pneumonia. He has been here for four months."

Richard was *staffed*, which means that his case history, medications, x-rays, medical treatment, and change in attitude were presented to the attending physician by the residents and nurses who were a part of Richard's medical team. Following a multidisciplinary discussion, the staff recommended that Richard receive a mother from the mother bank. The *mother bank* was made up of older women who volunteered to be surrogate mothers. They came to the hospital five days a week for eight hours a day to create a connection with one child who had no family to visit.

The following day, Richard received his surrogate mother. What do you think his response to her was? He silently screamed all day for four days. His "mother" just held and rocked him. All medications and suctioning took place in her arms while she was with him. He was furious again; however, he was also responding. After the fourth day, he began to quiet down and nestle more comfortably in the woman's arms. She said, "I cannot take the weekend off; it will put him back to where he was." She stayed on over the weekend, and by the end of the next week he was responding to her, gazing at her, and silently babbling like a normal six month-old. By the time she had been with him for two full weeks, he began to put on weight and smile and silently coo at the nurses who were most familiar to him. All of Richard's treatments were the same. The only difference in his medical treatment was his surrogate mother. He rapidly began to improve, and after one month his tracheotomy tube was removed. When his birth mother came to get him, she and the surrogate mother both took turns holding him so that he could more easily make a transition to his own mother before returning home.

Description of the Negative Complex

Richard experienced a series of disintegrative events: an absence of his primary caretaker; loss of familiar sounds and smells; repeated illnesses, including great difficulty breathing; multiple new caregivers; and invasive, painful medical procedures. When Richard was touched, he was often tortured by the necessary medical treatments. In Richard's case, the repeated experience of touch that was sometimes *good* and sometimes *bad* produced high levels of disintegration, demonstrated by his tactile defenses (blowing the inner part of the tracheotomy tube across the room). In the first year of life, the most predominant pattern of mediation of the archetypal/developmental processes is symbiotic because the infant shares ego functions with the caretaker.

One of the founders of the interpersonal theories of psychiatry was Harry Stack Sullivan (1953). In *The Interpersonal Theory of Psychiatry*, he described three aspects of the interpersonal cooperation that create the socialization of the infant and the conception of I/"my body." These are "good-me," created by experience of the pleasure of the caregiver with the infant; "bad-me," created by tenseness in the caregiver causing states of higher levels of intensity and duration of affect; and "not-me," created by misattunement of the archetypal/developmental processes with prolonged, repetitive experiences of disintegration (1953, 161–164). The experience of "not me" is associated with the pathological complex and the inability to be aware of it or verbalize the experience of being constellated.

Ego Functions

Richard's strongest function was affect. He let people know he was angry and demonstrated that in his behavior. He remembered the traumatic treatments, and he experienced repeated invasion of his body. As he experienced repeated trauma, affect was reduced until Richard stopped responding. The difficult dilemma of his medical treatment was either treat the illness and allow psychological damage with the hope that it could be reversed, or not treat the illness at all and let Richard die.[5]

Archetypal/Developmental Processes

During his hospitalization, the archetypal/developmental processes were poorly mediated because Richard did not have one constant caregiver. He was underweight and did not respond like a normal six-month-old infant. The only archetypal/developmental process still active was *being*, and without a caregiver, Richard could not survive.

Patterns of Mediation

Richard made screaming faces when anyone touched him because he associated touch with disintegration and annihilation. When the surrogate mother held Richard, he moved from apathy to screaming. She attuned to him and provided containment; and as he began to respond to her, she mediated all of the archetypal/developmental processes and Richard responded.

Cycles of Nature

Richard was caught in a pattern of death and imbalance. Transformation occurred after he experienced and endured the chaos of being held and nurtured. We could say that he emerged from a profound experience of disintegration and dissociation into a state of new life.

Defenses of the Self

The defenses of the Self were fully operative, and eventually Richard stopped responding. In this case especially, it is easy to understand how the defenses of the Self operate in service of survival. Richard's screaming expressed his discomfort at being touched. However, because he was contained, he moved through the repeated experiences of annihilation back into life. The defenses of the Self stopped operating, and the rudimentary components of ego consciousness started to operate again.

The Fantasy Bond

Richard was not old enough or conscious enough to form a fantasy bond. He was totally dependent on other human beings to give him the containment he needed.

The Imago

Richard was the most powerful example of the constellation and healing of a pathological complex that I have ever witnessed. The repeated experiences of being held and invaded formed an imago that moved Richard away from human contact, the very thing he most needed to survive. The absence of a surrogate caregiver created the problem, and the presence of a surrogate caregiver solved the problem.

Patterned Form of Attachment

The patterned form of attachment was avoidant. Richard was going to die because he needed to be held by one person who consistently attuned to him and mediated the archetypal/developmental processes on a daily basis. This need was not sexual, and no internal fantasy appeared to support him. The hospital already had a staff of volunteers ready to deal with the problem.

I have seen and cared for hundreds of children with chronic illnesses who continually require invasive medical treatment and who die early in life. Each was usually terrified of medical personnel, yet each remained deeply connected to parents who were nurturing and empathic. The children who were old enough to know they were going to die and who had honest, attuned parents developed a closer connection with their dreaming body, the collective unconscious, their soul, and their spirit. They often drew pictures that demonstrated this connection. Perhaps the unconscious was compensating the problems in the physical body with a greater awareness of the subtle body.[6]

TREATMENT SUMMARY

The surrogate mother from the mother bank served as a catalyst to interrupt the experience of pathological mediation of the archetypal/developmental processes and restore normal processes of compensation through proper attunement and mediation. I am told that these mother banks still exist today, saving lives and performing little miracles everyday.

CASE #3: VIVIAN

DSM-IV DIAGNOSIS

Axis I: 300.3 Obsessive compulsive disorder
 300.4 Dysthymia with atypical features
 307.50 Eating disorder NOS

Axis II: V71.09 No diagnosis

Axis III: 244.9 Hypothyroidism acquired

Axis IV: Relational problems with primary support system

Axis V: GAF: 58

Vivian was a 43-year-old woman who entered therapy because of depression, anxiety, and binge eating. She had recurring nightmares involving her mother driving her car and having a terrible accident that severely injured her for the rest of her life. She also woke in the middle of the night from dreams of volcanic eruptions that devastated the earth as far as she could see. She was referred for therapy by her psychiatrist and had just been placed on medication for depression and mild obsessive-compulsive disorder.

History

When Vivian was born, her birth mother signed papers so that Vivian could be adopted. No information was available about the birth mother. Vivian was adopted when she was six months old. Until that time, her primary caregivers were the nursing staff. Vivian's adoptive mother wanted a little girl that she could dress in pink and who would be beautiful, talented, and bright. Her adoptive parents were in their mid-forties and had been married for more than 20 years. They were quiet, religious people who were very involved in their church—a very strict, fundamentalist Christian sect. Both of her parents operated out of a strict behavioral code that weighed even minor actions as good or bad and believed that any expression of affect, disorderliness, loud talking, or exuberant play was against the laws of God. Her parents had a difficult time with a busy six-month-old baby who was much more lively than the little doll they imagined.

When Vivian eventually entered therapy, she and her husband and their two children lived in Vivian's parental home. Her father had been dead for 11 years, and her 85-year-old mother lived with Vivian. With the exception of binge eating, being overweight, and feeling depressed, Vivian described herself as "just fine." She was a good mother, a happy wife, a respected professional accountant, and a giving member of her church community. She wanted her boring symptoms to disappear as soon as possible because she simply did not have time for them.

About four months into the therapy, Vivian started to call me between sessions, remembering things I had said to her that sounded critical and painful to her. I asked her to tape our sessions and listen to the tapes between her visits in order to locate the problem areas so that we could explore them together in order to understand her experience.

When a patient has difficulty with things I have said in previous sessions, it is often quite difficult to remember the actual context and exact words that have been used. I ask the patient to bring a tape recorder to each session, record the entire encounter, and listen to the tape during the week to locate the context and the words where I might have been insensitive and nonempathic. The patient plays the tape in the following session, and we listen to it together to gain a better understanding of what the problem is. I have found this exercise useful for (1) building an observing ego for both the patient and myself in order to understand how our pathological complexes are creating problems with communication; (2) using real data to develop a better understanding of transference/countertransference dynamics for both the patient and myself; (3) developing the habit of clarifying misunderstandings as they occur so that both of us feel more comfortable exploring difficulties in the relational field; and (4) facilitating an understanding of distortions in the relationship that may be due to the patient's pathological complex.

As Vivian listened to the tapes, she began to notice a discrepancy between her perceptions of what she believed she had heard and what was actually said on the tape. Gradually, as she reviewed the tapes, she started identifying sensations and feelings in her body during our sessions when she perceived me as being rejecting, shaming, and overcontrolling. These sensations were not congruent with my voice or my words. As we began to speak of her negative reactions to me, I listened carefully and attempted to understand what was happening for her in order to attune to her. She was very frightened by the difference between what was on the tape and what she was experiencing.

However, by this time her medications were beginning to alleviate her anxiety, her depression, and the obsessive-compulsive disorder. As the medication began to work, her symptoms began to abate and she was able to link the binge eating with suppression of her feelings, especially anger at her mother for being overly controlling. This anger was accompanied by a feeling of anxiety that she had not done enough to help her mother. The two of them often had arguments that ended in weeks and months of cold silence. The silence would be over when Vivian apologized to her mother.

Gradually, she began to realize that something was operating in our relationship that was more like her relationship with her mother than her relationship with me. This awareness came as a terrible shock, and the assurance that the distortions were important information about inner hurts that she could not consciously remember, was useful for her. We both spent a great deal of time exploring her experiences of me in order to understand how I had stimulated her patterned form of attachment. She discovered that she was very angry with me because I was not giving her any cues about how she should be a good patient, what she should do to become a good patient, and a list of things to do to become "normal." The lack of cues felt like the cold silence that existed in her relationship with her mother.

As we explored the parts of that anger, Vivian discovered that her rage was made up of several different parts. One part was a mean-spirited, sadistic, critical glance that she called the "evil eye" that made her want to shake me to get me to tell her what she had to do and be in order to get over her problems. Another part was a frightening, raging, chaotic black hole that had no words. And a third part wanted to learn more about what was going on within her.

"Evil eye" was the imago: a combination of Vivian's own disintegrative, primitive terror and rage experienced during mediation of the archetypal/developmental processes combined with the numinous gaze of an adoptive mother who shamed her. Vivian's mother was not able to help Vivian develop containment or support her self-expression. Vivian found a space in the office to enact her mother part. She preferred an enactment to sand play, drawing, painting, or work with clay. After she enacted her mother part, Vivian experienced this part of her as "bigger than her mother" (an introjected structure) rather than exactly like her mother. The tension in our relationship finally decreased.

"Evil eye" was connected with numinous archetypal/developmental energy, and gradually we came to understand that part of "evil eye" as a daimonic[7] guardian that kept her attention outwardly focused in order to protect her from having an inner experience of affective hell: a black hole of rage, terror, chaos, and death. "Evil eye" always told Vivian what she should and should not do, focusing her attention outward to avoid her internal experience, helping her avoid any hint of anger or rage. The avoidance produced binge eating and obsessive ruminations.

My work was to attune to her, understand her, and tell her the truth and to accept "evil eye" as another patient, an important and vital part of Vivian's pathological complex. As our work progressed, Vivian became aware of a terrible pain in her stomach area. She saw her physician and after a thorough examination, nothing was found. We sat together with the pain in her stomach while she drew it, had a dialogue with it, and experienced her terror and rage while she tried to understand and accept it. This process took over a year.

Eventually she had the following dream: "I am in a zoo with a woman who is teaching me how to handle big poisonous snakes. (Snakes had always terrified Vivian; she was unable to look at a picture of one without experiencing high levels of anxiety.) The woman and I move down into a temple that is far beneath the ground and very ancient. In that place, the woman begins to show me how to move the snakes onto pillars that are very high. The pillars are high so that they can sit in the light. I am not afraid; I know how to do this." Vivian experienced the dream as sacred. She felt as if she had stood in the presence of God, and as she and the woman performed the ritual with the snakes, a sense of deep peace and nurturing flowed over both of them. She interpreted the dream and the numinous experience that accompanied it as a bringing of her body and her emotions into the light, that somehow she had birthed the pain that was held inside of her.

We explored the meaning of the dream through her associations to her relationship with her mother and through amplification, using mythological motifs containing snakes. We both began to understand that images of the "great mother," a basic experience of all humans of mothering and being mothered, had stepped into Vivian's dream as a presence who had chosen her and would always show her the way.[8]

In Vivian's case, we could think about "evil eye" as the imago, which shamed her with its glance, frightening and enraging her and directing her attention outward to an idealized, external authority who would tell her how to be and what to do. When Vivian began to experience her shame, rage, or terror, the imago helped her soothe herself with food.

Ego Functions

Vivian's strength was her dreaming body—her connection with the collective human memory and her soul. Many of her dreams were filled with numinous images, and she found meaning in singing in a church choir and playing several musical instruments. Her affect, memory, physical body, spirit, and behavior were locked into her pathological complex of adapting herself to what she believed her projected/idealized authority wanted her to do.

Archetypal/Developmental Processes

Vivian's strength was thinking. She and her father had played puzzles, chess, and mathematical games. She was in all of the gifted programs at school. Her dad was very supportive of her intelligence and her academic success. She graduated summa cum laude in accounting.

Vivian's pathological complex distorted the archetypal/developmental processes of being, doing, identity, and creativity. She could not be, do, or define herself without an external glance of approval from a perceived authority. Her right to be, do, create, and define herself always had to be weighed against what other people might want or think.

Mediation of the Archetypal/Developmental Processes

Vivian's strength was a healthy experience of educating patterns of mediation. However, all other patterns of mediation were distorted. She had had multiple caregivers for the first six months of her life and no contact with her birth mother. This experience distorted normal symbiotic mediation, creating a deep black hole and an internal hell that kept her symbiotic with perceived authorities, providing fertile ground for the development of her pathological complex.

Vivian's mother thought of her as a "perfect little doll" and only had to look at Vivian with hatred to shame her into conformity. This was a severe distortion in the directing form of mediation because the mother replaced Vivian's sense of her own experience by becoming the greater authority, teaching Vivian to fulfill other peoples' expectations. Cooperation was not a part of Vivian's experience. Both parents disapproved of any expression of affect, which damaged Vivian's ability to contain and reflect upon her experience. Confirming and empowering forms of mediation only operated when Vivian conformed to parental expectations.

The Cycles of Nature

Vivian's pathological complex appeared to move in its own cycle. As she adapted to the perceived wishes of outer authorities, she lost touch with her body, her behavior, her spirit, and her memory. As she dismissed her own experience, rage and terror began to accumulate within her body, creating a sense of anxiety and imbalance. Vivian managed her anxiety by creating order within her household in an obsessive kind of way, shopping for bargains that she didn't use and compulsively ordering material goods, which accumulated over the years. If her anxiety rose beyond a certain level, Vivian ate until she felt soothed, briefly stopping the cycle. However, after she binged, she experienced a sense of shame and the "little death"[9] of falling into an empty black hole. She eventually climbed out of the hole by finding an authority to tell her how she should be or what she should do about her problem. She "forgot" about her symptoms and "felt fine."

As Vivian faced her anxiety and "evil eye" she finally allowed herself to enter her black hole through the pain in her stomach. She began to become aware of her terror, rage and shame and she accepted the "little death" they brought her. She endured the chaos of emerging affect and her terror of being "so bad that she would be abandoned." Her perseverance and willingness to endure her pain opened a space between the ego and the imago that brought forth the dream along with an internal sense of a timeless "great mother" who loved her unconditionally.

Defenses of the Self

All of the defenses of the self were operating when the pathological complex was constellated. Vivian's therapeutic work began with the uncovering of the imago, the introjected structure she called "evil eye." It continued through her confrontation with the pain in her body (denial and splitting). The last defenses that Vivian became aware of were her projection and positive idealizations of authority figures that accompanied her negative beliefs that she was "bad and evil." When Vivian's patterned form of attachment was operating with perceived authorities, she went against her very nature, creating a cycle of self abuse to numb herself against repeated early experiences of abandonment.

The Imago

The imago appeared as the numinous image of "evil eye." It expressed itself in an internal, hate-filled glance that constantly forced Vivian to turn outward and adapt to the perceived demands of others in order to avoid feeling the deep hole of abandonment, rejection, and annihilation.

The Patterned Form of Attachment

The patterned form of attachment was anxious/adaptive. By that I mean that Vivian experienced anxiety most of the time. In order to feel secure, she focused on any perceived authority and looked for verbal and nonverbal cues to adapt to what she perceived the authority wanted her to be, to do, what might please that authority, and how she should define herself.

The Fantasy Bond

Vivian's fantasy bond created a connection with those idealized, outer authorities that could confer acceptance, approval, and justification for her existence. This bond created a sense of safety for Vivian and protected her from experiencing the rage and shame that was locked in her body. When she received the approval of outer authorities, the fantasy bond protected her from experiencing high levels of anxiety.

Dialogue

Vivian: "I binged again and I was so upset afterward that I couldn't sleep."
Therapist: "That sounds painful. What was happening inside, Vivian?"
Vivian: "I was hoping that you would tell me. I don't understand any of this stuff. I haven't binged like that in two months. I did all that work with 'evil eye' and now I'm eating again. The therapy isn't working at all. What do I have to do to make this stuff stop?"

Therapist (internal experience): If I tell her what to do, I am caught in becoming another directive authority. If I try to slide away from her question with a question, I will slip out of the relationship. I feel frustrated, as if I am not doing a good job as a therapist (my complex) and really caught in a double bind. I will return her dilemma to her.

Therapist (to Vivian): "I am stuck. If I tell you what to do, I reinforce your complex. If I don't answer you, I am being rude to you. I don't know how to answer you, can you tell me more about what you are experiencing?"
Vivian: "I am really frustrated with myself and so angry. Just when I thought I was really making progress, I binged. I am disappointed and angry with myself. I am ashamed to tell you I binged, like I have failed you or something."
Therapist: "That is a lot of pain. It sounds as if your pain might have parts. Is that right?"
Vivian: "Well, there is a big part of me that wants to quit therapy because I am so frustrated. There is another part trying to figure out what is going on. That last part wants to run away when I have to have you look at me while I tell you I binged."

Therapist (internal experience): We are right here in the middle of the muddle in our relationship.

Therapist (to Vivian): "A part that is really frustrated and wants to quit, a part that is really ashamed of being seen by me, and another part that is working hard to understand what has happened. What is the part that is most present right now?"

Short silence.

Vivian: "I can't look at you. I feel like running away."

Therapist (internal experience): A lot of shame for her, so painful. I hope we can contain this. I hope she feels safe enough with me to take in a little nourishment.

Therapist (to Vivian): "Can you look at me a little bit and tell me what you see?"
Vivian: "I can only look at your chin and your mouth, not your whole face. This is really hard."
Therapist: "What do you see at my chin and my mouth?"

Vivian: "I see your smile." *(Vivian begins to sob, and we sit together and "be" with her sobbing until she is finished.)*

Vivian: "I can't believe how hard and how beautiful that was. What happened?"

Therapist (internal experience): I feel as if we really connected somehow. I don't think she and I need to put it in words and tear it apart.

Therapist (to Vivian): "I think it was a sacred moment that doesn't have words yet."

TREATMENT SUMMARY

Vivian's psychiatrist referred her for therapy after she was placed on medication. Vivian was so filled with anxiety that her observing ego was weak. Her memory and affect were blunted; she had little physical strength and no sense of being embodied. She dreamed regularly, remembered her dreams, and sometimes wondered what they meant. She never wrote her dreams down until she came into therapy.

The focus of the treatment was on uncovering and containing Vivian's complex in a way that was nondirective. The dilemma presented by the transference of "evil eye" onto the therapist was avoiding the unconscious pressure to become an overly directive, therapeutic authority that Vivian could adapt to and obey and at the same time containing the rage that surfaced in the relational field without shaming her when the projection failed.

Medication relieved a great deal of the anxiety and depression that she was experiencing when she came into therapy, giving her enough internal relief and space to begin developing an observing ego. Taping her sessions gave her a sense of her own authority, empowering her to have the right to call me to account if she did not like what I said. Her dreams came directly from her own experience and provided a wonderful opening in the transitional space.

Many books were suggested for her to read in order for her to amplify her own dream images. Because her thinking was so well developed, she found dream amplification interesting. Even as a child, Vivian had loved puzzles and strategy games like chess and bridge. She dreamed often and kept a record of her dreams. She was also very good at discussing how the dreams made her feel, what she thought they meant, and whatever else came to her mind as we discussed a dream (association).

The numinous dream of snakes being moved up into the light, with someone showing her how to do it, created the turning point in her therapy.

Vivian had a lifelong experience of terror whenever she saw a snake or even a picture of a snake. The fact that she could move the snakes into the light with no fear at all and that another woman was helping her do that enabled her make the connection between her fear of snakes and her fear of her own primitive rage. Amplification of the image of the snake was quite useful in helping Vivian understand the numinous feeling of being mothered and at the same time being at peace with that experience. Gradually, she began to become aware of the experiences that triggered her binge eating and learned to prevent them by nourishing herself: taking time to do puzzles, eating five small meals a day, getting enough sleep, and exercising. She also sought help from an allergist/nutritionist and began to identify the foods that she was allergic to and avoid them. Even though she was on a diet and thyroid medication, Vivian did not lose weight. She was very frustrated and tired of being 40 pounds overweight. Eventually she and her physician discovered that if she consumed more than 800 calories a day she began to gain weight. After much reflection, Vivian chose to nourish herself on 1,200 calories a day and exercise four times a week, and she went off all medication except her thyroid pills.

Vivian's therapy lasted for more than four years. During the last year and a half of therapy Vivian began to realize how angry she was with her husband. They began marital therapy with another therapist about a year before Vivian stopped seeing me. For a while, she felt as if she were going backward in her individual therapy because the symptoms that originally brought her into therapy had surfaced again in couples therapy, and she had to go back on all of her medications.

It was very difficult for her to accept the fact that her pathological complex was a psychological reality that would be with her for the rest of her life. Unconsciously she believed that therapy would bring her into a state of perfection and enlightenment, of living a happily-ever-after, symptom-free life. As the marital therapy progressed, she began to understand how pervasive her complex really was and how she had lost herself in her marriage, her parenting, and her relationships at church.

Coming to grips with the reality of her complex was terribly painful for Vivian. She believed in a just and ordered universe with a loving God overseeing his people. She was horrified when she realized that she had had no part in the formation of the unconscious, pathological complex and that the only choice she really had was to continue to come to grips with that complex every day for the rest of her life. She was quite angry because her pathological complex was so unfair. I encouraged her to explore human experience in all its diversity in whatever way she chose in order to understand how God operated in other lives. I suggested that she begin with the study of her mother's life.

Vivian's self-importance began to fade as her mother told Vivian her own life story. She began to understand that her parents were just people who had done the best they could with her and that they came from a long line of caretakers who passed on their own pathological complexes to their children.

She experienced gratitude for what she had received from her parents because she knew that they had been better parents to her than their own parents had been for them. What was most wonderful and distressing for her was that she no longer cared what anyone thought about her or wanted from her. She understood she was responsible for her impact on the world around her. She was quite confused about God, and as she sat with her confusion and worked with her dreams, it began to be clearer to her that there was a kind of internal authority guiding her life. She decided to remain in her church with her changed outlook.

Both Vivian and her husband discovered that they really liked each other in spite their neglect of each other and their poor communication. They discovered that they were both locked into the relentless pressure of making enough money to meet their expenses and also invest. They both hated their jobs and decided to invest in each other. They both returned to graduate school part time and became attorneys, she in forensic accounting and he in patent law.

CASE #4: MICHAEL

DSM-IV TR DIAGNOSIS

Axis I: 300.00 Anxiety disorder not otherwise specified

Axis II: V71.09 No diagnosis

Axis III: None

Axis IV: Partner relational problem

Axis V: Gaf= 62

History

Michael entered therapy because of generalized anxiety, insomnia, and random panic attacks. He had nightmares about atomic bombs bringing about the end of the world, being tied up while hang gliding, and being chased and fatally wounded by police.

Michael was a successful investment banker and was married with one child, a little boy ten months old. Several months before he came into treatment, he began having an extramarital affair with a woman in the same profession who supported him emotionally as he took greater financial risks at work. She helped him learn to trust himself. He believed that his mistress gave him a center and a ground he had never experienced before. Yet instead of being happy, Michael felt as though he was falling apart and was desperate from anxiety because he was being unfaithful to his wife.

His home was a stable place to be–a place to be safe and numb. Sometimes he became anxious at home and felt locked up. When that happened he went hand-gliding, deep sea diving, or riding on his motorcycle.

Home for Michael was linked with a part of him that felt safe, cared for, and enclosed. He described his wife and his home as his cave, his safe haven. After a time, Michael would begin to feel smothered and have to get "out." "Out" was a place that contained high excitement and a lot of stimulation. After awhile, however, "out" became overwhelming, and Michael would feel the need to return home and feel "safe." Michael was not alternating between anxiety and depression; he appeared to move from numb to high levels of excitement with anxiety about the entire experience.

As we sat together, he and I noticed that his ability to talk about his feelings was quite impaired. He was not even physically aware of them. He knew that when he was at home he felt numb; and as the numbness built up, he moved out of it into experiences of high intensity that made him feel alive.

As part of his therapy, I asked him to ask his mother about his early childhood. Upon doing so, Michael discovered something he had never known. When he was four months old, his mother developed tuberculosis. She was treated surgically in a sanitarium and then returned home to rest and take her medication. She was not allowed to do much. The older children were sent to live with Michael's aunt, but Michael, the baby, was returned home to be with his mother. Even though his mother could perform only limited activities, she could hold, feed, and change him. However, he was a very athletic little boy, and by the time he was a year old his mother told him that she had to keep him in a plywood-covered playpen because she simply could not keep up with him. When his father came home late at night, Michael was let out of the playpen for a short time while his dad watched him explore the world.

That information cast an entirely new light on his experiences of numbness and safety alternating with cycles of seeking high intensity experiences. He and I began to imagine the wall of the playpen as the space between "out" and "in." "Out" was a stressful job with high-level investments that kept him teetering on the boundary between excitement and panic, wealth and financial ruin. His mistress was someone who helped him to slow down, contain, reflect, and explore his own inner experience of being "out" and begin to trust what he experienced in a gradual and contained way. "In" was the place his beloved wife and his brand new son lived; and "in was a place of warmth, safety, nurturing, and peace.

At the time he started treatment, Michael was parenting his year-old-son who was very busy exploring the world. Michael dearly loved his son and enjoyed following him as he tasted and touched the world. In order to attune to his son, Michael had to regress to his own early experiences of the archetypal/developmental process of doing, and experience the anxiety associated with dysfunctional mediation during this time. Michael loved his wife and felt guilty and ashamed for being emotionally unavailable in their relationship. He felt committed to his marriage. He also loved his mistress, who was deeply attuned to him and contained and mediated his primitive feelings for him. As Michael sat with his experience he began to become aware of the shadow of having what he called "the best of two worlds" with no emotional accountability to his wife and no financial commitment to his mistress. Michael believed he received the best each woman had to give him and neither woman was receiving his best.

Michael wanted me, his therapist, to tell him what to do about his relationships. I had no idea at all about what he should do. I asked him if instead of worrying about being "in" or "out," he would be willing to explore those spaces as different parts of himself. Gradually, our work became an exploration of his parts as he spoke from each of them and wrote poetry to describe them. The "wall" was the barrier that split Michael's experience into "out," a search for high intensity activities; and "in," tired, nourished, curled up, and withdrawn who eventually felt a desperate need for stimulation that pushed him into going "out" again. The imago was an unconscious, numinous "wall" that split ego consciousness into two parts, "in" and "out, " creating anxiety about the archetypal/developmental process doing.

Description of the Negative Complex

Michael was a high functioning and successful investment banker. When his negative complex emerged after the birth of his son, the affective theme of the complex, one of increasing anxiety, seemed to split him into two different attachments and two partial identities. Even though he could identify these parts of himself consciously, he was unconscious about how they operated and could not control the high levels of anxiety that caused him to shift back and forth between them.

Ego Functions

When the pathological complex was operating, Michael had a good memory; however, his affective range shrank into an uncontainable anxiety/terror/panic. His body was healthy, and he took care of himself to keep himself physically fit. His behavior was split between two different kinds of lives. Michael told me that he "never remembered his dreams." He found great meaning in his life in his relationships with his wife, his mistress, and his son. Michael was so confused and ashamed of his duplicitous behavior that he described himself as feeling spiritually bereft and that the "Holy Spirit" who had always lived within him had left him because of what he was doing.

Archetypal/Developmental Processes

Michael's capacity to go out and explore the world around him and return to a safe center (in the form of a caretaker) was impaired. As a result of his mother's illness, Michael was not allowed to explore until his father came home. Then he was allowed to explore to the point where he became overstimulated. We knew this because both of his parents talked about how difficult it was for them to get him to go to sleep at night. Somehow this split in the mediation of the archetypal/developmental process of doing created enough experiences of disintegration both to affect Michael's doing and to influence his identity, creating two partial personalities. Michael believed that the split had always been there and that when he began parenting his infant son, the high levels of anxiety embedded within the pathological complex emerged causing him to begin his affair which helped him contain his anxiety.

Patterns of Mediation and the Archetypal/Developmental Processes

Mediation of the archetypal/developmental processes of doing and identity were split between a lack of stimulation and overstimulation. Somehow the difference between these two experiences produced enough repeated experiences of disintegration to create an affective theme of high anxiety mixed with terror. The pathological complex was always there, however it was activated when Michael became a parent who had to mediate these archetypal/developmental processes to his son in an attuned way. In order to attune to his son, Michael had to partially regress to his own experience of mediation of these processes.

Cycles of Nature

Michael was locked into a pattern of movement and imbalance that fluctuated between two poles and two relationships with significant others, preventing change, death, and transformation.

Defenses of the Self

The predominant defenses visible in Michael's pathological complex were denial, introjection and splitting. Identification fluctuated with Michael's anxiety as he moved between "in" and "out."

The Fantasy Bond

Michael's fantasy bond was connected with both his wife who supported "in" and his mistress who contained "out. Each in her own way provided safety and support for the partial personalities created by his pathological complex. His wife provided the familiar sense of being overly contained, safe, and close. His mistress provided an attuned and supportive center for him to explore new experiences and feel contained. Michael's fantasy bond was split between the two women reinforcing the imago and the pathological complex.

The Imago

As Michael became aware of "the wall" (his experience of the imago), he experienced high levels of anxiety and terror. He was able to connect these feelings with a physical experience that tightened his chest and squeezed his lungs so that he had difficulty breathing. As he endured the physical sensations of affect, he was able to draw them with colored markers. Gradually, the physical experience of being unable to breathe emerged as two different kinds of affect. One was a sense of gradually becoming constricted and held back, accompanied by frustration and rage. The other was a sense of excitement and joy that gradually turned into an experience of high anxiety, "having no gravity to support him."

Michael began a dialogue with the "wall" using a technique developed by Jung called "active imagination" (CW 6, 1935, 1977, 433n.). Using this technique, Michael visualized the "wall" and spoke with it as if it was another person. The unconscious responded to Michael by speaking back to him as "the wall."[10] Gradually, the wall became a door that opened into the unconscious, creating a bridge (the anima) between ego consciousness and the Self, giving Michael an unlimited internal world to explore.

The Patterned Form of Attachment

Michael's patterned form of attachment was split between being "in" with mother and being "out" with father. Both parts were separated by feelings of anxiety and disorganization created by the imago.

The Fantasy Bond

Michael's fantasy bond was created by his need for containment when his son was born. His mistress helped him begin to learn how to contain his anxiety and encouraged him to seek therapy. Her love for him gifted him with a new life.

Active Imagination in the Clinical Setting

Michael: "I feel as if I am looking through the broken wall to a world beyond it that I never knew existed."
Therapist: "What do you see?"
Michael: "It's so dark it's hard to see. There is something coming toward me. Oh God, it looks like that Baron Harkonnen in *Dune*. I am so scared."
Therapist: "What would you do if this happened in real life?"
Michael: "I have to speak with him. He is bouncing all over and leering at me. Who are you? What do you want from me?"
Michael: "He wants to hug me and give me his diseases. This is disgusting."
Therapist: "He is asking your permission."
Michael: "I don't want you to touch me. You are ugly and diseased. Why are you here?"
Michael: "He says he is me. He says he is a big ball of power and ugly because I am that way. If I touch him I will know him. If I know him, he will give me his heart. I have to eat it. Oh God, this is so hard. I know I have to do it. He is me. He is me and all the ways I have used people. All the ways I have cheated people. All the ways I have manipulated to get money. Oh, I am going to be sick."
Therapist: "Michael, there's a waste basket right here. It's okay if you get sick."
Michael: "He is making me remember all the things I have done. All the rotten things I have ever done. It is like he is pouring out the memories because I touched him. Long pause. I will turn into him if I keep going the way I am. He is showing me the real me. What I have chosen to be. I am remembering all of it and being cleaned out." *(Michael begins to cry.)* "I have to quit my work. This is where the anxiety came from. I am like

Harkonnen. I really hated him in that movie and he is me." *(Michael appears to be quite shaken. He looks gray.)*
Therapist (to Michael): "It is so terribly painful to be confronted by the 'shadow.'"
Michael (crying): "I have no words. This is so painful."
We sit together for a long time.
Therapist: "Our hour is up, Michael. What will you do until the next time I see you?"
Michael: "I am going home to be with my wife and play with my son. I already know what to do. It's what you have said to me before. "Let yourself be overwhelmed and don't fight it. Be patient and kind to yourself while you wait. It will pass. I will see you the day after tomorrow."

TREATMENT SUMMARY

At the beginning of therapy, Michael was referred to his primary care physician for a full physical examination to rule out any biological cause for his generalized anxiety disorder. His doctor told Michael that he was in excellent health and referred him for a psychiatric evaluation. The psychiatrist prescribed several combinations of medication, however, none were effective at reducing anxiety in Michael's case.

In the beginning of therapy Michael felt out of control and asked me to give him specific techniques that he could use to alleviate some of his anxiety. I was directive with him and shared techniques with him for deep breathing, relaxation, and self-hypnosis to help him regain a sense of control over himself. In addition, I encouraged him to do one hour of physical exercise, at his level of endurance, six days a week so that he could sweat and release the chemicals that had built up in his body from his ongoing anxiety. Michael decided to bike eight miles a day and come to therapy twice a week.

My office provided a space of containment for him because of the regularity of the day, time, length of visit and the presence of an empathic listener who attuned to him and used techniques of mediation that were directive, educating, cooperative, confirming, educating and empowering. Gradually, Michael began to experience the containment of the therapeutic structure and to develop a space within himself from which he could observe his experience. This process took over two years. In Michael's case, his anxiety was so debilitating that it was quite difficult for him to contain and separate from it.

As he became better at containing and exploring his anxiety, Michael was able to slow down his patterns of reactivity when he became anxious and gradually observe the shifts taking place within him.

Michael lost a great deal of energy when his pathological complex was constellated. Because he was a very honest man, he suffered. As he said, "I have the best of both worlds because I am so dishonest." He was quite open to a dialogue with the unconscious, and as his observing ego became stronger his anxiety lessened because he contained it rather than reacting to it. He was able to move into the transitional space: enacting parts, drawing feelings in color, and finally, performing active imagination.

My task was to balance being directive with the other forms of mediation of the archetypal/developmental processes. Michael was gradually able to identify and enact the many parts of himself that composed the basic split between "in" and "out." Often he would move from one part of the room to another and then back again as his internal awareness shifted and he identified which part was cathected (energized) at that particular moment. Gradually, the "wall" (imago) part emerged as an impersonal, godlike force that threatened to totally annihilate him no matter which side of the "wall" he was on. Michael experienced chaos and was unable to work at all for several weeks.

When a patient has done parts work with the imago for a long enough time to develop a solid observing ego and containment and yet the imago appears to become stronger, it is a sign that the imago is beginning to crumble. At that time several things begin to occur: the patient may feel as if his or her entire life has become chaotic because the protection of the imago is fading; the sense of annihilation connected with the defenses of the Self begins coming into conscious awareness; the affective theme of annihilation produces mental, physical, and emotional chaos; the patient may experience regression to unconscious archetypal/developmental material in the form of numinous images, voices or fantasies, and the patient reexperiences annihilating patterns of mediation.

During that chaotic time, Michael came to therapy three times a week and did active imagination within the container of the relational field. As his process continued, Michael developed the ability to define himself in his dialogue with the unconscious as he struggled to be a nurturing father who would give his son a balanced center to go "out" from and return "in" to. Gradually the sense of chaos reordered itself as Michael's perceptions organically shifted his conscious awareness into a different way of perceiving the world that was much freer of anxiety. He made the decision to remain with his wife and his son. He also decided that he would leave the investment-banking field and go back to school to get a graduate degree in international finance.

Michael knew he had used his mistress and felt that he could never make reparation. However, he met with her to tell her how she had helped him and what had happened to him. He felt terribly guilty and knew that he would carry that guilt for the rest of his life. This entire therapeutic process took four years.

THE BENEFITS OF USING FIGURE 15 WITH THE DSM-IV

Differentiating Between the Need for Short-Term or Long-Term Therapy

Figure 15 (p. 179) can be used to assess the pervasiveness of the pathological complex.

When a patient is deeply embedded in a pathological complex that affects every area of the bio-psycho-social-spiritual systems in his or her life, short-term therapy is recommended because symptomatic relief will increase the patient's level of self-esteem and provide a sense of hope that life can be better.

Questions that a therapist might ask as part of an assessment to differentiate between the need for long and short-term therapy are:

- Does the patient have the capacity to develop an observing ego?
- Can the patient develop the ability to contain painful material?
- Is the patient capable of interrupting and exploring his or her reactivity?
- How often and to what extent does the patient regress?
- How capable is the patient of tolerating a relationship with the therapist?
- How willing is the patient to be educated?

Educating the Patient

Figure 15 can be used to educate the patient about the different aspects of the pathological complex including how it was formed and how it operates in the here-and-now.

Patient Referral

A pathological complex affects the bio-psycho-social-spiritual aspects of the patient's life. Therapy alone is often not enough to help the patient create changes in all of these areas of his or her life. It is important for a therapist to have a network of referrals that include psychiatrists, primary care physicians, career counselors, other therapists with special expertise, priests, ministers, and services from the local hospitals such as psychological testing, physical therapy, and exercise facilities just to name a few.

Communication

Therapists can use Figure 15 to identify and rank the patient's symptoms in order to enhance reports, provide information for staffings, and facilitate communication with other health care providers.

QUESTIONS

1. Review two cases you are working with. How might you use Figure 15 and the DSM-IV diagnosis with each patient?
2. Use Figure 15 and map your own pathological complex.
3. Reread the patient/therapist dialogue in each case. How would you respond to the patient using your own style? What mistakes did the therapist make?

ENDNOTES

1. The DSM referred to in this chapter is the DSM-IV-TR, fourth edition, published in 2000 by the American Psychiatric Association.
2. The diagnostic criteria for 296.89 Bipolar II Disorder are: (a) the presence (or history) of one or more Major Depressive Episodes; (b) presence (or history) of at least one Hypomanic Episode: (c) there has never been a Manic Episode or a mixed Episode: (d) the mood symptoms in Criteria (a) and (b) are not better accounted for by Schizoaffective Disorder and are not superimposed on Schizophrenia, Schizophreniform Disorder, Delusional Disorder, or Psychotic Disorder not Otherwise Specified: (e) the symptoms cause clinically significant distress or impairment in social, occupational, or other important areas of functioning (DSM IV-TR 2000, 359–62).
3. Identity is linked with the physical gender, which is like that of the same-sex caregiver. A child has no choice about his or her physical gender, and even in early life there are big differences between toddler boys and girls. Caretakers mediate the archetypal/developmental process of identity and influence it. Shirley's sense of identity was impaired because of being made to observe the sexual abuse of her sister and being shamed for being ugly by her stepfather. In addition, unconsciously Shirley did not respect her mother for abandoning her children, acting helpless, and becoming totally dependent upon a man who was an abusive tyrant.
4. Jungian analyst John Beebe presented a lecture on typology at the Jung Institute of Chicago in 1985. This comment was an answer to a question on sexual preference and typology.

5. Rene Spitz (1945) discussed the kind of disintegration Richard experienced in "Hospitalism: An inquiry into the Genesis of Psychiatric Conditions in Early Childhood," in *The Psychoanalytic Study of the Child*, 1:53–74.
6. Susan Bach (1990) did extensive research on the drawings of severely ill children and demonstrated the connection between the physical and subtle bodies.
7. In ancient Greek belief a daimon was a spiritual power that guided a person's actions and was their fate. It was both positive and negative, good and evil embodying the talents, capacities and a fate that a human being had to wrestle with to move toward good or toward evil (Diamond, S. (1996, 66-67).
8. Amplification is a technique in which the patient is requested to study in order to develop an understanding of dream images through the study of cross-cultural mythology, fairytales, and ancient symbols. The authors who were most helpful to Vivian were M. Gimbutas *The Goddesses and Gods of Old Europe* (1986); R. Graves, *The White Goddess* (1982); and B. Walker, *The Woman's Encyclopedia of Myths and Secrets* (1983).
9. Elisabeth Kubler Ross spoke to me at length about the fact that life is full of pain and loss, as well as joy and beauty. She believed that in order to live life as fully as we can, we must endure the "little death" of pain and loss and allow it to transform us (personal conversations 1979–80).
10. The process of active imagination is defined and more fully discussed in the glossary of terms at the end of Chapter 6.

Chapter 6

DEVELOPING CLINICAL SKILLS: INDIVIDUAL EXERCISES

The basics of complex theory have been presented. This chapter will focus on putting these theories into practice. There are several areas used by therapists to develop clinical skills in addition to study, including one's own therapy, supervised clinical experience, and practicing skill development with colleagues. This chapter will present exercises for individual skill development as well as exercises for a group of colleagues who have decided to work together on skill development.

INDIVIDUAL SKILL DEVELOPMENT

The Complex Awareness Measure[1]

This measure is designed to assist you in becoming more aware of your own complexes through recognizing your patterns of reactivity. Don't spend a lot of time on each answer. Simply answer each statement with a few words that are descriptive and meaningful to you. For best results, begin with item one and proceed sequentially from page to page. There is no right way to fill out this measure; your own answers will provide the data.

DESCRIBE YOURSELF

1. Use four words to describe yourself. I am a person who is:

    A.   B.

    C.   D.

2. I am a person who has both strengths and weaknesses. Use four words to describe each.

    A. Strengths   B. Weaknesses

    1.   1.

    2.   2.

    3.   3.

    4.   4.

3. Living has taught me four things about life:

    A.   B.

    C.   D.

4. The four things, events, learnings, people in life that have given me the greatest satisfaction are:

    A.   B.

    C.   D.

5. Name up to three psychological roles (e.g., scapegoat, peacemaker, listener) that you played for each of the following people:

    A. My mother:

    1.   2.   3.

    B. My father:

    1.   2.   3.

    C. My siblings:

    1.   2.   3.

6. If I could do anything in the world I wanted to, knowing that I would not fail, I would:

   A.   B.   C.

DESCRIBE YOUR FAMILY

7. Describe your father:

   A. List his five most positive qualities:

   B. List his five most negative qualities:

   C. In what ways are you like him?:

   D. In what ways are you different?:

   E. Use one word to express how he described you as a child, an adolescent and an adult.

   Child   Adolescent   Adult

8. Describe your mother:

   A. List her five most positive qualities:

   B. List her five most negative qualities:

   C. In what ways are you like her?:

   D. In what ways are you different?:

   E. Use one word to express how she described you as a child, an adolescent and an adult.

   Child   Adolescent   Adult

9. Name each of your siblings:

   a.   b.   c.   d.   e.   f.

Name the most positive quality of: Name the most negative quality of:
   Sibling a: Sibling a:
   Sibling b: Sibling b:
   Sibling c: Sibling c:
   Sibling d: Sibling d:
   Sibling e: Sibling e:
   Sibling f: Sibling f:

Name one way you are like: Name one way you are different from:
   Sibling a: Sibling a:
   Sibling b: Sibling b:
   Sibling c: Sibling c:
   Sibling d: Sibling d:
   Sibling e: Sibling e:
   Sibling f: Sibling f:

10. How do your siblings as a group describe you as a child, an adolescent, and an adult?

   Child   Adolescent   Adult

11. Name four ways you influenced people in your family to get what you wanted:

   A.   B.

   C.   D.

12. Name three ways you were labeled or perceived by your family members that was inaccurate and painful:

   A.   B.   C.

13. Use four adjectives to describe what your life will be like five years from now:

   A.   B.

   C.   D.

Developing Clinical Skills: Individual Exercises 235

14. On the back of this page record any recurring dreams or enduring impressions you remember from your childhood. Note the images in the dream that were most meaningful to you and any impact the dream or the enduring impressions had on you, e.g., emotional reactions, insights, etc. Take the space below to summarize your responses in as few words as possible.

15. If you could change anything about yourself by wishing, what would it be? List up to four things:

    A.   B.

    C.   D.

16. How would your friends describe you? Use four adjectives:

    A.   B.

    C.   D.

17. How would your enemies describe you? Use four adjectives:

    A.   B.

    C.   D.

18. What are the feelings you never want to feel again?

    A.   B.

    C.   D.

19. If you knew you were going to die soon and you could do anything you wanted to do, what would it be?

20. When you reflect on what it was like for you growing up in your family, what do you:

    A. Feel: B. Remember:

    C. Imagine: D. Physically experience:

21. Name up to four subjects that were hard to discuss in your family:

    A.   B.

    C.   D.

22. Name three things that you are most ashamed of about your family:

    A.   B.   C.

23. Name three things you are most proud of about your family:

    A.   B.   C.

DESCRIBE YOUR RELATIONSHIPS

24. List three people who have been influential in your development, excluding the family members mentioned above:

    A.   B.   C.

25. List the positive traits for each person:

    A.   B.   C.

26. List the negative traits for each person:

    A.   B.   C.

27. List the positive traits brought out in you by each person:

    A.   B.   C.

28. What would you have liked to receive that you were not given by each person:

    A.   B.   C.

29. Describe your reaction when (the above, # 28) happened, with each person:

    A.   B.   C.

30. List the ways you tried to use your influence to get what you wanted from each person:

   A.   B.   C.

31. List your most positive feelings about each person:

   A.   B.   C.

32. List your most negative feelings about each person:

   A.   B.   C.

33. How did you react emotionally, physically, and behaviorally when you had negative feelings about each person?

   Emotion:

   A.   B.   C.

   Physical sensation:

   A.   B.   C.

   Behavior:

   A.   B.   C.

34. How did you react emotionally, physically, and behaviorally when you had positive feelings about each person?

   Emotion:

   A.   B.   C.

   Physical experience:

   A.   B.   C.

   Behavior:

   A.   B.   C.

238   *C. G. Jung's Complex Dynamics and the Clinical Relationship*

35. On the back of this page, record any ongoing positive and energizing pattern of interaction and communication that appears in your dreams and fantasies about any of your relationships. Record the feelings, memories, physical sensations, behaviors, and images that are most meaningful to you about this pattern.

Feelings:

Memories:

Physical sensations:

Images:

Behaviors:

Meaning:

PATTERNS OF REACTIVITY

To complete the following statements, look back to the numbers and the descriptions you gave of yourself, your family, and your relationships on the previous pages. In the space provided after each statement, place the answer you previously gave for each question number as indicated. After you have written your previous responses, use two or three words to summarize what they mean when added together.

1. When I form a deep relationship with someone, his or her positive qualities are:

   3 _____   4 _____   7A_____

   8A_____   9-1_____   23 _____

   25 _____   **Summary of responses** _____

2. They bring out these positive things in me:

   1 _____   2A_____   4 _____

   6 _____   7A_____   8A_____

91_____   16_____   27_____

31_____

Summary of responses: _____

3. Because of these positive things, I experience myself as:

   1 _____   2A_____   2B_____

   5A_____   5B_____   5C_____

   9-4_____ 10_____   12_____

   16_____   20_____   22_____

   23_____   22_____   23_____

   27_____   30_____   6 _____

Summary of responses: _____

4. My best feelings in a relationship are:

   4 _____   7A_____   8B_____

   9-1_____ 16_____   27_____

   31 _____   5 _____   23_____

Summary of responses: _____

5. My worst feelings in a relationship are:

   7B_____   8B_____   11_____

   12_____   17_____   8E_____

   22_____   26_____   28_____

   32_____   10_____   7E_____

Summary of responses: _____

6. When I believe that I have good intentions and yet my actions and/or words are misunderstood, I feel as if I am being perceived as:

   2B_____   11 _____   12_____

   7E_____   8E_____   10_____

   Summary of responses: _____

7. When I am feeling as if I am being misperceived, I react by:

   11A_____   11B_____   11C_____

   11D_____   30 A_____   30B_____

   30C_____   32A_____   32B_____

   32C_____

   Summary of responses: _____

8. The meaning my life holds for myself and others I relate to is:

   4 _____   6 _____   13 _____

   19 _____   34 _____

   Summary of responses: _____

Take the summaries from numbers 1 through 8 above and place them in numerical order at the end of the following statements:
I am attracted to people who are:
   Answer from 1: _____

My positive qualities are:
   Answer from 2: _____

I have learned to experience myself as:
   Answer from 3: _____

My best experiences in relationships are:
   Answer from 4: _____

My most painful feelings in relationships are:
   Answer from 5: _____

When I feel I am being misperceived I believe that I am seen as:
   Answer from 6: _____

When I believe I am perceived that way, I react by:
   Answer from 7: _____

The meaning life holds for me and the way my relationships support that meaning is:
   Answer from 8: _____

Answer the following questions based upon your own experience of filling out this measure, in order to become more aware of, and start to step out of, your complexes. When I am caught in a complex, my pattern of reactivity is:

I experience tension in my body in the following places:

I feel:

I remember:

I react by:

The things that hold the most meaning for me then are:

The images I have are:

My experience of myself when I am having dreams that contain these images, feelings and memories is:

My choices are limited by:

The rules and laws I obey are:

The ways I perceive myself and the world around me are:

My center of authority resides in:

What I most want from another human being is:

What I most need to do to take care of myself is:

What I realize now, after filling out this measure, is that many of the physical experiences, memories, feelings, and behaviors I have identified in the pages above are ongoing, predictable, reactive, and part of my negative complex. Write down your response in your journal.

Over time your awareness of your complex and patterned form of attachment will change. If you take the measure every 18 months and continue to journal your responses, you may observe changes in your life that include increased energy and a wider range of options for life.

COMPENSATION

This exercise should be done with a journal or sketchbook. Find a place that is in or close to nature or a place that seems attractive to you. If the place is in nature, ask the place if it will welcome you. You will receive a sense of comfort within or a sign from nature that you are welcomed. If you are welcomed, stay there and quiet your mind. If you do not feel comfortable, find another space and repeat the same process until you have found the right space. Then let go of the tension in your body, relax, and smile a little *Mona Lisa* smile. Remember that as you relax all of the parts of your body are working, even when you do not think of them. Look within and visualize each part of your body: bones, muscles, organs, lymph, blood, tendons, nervous system and brain. Smile and thank each part of your body for nourishing you from the time you were in the womb. Let each part of your body smile back at you. Each part enjoys the work it does. Allow yourself to sink into a state of pleasure and gratitude for your body and all of its parts that work so hard for you.

Stand up and walk counterclockwise in a circle to create a Sacred Space. (Moving counterclockwise aligns personal energy with the movements of the earth.) As you walk, ask all of the parts of nature to come into your circle: plants and trees, bushes and grasses, mountains and earth, animals and humans, and all of your ancestors who have loved you since always. Ask them to come to help you grow in wisdom and understanding. Thank them for coming into your circle, and ask that any energy that is not helpful in this process move out into the universe into the places where it will be useful.

Sit down facing the South. When you are ready, ask the question: *What in my life gives me the most energy?* Listen for an answer. Something will come to you internally or externally. It may be a thought, an image, or something that happens externally that is meaningful. Accept your experience and write it down or draw it in your sketchbook.

When you are finished, move counterclockwise and sit quietly in the circle, facing the West. Quiet yourself and return to your smiling meditation. When you feel relaxed, ask the question: *What holds me together?* Listen and wait for the answer. Allow an experience to come to you without expectations or rules about what may or may not appear. Whatever occurs is the answer. Write down the image or draw it in your sketchbook. Trust what happens. After you feel that you are finished, move counterclockwise and sit facing North.

Quiet yourself again. When you have relaxed into your sense of pleasure, ask your next question: *What must I remember?* Repeat the same process used above. When you are finished, move counterclockwise and sit facing the East.

Quiet yourself and relax again as you sit facing the East. When you are ready, ask the question: *Are my actions helping me or hindering me on my life path?* Repeat the process performed in the other three directions. When you are finished, thank the sacred space that has opened to allow loving energy to enter there so that you could learn. Stand up and walk clockwise, closing the circle as you thank your ancestors for coming and loving you enough to help you. To show your gratitude, go outside or to a window and put a little tobacco on your hands, allow the wind or your breath to send the tobacco out into the air. Spend some time praying for continued growth and healing for the members of your family, for your friends, and for the world.

THE IMAGO

Use your sketchbook to put down what you discover.

Recall three of your most painful relationships. Suspend your judgment and your emotions, while focusing on experiencing the sensations in your body.

- Who were they with?
- What made the relationships so difficult for you?
- What are the feelings from those relationships that you never want to feel again? What did you do to get through the pain?

After reflecting upon these experiences, notice the tension in your body;

sense those places that are tight and constricted. Use your sketchbook and draw the colors, shapes and images connected with your physical constriction. Do at least five drawings, each on a separate page, without referring to the previous drawings. Draw a picture of your worst nightmare in a relationship on the last page.

Sit for a moment and reflect on what you have just experienced. What are your feelings? Draw them.

- What are the images that accompany your feelings?

Let yourself relax into the feelings and the images that accompany them. They are an important part of your life experience. Draw them and thank them for helping you survive and become strong.

- What were the things you did in each relationship that were most hurtful to you?
- What were the things you did in each relationship that were most hurtful to the other persons?

Focus on your behavior and the behavior of each of the other three persons.

- What was similar about your behavior in all three relationships?
- What was similar about the behavior of each of the other three persons involved in the relationships?
- Write the common themes you have discovered in your sketchbook.
- What was your fantasy about each relationship?
- What might the other person's fantasy have been?
- What were the patterns of mediation of the archetypal/developmental processes you most needed and didn't receive?
- What were the patterns of mediation of the archetypal/developmental processes you received from the other persons?

Return to your drawings and look at them again. You may find images and feelings that describe the feelings and actions of both a victim and a predator.

- What have you learned about your imago?

ARCHETYPAL/DEVELOPMENTAL PROCESSES

Being

Sit by yourself in silence for 15 minutes. Close your eyes and relax into a state of pleasure. Let your thoughts flow around you and past you. Afterward, describe your experience or draw an image that expresses the experience in your sketchbook. Next, ask yourself the questions:

- When you are upset what are the ways you use to settle yourself down?
- How does your body let you know when you are hungry, lonely, tired, or overwhelmed?
- What are the ways you nourish yourself?

Doing

- Explore a new idea, activity, hobby, or form of experience that captivates your interest and don't know anything about.
- What is it like for you when you explore or experience new situations?
- What is your safe place that you go out from and return to after a hard day?
- What happened when you set out to explore something? Was it easy? Was it difficult? How did you nurture yourself as you explored something new?

Record that in your sketchbook.

Thinking

Name the biggest problem in your life right now. Draw a large image with crayons or markers of what your experience of the problem is like. Cut up the drawing to create pieces that look like pieces of a puzzle. Turn the puzzle pieces over and mix them up. On each piece write out one part of what you must do to solve the problem. If the problem is not solvable, use each piece of paper to write one part of what you must do to take care of and nurture yourself as you endure the problem. Put the pieces of the puzzle together upside down (with your original image face down). Look at the messages on each piece and prioritize that message into an order that goes from easiest to most difficult to do. Create a list of priorities from easiest to most difficult. Begin with what is easiest to solve and slowly move toward what is more difficult. Record each step in your sketchbook along with those things you didn't expect to happen. Record how you nourished yourself during this process and what you learned.

Identity

Change your identity by dressing up in clothes that are different from your everyday wardrobe. Dress down and go shopping at a very fancy store and have a salesperson in the store help you look for something. Dress up and go to a bargain store. Have a salesperson help you look for something.

Repeat the experience, but this time, dress up in your worst clothes. Return what you bought from the fancy store, or ask someone for help. Wear your best clothes and return to the bargain store. Purchase something and/or ask for help.

What did you learn from this experience? How can you use your natural gifts to create new roles for yourself and develop your understanding of how others influence your identity? Record your experience and observations in your sketchbook.

Assume the identity of your favorite fictional character. What is it like to become someone else? Have a dress-up party and invite your friends to come as their favorite fictional character. Remain in your roles until everyone has introduced themselves as their character. Record your observations and your experiences in your sketchbook.

Creativity

Ask yourself this question: What do I do when I play? Each person plays. Some of us play in destructive ways. Some of us play in ways that bring pleasure and energy into our daily life. The possibilities for play are unlimited: rearranging our surroundings; challenging ourselves to learn something new and interesting; playing the usual adult games of cards, golf, tennis, baseball; etc. Do I like playing by myself? Do I prefer playing with others? How can I bring play into my everyday life?

Here are some examples of ways in which to incorporate play: walk backwards, change routines (e.g., the order of personal grooming), find ways to challenge yourself at work (e.g., standing or sitting in different positions, using a different hand or foot), bring a sense of smiling relaxation to whatever you do, pursue your interests and find a way to blend your interests with your work, practice maintaining a sense of pleasure within yourself.

Each of these examples is designed to help you gain a sense of pleasure and ease in your performance. Creativity has everything to do with pleasure, ease, and enjoyment. Life is a difficult school. We can choose to make a space in our life within ourselves that holds the potential for unlimited experience; we need only develop and protect it. Both positive and negative experiences can be teachings for us that we can use to develop our creativity. Choosing to relax and not react expands our creative space and protects it.

PERFORMING ACTIVE IMAGINATION

1. Create a sacred space in whatever way seems comfortable for you.
2. Empty the mind.
3. Let an unconscious image enter into the field of inner attention, or pay attention to a constricted or painful place in the body and allow an image to arise from this experience.
4. Draw, sculpt, paint, or write a description of the image.
5. Begin a dialogue with the image or images that arise just as you would with events or persons in everyday life. The images will change or perhaps speak back to you. (This dialogue is active imagination). Do not perform active imagination with a person that you have a relationship with in the outer world to influence that person or your relationship with them in a negative or positive way. That is what practitioners of magic do. Active imagination is a dialogue with contents of the unconscious. Practitioners of magic use their imagination and will to influence persons and events in the outer world.
6. Ego consciousness must be directly and ethically involved, for the unconscious is the inner guide. True active imagination looks for the truth of oneself. If it is used for ego gains or selfish purposes, the pathological complex is reinforced.
7. Whatever is learned or experienced must be made material through writing, drawing, painting, poetry, physical movement, or any kind of material expression that locates the experience between ego consciousness and the unconscious in the material world. When the experience is not expressed materially, it gradually falls back into the unconscious and it is as if nothing has happened.[2]

When a person experiences transformation, consciousness develops. Gradually the energy of ego consciousness is increased, creating the possibility for the person to have a greater impact on the material world. It is my belief that people who possess higher levels of energy within the components of ego consciousness behave quite differently from people with lower levels of energy within the components of ego consciousness.

GROUP SKILL DEVELOPMENT STRUCTURE

Form a "working group" of six to nine people. I recommend that participants agree to abide by the following structure:

1. Meet at least once a month for two hours at the same place.

2. Decide what skill to work on before each meeting.
3. Structure the group meeting as follows:

   - Brief check in: each member checks in about what is going on in his or her practice and one question he or she has about a patient
   - Skill building for 50 minutes
   - Client enactments for 50 minutes
   - Brief check out: each member says a little about what he or she has learned

4. Confidentiality: nothing that occurs or is discussed during the group is discussed with anyone outside the group.
5. Interpersonal difficulties are discussed and worked through within the group, and if necessary, an outside consultant can be hired to facilitate communication so that difficulties can be worked through within the group.

THE RELATIONAL FIELD

The entire group sits in a circle. One therapist leads the group, guiding the rest of the group into a state of relaxation and an inner safe place. The following exercise is a suggestion for the leading therapist to use to assist people to relax and discover an inner safe place.

Close your eyes. Take a deep breath then let it go. Relax then tighten your body. Let go of the tightness and let yourself relax more deeply. Relax your face and just lift the corners of your lips into a smile. Allow yourself to feel a sense of gratitude for your body. Let your attention sink into your bones. Begin with your toes and allow your attention to move up your legs. Smile at your toe bones and your leg bones. Let them smile back. Allow your attention to continue up your body into your hips, pelvis, and tailbone. Smile at your hips, pelvis, and tailbone and let these bones smile back at you. Allow your attention to move up your backbone and through your ribs. Smile at your backbone and your ribs. Allow them to smile back at you. Return your attention back to your backbones, neck bones, and skull. Smile at your backbones, your neck bones, and your skull and allow these bones to smile back at you. Remember your shoulder bones, your clavicle, and your arm and finger bones. Smile at them and allow them to smile back at you.

Now allow your attention to wander over your body watching your tendons and muscles. Smile at those muscles and tendons that feel tight and let them smile back at you. Allow yourself to pay attention to the blood and lymph flowing through your body, bringing in what you need and letting go of what you do not need. Smile at your blood and your lymph and while they flow, let them smile back at you. Feel your lungs taking in and letting go. Smile at your lungs. How many breaths have they taken since you were born? Let your lungs smile at you. Sense your heart beating and smile at your heart as it beats. Allow your heart to smile back at you.

Allow yourself to imagine the rest of the organs in your body. Slowly smile at the liver, spleen, pancreas, gall bladder, kidneys, digestive system, and the nervous system. Smile at each one. Let each one smile at you. Allow yourself to become more deeply relaxed. Don't forget to thank your reproductive organs; your skin, your hair, your eyes, your ears and your nose. Allow each of those parts to smile back at you. Let yourself sink into a deep state of pleasure and gratitude for being alive. Take ten relaxed breaths.

Now you are more deeply relaxed. Imagine that there is a door in front of you. While maintaining your deeply relaxed state, open the door and step through to a beautiful place, outdoors in nature. It may be a place you have been, it may be a place you have always wanted to go. It may be a place of water, mountains, sunshine, clouds, trees, sand, and grass. It is a beautiful place filled with the light of the Creator. All of the energy that is not useful for the health of your mind, body, soul, and spirit has been sent out into the universe where it can be useful. Lie down in your safe place and take time to feel the quiet and the safety; let yourself become more deeply relaxed. Take twenty relaxed breaths. At the end of that time open your eyes and slowly rise from where you are lying. Look at the beautiful scenery around you so that you can remember this place and return to it whenever you wish, just by relaxing your face and smiling. Take a deep breath, turn and open the door. Take another deep breath and slowly open your eyes, feeling a sense of pleasure and gratitude for being alive.

When the relaxation exercise is finished and everyone has opened their eyes, ask one person to sit in the center with the other group members around him or her. The people in the circle look at the person in the center and imagine his or her beauty and health while accessing their own sense or pleasure and relaxation. The person in the center closes his eyes and takes in the positive attitude of those in the circle. After two minutes, the person in the center shifts to the circle and another person from the circle enters the center. The exercise continues until everyone in the group has been in the center. When everyone has experienced being in the center of the circle, the exercise is complete. Take time for group members to discuss and share what each has learned from the experience.

TRIADIC ROLE-PLAY

Triadic role-play is an enactment that involves three different people enacting three different roles: the patient, the therapist, and the observer. Each role represents one portion of the therapeutic encounter.

The clinician who plays the role of the patient enacts, to the best of his or her ability, an actual patient in his or her practice or uses one of the examples suggested below. The purpose of enacting a patient is to develop a deeper level of attunement with the perceptual framework of that particular patient's patterned form of attachment and pathological complex.

The clinician who plays the role of the therapist is practicing in order to develop or increase a clinical skill.

The clinician who plays the role of the observer functions as an *observing ego* and pays attention to the body language of both the "patient" and the "therapist." In addition, he or she grounds the clinical experience with part of the theory presented in the book. For example, highlighting the patient's patterned form of attachment or the "fantasy bond," or noting a regressive part of the patient's pathological complex. The observer offers feedback after the enactment is completed.

Role-plays are time limited, lasting from about 8 to 10 minutes. Since they are a form of learning and play, it is especially important that group members protect, empower, and give one another permission to be dramatic and reactive during the role- play itself.

The following exercises are suggested as ways group members can begin to work together to develop their skills and learn. They all use triadic role-play unless otherwise stated. A patient with a brief history will be presented with each exercise as a suggestion for the role-play. The participants can also use any one of the cases presented in Chapter 5 or someone from their own practice.

FOCUS

Clinical work requires the therapist to be in a state of focus. What does that mean? A focus is a central space where diverging lines meet. If we think of the relational field as a place where hundreds of lines of information exist at any one point in time, then to be focused means to be in a physical and mental state where these diverging lines can meet and be held by our attention. In order to become focused, the therapist can relax the bones, muscles, and organs of the body while letting go of all theories, opinions, ideas, and affect so that he or she feels calm, unhurried, grounded, and happy. As physical relaxation occurs, mental awareness can sink into a state of pleasure in order to focus the mind so that more information can be received and processed.

Clinical Exercise: Triadic Role-Play: Focus

In this exercise one person enacts the patient, another the therapist and another enacts the observer. The exercise is designed to help the participants focus on both their internal and external responses to a patient when his or her patterned form of attachment is constellated during the clinical hour.

SUGGESTED PATIENT ROLE: The patient is a middle-aged man who has lost his job and has begun to search for a new one. In this particular hour he talks about how his wife doesn't work and is spending their savings. He wants the therapist to help him say something to her to get her to stop spending money. He has asked her to see a financial planner with him and she has refused.

Before the role-play begins, the person enacting the therapist relaxes physically and mentally.

The person role-playing the patient begins the enactment by being mildly constellated in the patient's avoidant patterned form of attachment.

THERAPIST SKILL BUILDING: The therapist begins to attune to the patient's concerns about money. The patient avoids discussing his own experience by focusing on what to say to his wife and how to get her to change. The therapist continues to attune to the patient and then begins asking him how he feels about all of this. The patient discusses his feelings but blames his wife for creating his affective discomfort. The therapist's goal in this exercise is to stay attuned and have the patient shift his focus to his own experience rather than trying to find ways to change his wife.

SUMMARY: When the exercise is completed, each participant gives a brief summary of his or her ability to remain relaxed and focused during the exercise. The observer adds any theoretical material he or she noted during the exercise.

LISTENING

Clinical Exercise: Listening

This exercise is done using triadic role-play. The focus is on listening.

SUGGESTED PATIENT ROLE: The patient is a 30-year-old married woman with two children. She works full time and gives all the money to her husband, who manages the household finances. For the past six months she has felt anxious and depressed, has had difficulty sleeping, and has had suicidal thoughts along with feelings of hopelessness and helplessness. She describes her children as successful in school and her marriage as a happy one. She has sought therapy because she cries all the time and doesn't know why she is unhappy.

THERAPIST SKILL BUILDING: Attune to the patient by mirroring her posture. Use the patient's descriptions and words to begin to develop a shared language with her. Gather a history of the problem and ask questions to develop a better understanding of the patient's experience and her goals for therapy. At the end of the exercise, shift your physical posture and describe your own internal experience during the exercise.

OBSERVER SKILL BUILDING: Attune to the therapist by mirroring his or her posture. Summarize what the therapist has said about his or her internal experience at the end of the exercise

SKILL BUILDING FOR THE PERSON WHO ENACTED THE PATIENT: Describe your experience as the patient and summarize what you learned from the enactment.

FACILITATING THE DEVELOPMENT OF THE TRANSITIONAL SPACE[2]

The techniques of inviting the patient to draw, paint, role-play, and write poetry; and the therapist's use of similes, metaphors, imaging patterned forms of attachment, and facilitating parts work are all part of developing the transitional space. Techniques to develop the transitional space are presented below in four exercises: (a) inviting the patient into the transitional space, (b) using simile and metaphor, (c) imaging patterned forms of attachment, and d) facilitating parts work.

Clinical Exercise: Inviting the Patient Into the Transitional Space

This exercise is done using triadic role-play. The person playing the role of the therapist uses questions like: What is that like for you? What does that feel like in your body? Where is your body tight when you have that feeling? When you have that experience what do you remember? When do you remember first having this experience? Help me understand what that is like? Does that tightness or looseness in your body have a color, a shape, a smell, an image? Tell me more about that. Describe it by telling me how it sounds or looks. What you are telling me seems really important, is there more? What do you think you need right now, and what would that look like? What is it like not to know? Is there a picture for your experience? Invite the patient into the transitional space.

SUGGESTED PATIENT ROLE: The patient is a 50-year-old man who works as a mechanic. For the past two months he has been waking up several times at night with dreams that he made a mistake at work and someone has been killed as a result. He was so concerned about the dream that he came into therapy.

THERAPIST SKILL BUILDING: The therapist takes a history and discovers that the patient has no time for himself because he is too busy taking care of the mechanical problems of family, friends, and neighbors. The therapist invites the patient to draw a graph of his activities on the past Sunday using different colors for different activities including the activity of doing something for himself. The goal for the first clinical hour is to invite the patient into the transitional space by using colors instead of words.

SKILL BUILDING ENACTING THE PATIENT: The person enacting the patient assumes the role of a really nice guy who simply can't say, "no" other people's requests. The patient is the oldest of nine children and has never even considered taking what it might mean to spend time taking care of himself. He is an excellent mechanic and has asked a supervisor to double-check his work because of the dream.

OBSERVER ROLE: The observer listens to the history and identifies the imago, the "fantasy bond," or the patterned form of attachment at the end of the exercise

Clinical Exercise: The Use of Metaphor and Simile

This exercise is done using triadic role-play. Similes and metaphors express likenesses, comparing one thing to another and can be used in therapy to expand the range of meaning in an experience or a statement.

SUGGESTED PATIENT ROLE: The patient is a 28-year-old woman whose fiancé has cancelled their marriage. She does not know why he has cancelled the marriage and he seems to be unable to give her a satisfactory answer. She comes in for individual therapy because she feels angry, depressed and chaotic.

THERAPIST SKILL DEVELOPMENT: The goal for this exercise is for the therapist to attune to the patient by confirming the patient's experience and mirroring what he or she hears back to the patient accurately, using metaphor or simile when possible, e.g., "you sound as if you've been shaken by a tornado." The patient will respond positively if the simile or metaphor confirms his or her experience. In this case, the patient might say something like, "Yes, I feel like I am caught in a tornado with nothing to hang onto." The experience of being caught in a tornado with nothing to hang onto becomes a location in the transitional space that can be communicated, shared, and then explored.

OBSERVER SKILL DEVELOPMENT: At the end of the exercise, summarize the patient's patterned form of attachment or describe the imago or the "fantasy bond." If the patient presents a regressed part, identify the archetypal/developmental process involved.

Clinical Exercise: Imaging Patterned Forms of Attachment Through the Enactment of Fairy Tales

The purpose of this exercise is to assist the group members to develop the capacity to imagine patterns of attachment, patterns of mediation, the imago, and the fantasy bond.

Read the fairy tale together as a group. Group members individually volunteer to play one role for each of the characters of the fairy tale. Enact the fairy tale. After the enactment, have the group members take time to discuss what they have learned.

Textbook: *The Complete Grimm's Fairy Tales* (1972), trans. Margaret Hunt (New York: Random House).

Suggestions:

"The Frog King or Iron Henry" (pp. 17-20)
"The Story of the Youth Who Went Forth to Learn What Fear Was" (pp. 29-39)
"Hansel and Gretel" (pp. 86-94)
"The Fisherman and his Wife" (pp. 103-112)
"Little Red Cap" (pp. 139-143)

CLINICAL EXERCISE: Imaging Patterned Forms of Attachment

This exercise is done using triadic role-play with two patients and one therapist.

SUGGESTED COUPLE: The wife has requested therapy. She is very upset about the marital relationship and has decided that if things don't change she is going to get a divorce. The husband thinks that their relationship is just fine and simply does not understand why they need therapy or why the wife would think about a divorce.

THERAPIST SKILL DEVELOPMENT: The therapist asks the wife to give a brief history of what has brought the couple for therapy without using statements that blame the husband. When the wife is finished, the therapist confirms what he or she has heard the wife say. The therapist then asks the husband to give a brief history of what has brought the couple for therapy without using statements that blame the wife. When it has become clear that the husband and the wife disagree on the need for therapy, the therapist reflects this problem back to the couple with an image of the problem, e.g., each person is facing in a different direction and neither can really hear what the other one is saying.

At the end of the exercise, each person takes a few minutes to summarize his or her thoughts, feelings and ideas.

DEVELOPING THE PATIENT'S AWARENESS OF PARTS

In order for a patient to be able to do "parts work," he or she needs to be educated about "parts" by the therapist. It has been my experience that many patients are not comfortable enacting "parts" in the early phases of therapy because of the lack of development of a grounded connection between the patient and the therapist and the rigidity of the pathological complex. However, educating a patient about his or her parts as they appear in the clinical hour is a useful skill because it helps the patient feel understood as well as contained.

Clinical Exercise: Developing Awareness of Parts

This exercise is done using triadic role-play.

SUGGESTED PATIENT: The patient is a 30-year-old physician. He is unhappy with his marriage and has come into individual therapy to make a decision whether or not to stay married. He is very ambivalent about whether or not to leave the relationship. He is having an affair and his mistress is putting pressure on him to leave his wife and marry her. His wife is unaware of the affair and has refused to attend therapy because she does not believe there are problems in the relationship.

THERAPIST SKILL DEVELOPMENT: The goal of the exercise is to educate the patient about his parts after he discusses his ambivalence, e.g., "What I hear you saying is that you love you wife and want to stay with her and at the same time you love your mistress and want to marry her. Is that right?" The patient will agree that is correct and then the therapist can say something like, "You are feeling a lot of pain because you are being pulled in two different directions at the same time. Each direction is a part of you. By exploring and understanding your parts you and I can begin to understand the truth of all of your experience."

OBSERVER SKILL DEVELOPMENT: The observer develops an image of this patient's patterned form of attachment.

Each participant summarizes his or her thoughts and feelings at the end of the exercise.

Clinical Exercise: Facilitating Patient Parts-Work

This exercise is done using a triadic role-play.

SUGGESTED PATIENT: The patient is a 48-year-old woman married to an alcoholic. She has been married for 20 years and has two children, both of whom are in high school. Her husband drinks secretly and denies it. The children blame her for being cranky all the time and think that their father is wonderful because he is never crabby. During this session the patient is feeling anxious and confused about whether or not her husband is really an alcoholic.

THERAPIST SKILL BUILDING: The patient has a good relationship with the therapist and is developing an observing ego. She is aware that she has one part that feels crazy, bad, and wrong, and another part that is sure that her husband is an alcoholic. In a directive, educating, and attuned way have the patient identify a place in the room where she can place the part of her that believes her husband is an alcoholic. Have her identify another place in the room where she can place the part of her that feels crazy. Have her keep her usual chair for the part of her that will observe both parts. Have her decide which part she wants to speak from first, and then have her begin in that place and move to the next part when she feels ready.

THE OBSERVER ROLE: At the end of the exercise, summarize the patient's patterned form of attachment, the imago, or the "fantasy bond."

Each participant summarizes his or her thoughts and feelings at the end of the exercise.

THE IMAGO AND PARTS WORK

Exposing the imago is difficult because so much of the imago functions unconsciously. I have broken down some of the parts of the imago in order for the readers to educate their patients about the imago.

Clinical Exercise: Locating the Imago as an Inner Voice, an Internal Image, or a Sense of Physical Constriction When the Complex is Constellated

SUGGESTED PATIENT: Michael from Chapter 5. In this session, Michael is feeling discouraged and stuck. He believes that nothing has changed at all and that he is still doing the same things. He is frustrated because he has not been able to decide whether or not he wants to stay married or live with his mistress. His greatest frustration is the feeling of constant anxiety and not being able to settle down.

THERAPIST SKILL BUILDING: The goal of the exercise is to help Michael move into the feeling of anxiety and locate an inner voice, an internal image, or a sense of physical constriction and express it by describing or drawing the experience.

THE OBSERVER ROLE: State what he or she has learned from watching the interaction between the patient and the therapist.

Each participant summarizes his or her thoughts and feelings at the end of the exercise.

Clinical Exercise: Using Image, Simile, Metaphor, Drawing, Poetry, or Movement to Assist the Patient to Describe the Parts of the Imago

SUGGESTED PATIENT: Shirley from Chapter 5. In this session Shirley becomes aware that the imago is an internal experience that has nothing to do with Jacob.

THERAPIST SKILL BUILDING: The goal of the exercise is to help Shirley express her internal experience of the imago using an image, simile, metaphor, drawing, poetry or physical movement.

THE OBSERVER ROLE: To describe how Shirley came to the point where she could separate the imago from her perceptions of Jacob.

Each participant summarizes his or her thoughts and feelings at the end of the exercise.

Clinical Exercise: Identifying the Parts of the Imago that Reinforce the Pathological Complex

SUGGESTED PATIENT: Vivian from Chapter 5. In this session Vivian reports that she has binged twice since the last clinical hour. She is aware of "evil eye." During this session the therapist explores the experiences that constellated the bingeing.

THERAPIST SKILL BUILDING: The goal of the exercise is to explore Vivian's experience with her and discover whether or not she can link her experience of "evil eye" and being shamed with her bingeing.

THE OBSERVER ROLE: Summarize what he or she has learned from observing the clinical interaction.

Each participant summarizes his or her thoughts and feelings at the end of the exercise.

Clinical Exercise: The Imago and the Fantasy Bond

SUGGESTED PATIENT: Jacob from Chapter 5. In this session Jacob is complaining about not having a gourmet dinner, wine, music, and the intimacy he and Shirley experienced before the birth of the baby.

THERAPIST SKILL BUILDING: The goal of this exercise is to remain attuned to Jacob while encouraging him to sink into his feelings of longing for the way things were and attempt to gently expose the "fantasy bond" and more importantly how it functions to reinforce his withdrawal.

OBSERVER ROLE: Summarize what he or she has learned from observing the interaction.

Each participant briefly summarizes his or her thoughts and feelings about the exercise.

Clinical Exercise: Interviewing the Imago

SUGGESTED PATIENT: Vivian from Chapter 5. In this session Vivian is ready to enact "evil eye." She locates a place in the office for "evil eye" to sit and places a chair in that spot. She defines her usual place as the space for her "observing ego." Vivian decides to begin the work by enacting "evil eye."

THERAPIST SKILL BUILDING: The therapist interviews "evil eye" in the same way he or she would take a history from any other patient. The focus of the conversation is on understanding the imago and its point of view. It is this structure that has helped the patient survive,[4] and the therapist must not take what it says personally.

OBSERVER SKILL BUILDING: Identify and summarize the mythological motif that belongs to the imago, e.g., hero, villain, god, victim, etc.

Each participant briefly summarize his or her thoughts and feelings when the exercise is over.

ENDNOTES

1. The authors who have contributed to the development of the Complex Awareness Measure are:
   Berne, Eric. (1964). Games people play. New York: Grove Press.
   _____ (1961). Transactional analysis in psychotherapy. New York: Grove Press.
   Hendrix, Harville. (1996). Keeping the love you find: A workshop for singles. Winter Park, Florida: Institute for Imago Relationship Therapy.
   Jung, C. G. (1902/57). On the psychology and pathology of so-called occult phenomena, CW 1.
   _____(1906-1909/73). Studies in word association, CW 2.
   _____(1907/60). The psychology of dementia praecox, CW 3
   _____(1911/60). A criticism of Bleuler's theory of schizophrenia, CW 3.
   _____(1912/56). Symbols of transformation, CW 5.
   _____(1919/60). On the problem of psychogenesis in mental disease, CW 3.
   _____(1934/53). The relations between the ego and the unconscious, CW 7.
   _____(1948/60). A review of complex theory, CW 8.
   Levin, Pamela. (1974). Becoming the way we are: A transactional guide to personal development. Berkley, Calif.: Self-published.

McCormick, Paul. (1971). Guide: For use of a life-script questionnaire. Berkley, Calif.: Self published:
Steiner, Claude. (1974). Scripts people live. New York: Grove Press.

2. These concepts about active imagination were developed from Marie Louise von Franz (1979), Alchemical active imagination (Dallas, TX: Spring Publications).
3. Working with dreams, sand play, and active imagination requires special training from someone certified to teach these skills. For more information on where to receive training, call the C.G. Jung Institute of Chicago in Evanston, Illinois.
4. In cases where the imago is violent, the therapist needs special training in bodywork to facilitate the expression of violence in order to protect the patient and others involved in supporting the patient.

Appendix

DEFINITION OF JUNGIAN TERMS

The terms used in this manual are often difficult to understand because Jung's psychology has a distinct vocabulary. Each term will be defined as I understand it. Following the definition, the source of that understanding will be cited from Jung's *Collected Works*, with the volume number and the page where it was found.

ACTIVE IMAGINATION: An intentional dialogue between the ego and images that arise spontaneously from the unconscious and from dreams. It involves active participation in fantasies and has the effect of: (1) extending the horizon of consciousness through the acceptance and inclusion of numerous unconscious contents; (2) gradually diminishing the negative effects of the unconscious upon consciousness because the communications from the unconscious are being related to; and (3) bringing about a change in the personality through the transformation of the conscious attitude (*CW* 7, 1977, 212–226).

The purpose of active imagination is to restore a balanced relationship between the ego and the unconscious, creating a bridge (the *transcendent function*) between them.

AFFECT: A set of emotions wound together; a state of feeling characterized by marked physical excitation on the one hand and a disturbance of the ideational process on the other. It is a group of cumulative emotions and the physical responses produced by them. Affect is a psychic feeling state and physical enervation, one having a reciprocal effect upon the other (*CW* 6, 411). "Affect always occurs where there is a failure of adaptation" (*CW* 6, 1977, 470).

AIM OF JUNGIAN ANALYSIS: To restore the process of compensation between ego consciousness and the unconscious and to come to a place of real understanding and dialogue between the ego and the unconscious. It is of vital importance that the patient experiences the images and physical sensations that arise from the unconscious and truly understand them, not in an intellectual way, but in a relational way that eventually changes the totality of his or her experience (*CW* 7, 1977, 212–213). As compensation begins to be restored, treatment of the pathological complex becomes more and more of a dialogue with the unconscious. If a decision is right, it will be confirmed by dreams of progress; and in the other event, correction will follow from the side of the unconscious.

AMPLIFICATION: Jung's method for interpreting archetypal contents of dreams, images, and fantasies. Jung tried to establish the context of a dream through associations, which led to the discovery of pathological complexes embedded within the psyche that are derived from the personal history. Amplification connected the dream images with the imagery of the collective unconscious through the use of myth, history, fairy tales, and cultural parallels. Amplification is the process that begins freeing the archetypal material embedded within the pathological complex for gradual integration and individuation (Samuels et al., *A Critical Dictionary of Jungian Analysis*, 1986, 16).

ANIMA AND ANIMUS: The bridge between ego consciousness and the Self, meant to serve in the process of individuation. Persona, or the role carried in the outer world, depends to some extent upon the physical gender. The animus (male) and anima (female) compensate for the outer gendered role by being the opposite gender of the persona. That means a man has an anima (female) and a woman has an animus (male) that is supposed to serve and facilitate the process of individuation. However, culturally the genders are not equal; therefore, it is important that a man kneel and listen to the anima so that his individuation may progress, and that a woman stand and face the animus until he serves her individuation (*CW* 7, 1977, 210–211).

ARCHETYPE: The most ancient and universal underpinnings of all of human experience (*CW* 7, 1977, 44). Archetypes manifest themselves only through their ability to organize images, ideas, and human experience. By reflecting on our experience, these phenomena become visible (*CW* 8, 1981, 231). Archetypes are the premises or structuring forms that support physical and psychic functioning. The word *archetype* is a psychosomatic concept that links body and image. They structure all human experience into patterns that are reproduced throughout the world. Analysis involves a growing awareness of the archetypal dimensions of human life.

ASSESSMENT of a patient in order for the patient to benefit from ongoing, long-term treatment:

1. Ego strength: does the patient have the ability to contain and reflect upon experience; the ability to allow emotions to give energy; the ability to be mentally receptive and the ability to act in a way that is grounded and nonreactive?
2. How extensive is the operation of the defenses of the Self-denial, splitting, introjection, projection, identification, and idealization?
3. What is the quality and the extent of the ego/imago axis? How much influence does the imago have over ego consciousness?
4. What is the degree of pathology contained within the patterns of mediation of the archetypal/developmental processes?
5. How strong is the "fantasy bond"?
6. What is the level of rigidification of the cycles of nature embedded within the pathological complex?
7. Is there an observing ego? Is it possible to assist the patient in developing an "observing ego"?
8. Is the patient willing to learn and understand how he or she contributes to the pathological complex?

When the patient appears to have the ability to step back, interrupt, and observe the activity of a pathological complex, that patient is a candidate for long-term therapy. Patients who do not appear to have the ability to step back, interrupt and observe the activity of a pathological complex can benefit from short-term therapy that focuses upon one issue at a time.

ASSOCIATION: The spontaneous linkage of ideas, images, perceptions, fantasies, physical sensations, memories, and behaviors with an affective theme.

Jung maintained that by carefully following the patient's associations and returning to them again and again, the pathological complex and the imago at the center of the defensive system will emerge in the patient's awareness spontaneously, without interpretation. In analysis, associations lead to the personal history and those parts of ego consciousness, both conscious and unconscious, embedded within the complex (*CW* 2, 1973, 3–196).

COLLECTIVE CONSCIOUSNESS: The aggregate of the entire culture a person lives in and is surrounded by, including the beliefs, traditions, conventions, customs, prejudices, rules, and norms of the group. This includes the introjected *shoulds* and *oughts* as in Freud's concept of the superego, but it also includes all those things that pour in from outside to influence the individual (Jacobi 1959, 29–30).

COLLECTIVE UNCONSCIOUS: Universal and regularly occurring phenomena that have nothing to do with individuality. It contains impersonal components called archetypes, which have formed and structured human performance from the beginning of time. The archetypes influence human memory, acting in a compensatory way to create the seeds of future experience. The collective unconscious contains patterns of human memory and experience that have existed since the dawn of time, as well as the possibilities for future human development (*CW* 7, 1977, 77).

COMPENSATION: A balancing or homeostatic mechanism producing adjustments between the conscious attitude and the unconscious. In this regard there are three possibilities:
1. If the conscious attitude is one-sided, the dream, vision, or fantasy takes the opposite side.
2. If the components of ego consciousness are fairly balanced, the manifestations of the unconscious are satisfied and produce only variations in the dreams, fantasies, or visions.
3. If the components of ego consciousness are balanced and individuation is occurring, the dreams, visions, and fantasies coincide with those processes and emphasize those tendencies (*CW* 7, 1977, 139–155).

COMPLEX: A certain psychic situation, an attitude, and a splinter personality that is more akin to a fantasy than reality. It is strongly accentuated emotionally and is incompatible with the habitual attitude of consciousness. The complex has a powerful inner coherence, its own wholeness, and a relatively high degree of autonomy, which limits conscious control. It behaves like a foreign body in the sphere of consciousness. It can be suppressed; however, it will return. It has a wave-like character with the wave lasting a certain length of hours, days, weeks, or months (*CW* 8, 1981, 96).

CONSTELLATION OF A COMPLEX: An outward situation activates a psychic and physical process in which the unconscious complex overrides ego consciousness, taking a position in which an individual will act in a predictable way. Constellation of a complex is an automatic process that happens involuntarily and that cannot be stopped of one's own accord (*CW* 8, 1981, 94–95).

CONSCIOUS AND UNCONSCIOUS: The conscious mind is always directed toward the adjustment of the ego to the environment. The unconscious, on the other hand, is indifferent to the egocentric purposes; instead, it is objective like all of nature, and its sole purpose is to maintain the possibility for individuation or wholeness (Jacobi 1959, 35).

EGO: The ego is the center of consciousness, yet less than the whole of the personality. It is concerned with personal identity, being, doing, thinking, and creativity as well as continuity over time, mediation between the conscious and the unconscious realms, cognition, and reality testing. The foundations of ego consciousness are archetypal, forming an ego complex that has the capacity for affect/soul, physical and dreaming bodies, memory and a connection with the collective unconscious, and behavior/spirit. Each component of ego consciousness is a form of energy that can be balanced or unbalanced. When the components of ego consciousness are balanced, individuation is occurring. The Self provides the total view of the entire personality, both conscious and unconscious and is therefore supreme. It is the function of the ego to challenge or fulfill the demands of that supremacy. Consciousness or awareness is the distinguishing factor of the ego. The greater the degree of ego consciousness, the greater the possibility for sensing what is unknown. The ego's role is to discriminate the opposites, withstand their tension until the tension is transcended, and then to protect what emerges. Defining the ego is difficult because it is constantly changing and shifting (Samuels et al. 1986, 50–53).

Jung uses four concepts when discussing ego consciousness:
The ego is a complex and is the center of consciousness (*CW* 18, 1980, 11).
The ego is not the center of the personality (*CW* 12, 1977, 98-99).
The ego is one aspect of the Self (*CW* 8, 1981, 224).
The ego can be viewed from a developmental perspective because of the shifting demands made on it during a lifetime (*CW* 8, 1981, 224).

IMAGO: a psychic structure that corresponds to an actual quality or qualities of persons in objective reality, for example, the parents (*CW* 8, 1981, 274). The imago is also built on those parental influences (patterns of mediation of the archetypal /developmental processes) that cause specific, subjective reactions within the child and are therefore intertwined with the psychic and somatic aspects of the archetypes adding *numinous* energy to the imago. The imago is unconsciously projected outward onto people in the environment and, when the parents die, is experienced as an internal ghost (*CW* 7, 1977, 127–128). The imago gives outer objects and persons energy that belongs to the individuation process. In addition, these outer objects often exert such an exaggerated influence on the person that they replace the Self, depleting the energy that is urgently needed for his or her own development (*CW* 8, 1981, 274).

INDIVIDUATION: Jung believed that marriage and/or analysis both promoted individuation, that is, these two experiences promote a relationship between the ego and the Self (the architect and blueprint for growth of wholeness of the personality). The aim of individuation is to allow the ego to separate from pathological complexes and observe the workings of the persona on the one hand, and relate to, rather than be overwhelmed by, the suggestive power of the archetypes on the other. Individuation means wholeness or an integration of the partial personalities of all of the complexes (*CW* 7, 1977, 174–175).

NUMINOUS: A term first used by Rudolf Otto (1958) in his book *The Idea of the Holy* to describe the awe-filled and the awful experience of the divine, the overwhelming mystery or mysterium tremendum (5–7). Jung talks about the archetypes as having a magical or numinous effect upon a person when they appear in dreams, which gives them an emotional intensity (*CW* 8, 1981, 205-206).

PERSONA: The persona is both an archetype and a complex. It is an archetype because it is universally human, and a complex because it is filled in with individual experience that is connected with ego consciousness. The persona is based on the physical gender and stands between the ego and the outer world. It is made up of the roles we carry in our relations with the outside world, e.g., mother, father, child, fireman, or artist. The persona is not identical with ego consciousness and is a compromise between the demands of the environment on ego consciousness balanced with the structures of the inner landscape. Its proper function is based on ego ideals, physical gender, the function of the individual within the culture, the demands of individuation, and the psychic and physical contingencies that limit or promote individuation (Jacobi 1959, 27).

PERSONAL UNCONSCIOUS: The part of the unconscious that contains repressed memories, painful experiences and feelings suppressed on purpose; subliminal perceptions that are sense perceptions not strong enough to reach consciousness, and contents not yet ripe enough for consciousness. It contains the personal memories of a lifetime that go all the way back to the womb (*CW* 7, 1977, 66). These contents are called *personal* because they have to do with an individual's personal past. They are the integral components of the personality; they belong to its inventory, and their loss to consciousness produces inferiority in one respect or another, which gives rise to a sense of resentment or entitlement. Whenever these manifestations of inferiority appear, they indicate an accumulation of energy within the unconscious that prevents the expression of personal growth and development and the deep need to assimilate an unconscious component (135–137).

PROJECTION: An unconscious process that throws contents of the unconscious out into the environment onto persons, things, values, ideas etc. Projection is a natural process. It occurs normally in children and adults when the conscious attitude is overcrowded and there is no means available for expressing the unconscious material. In this case, the unconscious has no alternative but to generate projections. When ego consciousness is exposed repeatedly to the threat of annihilation, projection becomes neurotic and is connected with the symptoms of the pathological complex (*CW* 14, 1976, 319–320). Projections consist of contents from both the personal and the collective unconscious (*CW* 18, 1980, 160–161). Personal contents and projections are dissolved through conscious realization. Impersonal contents, which belong to the structural elements of the collective unconscious, are not dissolved; they must be related to. Only the projection is dissolved, not the content.

PSYCHOID: defines the bipolar structure of the archetypes as being both physical and psychical. The science of physics shares the same theory when light is described as being made up of particles (matter) and at the same time waves (psychical). *Psychoid* refers to a level of the unconscious that is completely inaccessible to consciousness; it can be described but not comprehended; it is neutral, being neither psychological nor physiological, and it is the structural nature of the archetype (*CW* 8, 1981, 215–216).

SELF: The unknowable, self-regulating center of both consciousness and the unconscious, i.e., the entire personality. It serves as the architect and provides the blueprints (in the form of the archetypes) for human development and individuation. Jung developed the term *Self* as an empirical concept derived from his study of dreams, myths, fairy tales, cross cultural mythology, and the Word Association Test. The Self is neither good nor bad; it is simply the center and the circumference of all that we are. The ego is a reflection of the Self, and its function is to embody the Self in everyday life (*CW* 11, 1977, 259; *CW* 6, 1977, 340; *CW* 7, 1977, 221–222).

SYMBOL: This is what is perceived directly in the here and now when an archetype manifests itself. A symbol is only one facet of an archetype. Jung defines the symbol as the essence and the image of archetypal psychic energy, which cannot be perceived directly. Symbols are alive; they possess many meanings, and they arise from the unconscious to reconcile opposites. The conscious mind cannot create a living symbol. A true symbol transforms the conscious attitude and therefore can only arise from the unconscious. When one encounters a symbol in a dream, it is a powerful and numinous experience. Whether a thing is truly a symbol or not depends on the experience of the observing consciousness. When the tensions of opposing poles are tolerated by ego consciousness, a symbol will eventually emerge spontaneously from the unconscious, producing a transformation that integrates the antithetical parts into a new level of experience (Jacobi 1959, 119–121).

TRANSCENDENT FUNCTION: A phenomenon that Jung described as always appearing when opposing parts were contained and explored fully, allowing each part to express its own point of view without denying its opposite (*CW* 6, 1971, 480). It is the function that mediates internal, opposed parts. It facilitates the psychological movement from one point of view to another, expressing itself through symbols. "It is a natural process, a manifestation of the energy that springs from the tension of opposites and it consists in a series of fantasy occurrences which appear spontaneously in dreams and visions" (*CW* 7, 1977, 80). The transcendent function (or the capacity to transcend being pulled to only one part or another) always appears when opposing parts are contained and explored. "Consciousness is continually widened through [the appearance] of previously unconscious contents [that appear as waking visions or in dreams as *numinous* symbols] that give the patient the advantage [of using his or her] own resources" (*CW* 8, 1981, 90-91). The transcendent function gradually forms a bridge between consciousness and the unconscious that transcends the limited view of the pathological complex. It is a force of nature that will only express itself when there is a true dialogue between ego consciousness and the unconscious. The transcendent function is not a point for the ego to arrive at; rather, it is experienced spontaneously throughout a lifetime of containment, self-reflection, dreaming, and ongoing dialogue between ego consciousness and the unconscious.

TRANSFERENCE: The unconscious tendency of the patient to project parts of the imago, defenses of the Self, the *numinous* portions of the archetypal/developmental processes, and/or the patterns of mediation of the archetypal/developmental processes onto the therapist and to reenact these parts with the analyst/therapist. In actuality, transference takes place all the time and occurs every day in interpersonal interactions. However, the word *transference* is used primarily in the clinical setting to denote unconscious projections onto the analyst/therapist on the part of the patient.

UNCONSCIOUS: In addition to repressed material, the unconscious contains all those psychic components that have fallen below the threshold of consciousness as well as subliminal sense perceptions and all of the material that has not yet reached the threshold of consciousness. The unconscious is ceaselessly engaged in grouping and regrouping its contents. This activity should be thought of as completely autonomous (*CW* 7, 1977, 127–128). The unconscious has a causal sequence (as in the personal unconscious) and also a teleological orientation. This means that as we relate to the unconscious, containing and introspecting, disengaging from projections and dissolving pathological complexes, we become more whole. The unconscious does not think, as we understand *thinking*; it simply creates an image or physical experience that responds to the conscious situation (182–183).

WORD ASSOCIATION TEST: An experimental measure used to identify pathological complexes through associations to a stimulus word. Over and over, the results of the test support Jung's theories about complexes. "Jung distinguished different kinds of complexes, depending upon whether they were related to single, ongoing or repeated events; whether they were conscious, partly conscious or unconscious and whether they revealed strong charges of affect" (Samuels et al. 1986, 162).

The Word Association Test is administered to a patient using 100 stimulus words and a stopwatch. During the first part of the test, the person performing the test says one stimulus word at a time and asks the person taking the test to respond with the first thing that comes into his or her head. The person has 10 seconds to respond (Jung used a metronom.). The test is repeated, and the person taking the test is asked to remember the associations he or she made during the first portion of the test. The person taking the test has 10 seconds to respond. The tester notes any complex indicators such as failures to respond, lag in reaction time, giggling, signs of physical discomfort, or mistakes during both parts of the test. These *halts in awareness* are the complex indicators and will reveal the affective theme of the complex.

BIBLIOGRAPHY

Ainsworth, M. D. S., Blehar, M. C., Waters, E., & Wall, S. (1978). *Patterns of attachment: Assessed in the strange situation and at home.* Hillsdale, NJ: Erlbaum.

—— (1989). Attachments beyond infancy. *American Psychologist 44*, 709–16.

American Psychiatric Association (2000). *Diagnostic and statistical manual of mental disorders*: DSM-IV-TR., 4th ed. Washington DC: R.R. Donnelley & Sons.

American Psychological Association (1998). *Publication manual of the American Psychological Association*, 3rd ed. Washington DC: American Psychological Association.

Anderson, H. C. (1984). *Hans Andersen's fairy tales: A selection.* L. W. Kingsland (Trans.). New York: Oxford University Press.

Bach, Susan. (1990). *Life paints its own span: On the significance of spontaneous pictures by severely ill children.* Wilmette, IL: Chiron Publishing.

Bateson, G., & Bateson, M. E. (1988). *Angels fear: Towards an epistemology of the sacred.* New York: Bantam Books.

Becker, E. (1973). *The denial of death.* New York: Free Press.

Berne, Eric (1964). *Games people play.* New York: Grove Press.

—— (1961). *Transactional analysis in psychotherapy.* New York: Grove Press.

Bowlby, J. (1973). *Attachment and loss.* Vol. 2: *Separation.* New York: Basic Books.

—— (1980). *Attachment and loss.* Vol. 3: *Loss, sadness and depression.* New York: Basic Books.

—— (1982). *Attachment and loss.* Vol. 1: *Attachment.* New York: Basic Books.

Capra, F. (1991). *The Tao of physics: An exploration of the parallels between modern physics and eastern mysticism*, 3rd ed. Boston: Shambhala.

Campbell, J. (1970). *The masks of god: Primitive mythology.* New York: Viking Press.

—— (1970). *The masks of god: Creative mythology.* New York: Viking Press.

—— (1970). *The masks of god: Oriental mythology.* New York: Viking Press.

—— (1970). *The masks of god: Occidental mythology.* New York: Viking Press.

—— (1968). *The hero with a thousand faces.* New Jersey: Princeton University Press.

Castaneda, C. (1998). *The active side of infinity.* New York: Harper Perennial.

Demos, V. E. (1995). *Exploring affect: The selected writings of Silvan Tomkins.* New York: Cambridge University Press.

Diamond, S. A. (1996). *Anger, madness, and the daimonic.* New York: State University of New York Press.

Dieckmann, H. (1999). *Complexes: Diagnosis and therapy in analytical psychology.* Boris Matthews (Trans.). Wilmette, IL: Chiron.

Donahue, B. A. (1994). The way of the warrior: One metaphor for individuation. In *Psyche and Sports*, M. Stein & J. Hollwitz (Eds.). Wilmette, IL: Chiron.

Dreikurs, R. (1989). *Fundamentals of Adlerian psychology.* Chicago: Adler School of Professional Psychology.

Edinger, E. F. (1973). *Ego and archetype: Individuation and the religious function of the Psyche.* New York: Penguin Books.

Ellenberger, H. F. (1970). *The discovery of the unconscious: The history and evolution of dynamic psychiatry.* New York: Basic Books.
Eliade, M. (1958). *Patterns in comparative religion.* Rosemary Sheed (Trans.). New York: Meridian Books.
Erickson, E. (1950). *Childhood and society.* New York: W.W. Norton.
Erskine, R., Moursund, J., & Trautmann, R. (1999). *Beyond empathy: A therapy of contact-in relationship.* Philadelphia: Brunner Mazel.
Fierman, L. B., ed. (1965). *Effective psychotherapy: The contribution of Hellmuth Kaiser.* New York: Free Press.
Firestone, R. W. (1987). *The fantasy bond: Structure of psychological defenses.* Santa Barbara, CA: The Glendon Association.
Fish, B., & Dudas, K. (1999). The relevance of attachment research for adult narratives in psychotherapy. *Clinical Social Work Journal 27*, no. 1, 27–40.
Fordham, M. (1974). Defenses of the self. *Journal of Analytical Psychology 19*, no. 2. London: Society of Analytical Psychology.
Fordham, M., Gordon, R., Hubback, J., & Lambert, K. (Eds.) (1974). Technique in Jungian analysis. *Library of Analytical Psychology* 2. London: William Heinemann Medical Books Ltd.
—— (1976). The self and autism. *Library of Analytical Psychology* 3. London: William Heinemann Medical Books Ltd.
—— (1985). Explorations into the self. *Library of Analytical Psychology* 7. New York: Academic Press.
Fordham, M. (1978). *Jungian psychotherapy: A study in analytical psychology.* New York: John Wiley & Sons.
—— (1996). In *Analyst-patient interaction: Collected papers on technique.* Sonu Shamdasani (Ed.). New York: Routledge.
Freud, A. (1960). Discussion of John Bowlby's paper. *The Psychoanalytic Study of the Child 15*, 55–62.
Freud, S. 1961. *A general introduction to psychoanalysis.* Joan Riviere (Trans.). New York: Washington Square Press.
Graves, R. (1982) *The white goddess: A historical grammar of poetic myth.* New York: Farrar, Straus and Giroux.
Grossmann, K., & Grossmann, K. (1991). Attachment quality as an organizer of emotional and behavioral responses in a longitudinal perspective. In C. M. Parkes, J. Stevenson-Hinde, & P. Marris (Eds.), *Attachment across the life cycle.* New York: Tavistock/Routledge.
Guntrip, H. (1969). *Schizoid phenomena, object relations and the Self.* New York: International Universities Press.
Hall, J. (1991). The watcher at the gates of dawn. In N. Schwartz-Salant & M. Stein (Eds.), *Liminality and transitional phenomena.* Wilmette, IL: Chiron.
Harding, M. E. (1965/1993). *The parental image: Its injury and reconstruction,* 2nd ed. Boston: Sigo Press.
Hayman, R. (2001). *A life of Jung.* New York: W.W. Norton.
Hendrix, H. (1996). *Keeping the love you find: A workshop for singles.* Winter Park, Fl: Institute for Imago Relationship Therapy.
Hollis, J. (1996). *Swamplands of the soul: New life in dismal places.* Toronto, Canada: Inner City Books.
Jacobi, J. (1959). *Complex, archetype, symbol in the psychology of C. G. Jung.* Ralph Manheim (Trans.). Princeton, NJ: Princeton University Press.
Jung, C. G. (1963). *Memories, dreams, reflections.* Recorded and edited by Aniela Jaffe. R. & C. Winston (Trans.). New York: Pantheon Books.
—— (1975) On the psychology and pathology of so-called occult phenomena. In *Psychiatric studies, Collected Works,* Vol. 1, 2nd ed. R. F. C. Hull (Trans.). Princeton, NJ: Princeton University Press.

—— (1973) The associations of normal subjects. In *Experimental researches including the Studies in Word Association, Collected Works*, Vol. 2. Leopold Stein in collaboration with Diana Riviere (Trans.). Princeton, NJ: Princeton University Press.

—— (1973) The family constellation. In *Experimental researches including the Studies in Word Association, Collected Works*, Vol. 2. Leopold Stein in collaboration with Diana Riviere (Trans.). Princeton, NJ: Princeton University Press.

—— (1972) On the problem of psychogenesis in mental disease. In *The psychogenesis of mental disease, Collected Works*, Vol. 3. R. F. C. Hull (Trans.). Princeton, NJ: Princeton University Press.

—— (1972). The psychology of dementia praecox. In *The psychogenesis of mental disease, Collected Works*, Vol. 3. R. F. C. Hull (Trans.). Princeton, NJ: Princeton University Press.

—— (1972). A criticism of Bleuler's theory of Schizophrenia. In *The psychogenesis of mental disease, Collected Works*, Vol. 3. R. F. C. Hull (Trans.). Princeton, NJ: Princeton University Press.

—— (1979). The theory of psychoanalysis. In *Freud and psychoanalysis* (4th printing), *Collected Works*, Vol. 4. R. F. C. Hull (Trans.). Sir H. Read, M. Fordham, G. Adler, & W. McGuire (Eds.). Princeton, NJ: Princeton University Press.

—— (1974). *Symbols of transformation*, 2nd ed. with corrections. *Collected Works*, Vol. 5. R. F. C. Hull (Trans.). Princeton, NJ: Princeton University Press.

—— (1971). *Psychological types, Collected Works*, Vol. 6. H. G. Baynes (Trans.). R. F. C. Hull (Revised). Sir H. Read, M. Fordham, G. Adler, & W. McGuire (Eds.). Princeton, NJ: Princeton University Press.

—— (1977). On the psychology of the unconscious. In *Two essays on analytical psychology*, 2nd ed. *Collected Works*, Vol. 7. R. F. C. Hull (Trans.) Sir H. Read, M. Fordham, G. Adler, & W. McGuire (Eds.). Princeton, NJ: Princeton University Press.

—— (1977). The effects of the unconscious upon consciousness. In *Two essays on analytical psychology*, 2nd ed.. *Collected Works*, Vol. 7. R. F. C. Hull (Trans.). Sir H. Read, M. Fordham, G. Adler, & W. McGuire (Eds.). Princeton, NJ: Princeton University Press.

—— (1977). Individuation. In *Two essays on analytical psychology*, 2nd ed. *Collected Works*, Vol. 7. R. F. C. Hull (Trans.). Sir H. Read, M. Fordham, G. Adler, & W. McGuire (Eds.). Princeton, NJ: Princeton University Press.

—— (1981). A review of complex theory. In *The structure and dynamics of the psyche*, 2nd ed., *Collected Works*, Vol. 8. R. F. C. Hull (Trans.). Sir. H. Read, M. Fordham, G. Adler, & W McGuire (Eds.). Princeton, NJ: Princeton University Press.

—— (1981). Psychological factors determining human behavior. In *The structure and dynamics of the psyche*, 2nd ed., Collected Works, Vol. 8. R. F. C. Hull (Trans.). Sir. H. Read, M. Fordham, G. Adler, & W. McGuire (Eds.). Princeton, NJ: Princeton University Press.

—— (1981). On the nature of the psyche. In *The structure and dynamics of the psyche*, 2nd ed., *Collected Works*, Vol. 8. R. F. C. Hull (Trans.). Sir. H. Read, M. Fordham, G. Adler, & W McGuire (Eds.). Princeton, NJ: Princeton University Press.

—— (1981). General aspects of dream psychology. In *The structure and dynamics of the psyche*, 2nd ed., *Collected Works*, Vol. 8. R. F. C. Hull (Trans.). Sir. H. Read, M. Fordham, G. Adler, & W McGuire (Eds.). Princeton, NJ: Princeton University Press.

—— (1977). Archetypes of the collective unconscious. In *The archetypes and the collective unconscious*, 2nd ed., *Collected Works*, Vol. 91. R. F. C. Hull (Trans.). Sir H. Read, M. Fordham, G. Adler, & W. McGuire (Eds.) Princeton, NJ: Princeton University Press.

—— (1977). The concept of the collective unconscious. In *The Archetypes and the collective unconscious*, 2nd ed, Collected Works. Vol. 91. RFC Hull (Trans.). Sir H. Read, M. Fordham, G. Adler & W. McGuire (Eds.) Princeton, NJ: Princeton University Press.

—— (1977) Concerning the archetypes, with special reference to the anima concept. In *The archetypes and the collective unconscious*, 2nd ed., *Collected Works*, Vol. 91. R. F. C. Hull (Trans.).

Sir H. Read, M. Fordham, G. Adler, & W. McGuire (Eds.). Princeton, NJ: Princeton University Press.

—— (1977). Psychological aspects of the mother archetype. In *The archetypes and the collective unconscious*, 2nd ed., *Collected Works*, Vol. 91. R. F. C. Hull (Trans.). Sir H. Read, M. Fordham, G. Adler, & W. McGuire (Eds.). Princeton, NJ: Princeton University Press.

—— (1973). *Aion: Researches into the phenomenology of the Self*, 2nd ed., *Collected Works*, Vol. 92. R. F. C. Hull (Trans.). Sir H. Read, M. Fordham, G. Adler, & W. McGuire (Eds.). Princeton NJ: Princeton University Press.

—— (1969). Psychology and religion. In *Psychology and religion: West and East*. 2nd ed., *Collected Works*, Vol. 11. R. F. C. Hull. Sir H. Read, M. Fordham, G. Adler, & W. McGuire (Eds.). Princeton NJ: Princeton University Press.

—— (1969). Transformation symbolism in the mass. In *Psychology and religion: West and East*, 2nd ed. *Collected Works*, Vol. 11. R. F. C. Hull. Sir H. Read, M. Fordham, G. Adler, & W. McGuire (Eds.). Princeton NJ: Princeton University Press.

—— (1970). *Mysterium coniunctionis: An enquiry into the separation and synthesis of psychic opposites in alchemy*. *Collected Works*, Vol. 14. R. F. C. Hull (Trans.). Sir H. Read, M. Fordham, G. Adler, & W. McGuire (Eds.). Princeton NJ: Princeton University Press.

—— (1966). *The spirit in man, art and literature*. *Collected Works*, Vol. 15. R. F. C. Hull (Trans.). Sir H. Read, M. Fordham, G. Adler, and W. McGuire (Eds.). Princeton NJ: Princeton University Press.

—— (1966). Psychotherapy today. In *The practice of psychotherapy*, 2nd ed. In *Collected Works*, Vol. 16. R. F. C. Hull (Trans.). Sir H. Read, M. Fordham, G. Adler, and W. McGuire (Eds.). Princeton NJ: Princeton University Press.

—— (1970). Marriage as a psychological relationship. In *The development of personality: Papers on child psychology, education and related subjects*. *Collected Works*, Vol. 17. R. F. C. Hull (Trans.). Sir H. Read, M. Fordham, G. Adler, and W. McGuire (Eds.). Princeton NJ: Princeton University Press.

—— (1980). The Tavistock lectures. In *The symbolic life*. *Collected Works*, Vol. 18 R. F. C. Hull (Trans.). Sir H. Read, M. Fordham, G. Adler, & W. McGuire (Eds.). Princeton NJ: Princeton University.

Kalsched, D. (1996). *The inner world of trauma: Archetypal defenses of the personal spirit*. New York: Routledge.

Kaiser, H. (1955). The problem of responsibility in psychotherapy. In *Psychiatry 18*, 205–11.

Kalff, D. (1980). *Sandplay: A psychotherapeutic approach to the psyche*. Santa Monica, CA: Sigo Press.

Karen, R. (1994). *Becoming attached: First relationships and how they shape our capacity to love*. New York: Oxford University Press.

Klein, M. (1975). *The psychoanalysis of children*. New York: Free Press.

Kohut, H. (1977). *The restoration of the self*. New York: International Universities Press.

Kramer, H., & Sprenger, J. (1971). *Maleus malificarum*. M. Summers (Trans.). New York: Dover Publications, Inc.

Levin, P. (1974). *Becoming the way we are: A transactional guide to personal development*. Berkley, CA: Self-published.

—— (1985). *Cycles of power: A users guide to the seven seasons of life*. Deerfield, FL: Health Communications Inc.

Loevinger, J. (1976) *Ego development*. San Francisco, CA: Jossey Bass, Inc.

Loevinger, J. & Wessler, R. (1970) *Measuring ego development 1: Construction and use of a sentence completion test*. San Francisco, CA: Josey Bass, Inc.

Loevinger, J., Wessler, R., & Redmore, C. *Measuring ego development 2: Scoring manual for women and girls*. San Francisco, CA: Jossey Bass, Inc.

Lowen, A. (1971). *The language of the body.* New York: Collier.
—— (1976). *Bioenergetics.* New York: Penguin Books.
Main, M. (1995) Attachment: Overview with implications for clinical work. In S. Goldberg, R. Muir, & J. Kerr (Eds.), *Attachment theory: Social, developmental and clinical perspectives,* 407-74. Hillsdale, NJ: Analytic Press.
—— (1999) Epilogue. Attachment theory: Eighteen points with suggestions for future studies. In J. Cassidy & P. R. Shaver (Eds.), *Handbook of attachment: Theory, research and clinical applications,* 407-74. New York: Guilford Press.
McCormick, P. (1971) *Guide for use of a life-script questionnaire.* Berkley, CA: Self-published.
McNeil, J. (1976). The parent interview. *Transactional Analysis Journal.* San Francisco: TA Press.
Mudd, P. (1990). Death as a transferential factor. In *Journal of Analytical Psychology 35,* 125–41. London: Society of Analytical Psychology.
Mudd, P. (1998) Notions of gender: Jung's views and beyond. In *The Round Table Review of Contemporary Contributions to Jungian Psychology 6,* no. 2, pp. 1–10. New York: Port Washington.
Otto, R. (1958). *The idea of the holy,* 2nd ed. J. W. Harvey (Trans.). New York: Oxford University Press.
Parkes, C. M., Stevenson-Hinde, J., & Morris, P.(Eds.) (1991). *Attachment across the life cycle.* New York: Tavistock/Routledge.
Perls, F. S. (1971). *Gestalt therapy verbatim.* New York: Bantam Books.
Person, E. (1995). *By force of fantasy.* New York: Penguin Books.
Racker, H. (1982). *Transference and counter-transference.* Madison, WI: International Universities Press, Inc.
Sable, P. (2000). *Attachment and adult psychotherapy.* Northvale, NJ: Jason Aronson Inc.
Samuels, A., Shorter, B., & Plaut, F. (1986). *A critical dictionary of Jungian analysis.* New York: Routledge & Kegan Paul.
Scialli, J. (1982). Multiple identity processes and the development of the observing ego. *Journal of the American Academy of Psychoanalysis 10,* 387–405.
Selye, H. (1976). *The stress of life,* rev. ed. New York: McGraw-Hill.
Simpson, J., & Rholes, W. S. (Eds.) (1998). *Attachment theory and close relationships.* New York: Guilford Press.
Spitz, R. (1945). Hospitalism: An inquiry into the genesis of psychiatric conditions in early childhood. *Psychoanalytic Study of the Child 1,* 53–74.
Stein, M. (Ed.) (1982). *Jungian analysis.* The Reality of the Psyche Series. LaSalle, IL: Open Court.
—— (1995). *The Interactive field in analysis.* Chiron Clinical Series I. Wilmette IL: Chiron.
Steiner, C. (1974). *Scripts people live.* New York: Grove Press.
Stern, D. (1985). *The interpersonal world of the infant: A view from psychoanalysis and developmental psychology.* New York: Basic Books.
Stolorow, R., Branschaft, B., & Atwood, G. (1987). *Psychoanalytic treatment: An intersubjective approach.* Hillsdale, NJ: Analytic Press.
Storm, H. (1994). *Lightning bolt.* New York: Ballantine Books.
Tomkins, S. (1981). The quest for primary motives: Biography and autobiography of an idea. *Journal of Personality and Social Psychology 41,* 306–29.
Veith, I. (Trans.) (1972). *The yellow emperor's classic of internal medicine.* New ed. Berkley, CA: University of California Press.
Von Franz, M. L. (1973). *An introduction to the psychology of fairy tales,* 2nd ed. Zurich: Spring Publications.

—— (1980). *Projection and re-collection in Jungian psychology.* W. H. Kennedy (Trans.). The Reality of the Psyche Series. LaSalle, IL: Open Court.
—— (1979). *Alchemical active imagination.* Dallas, TX: Spring Publications.
Watson, J. B. (1928) *Psychological care of infant and child.* New York: W.W. Norton.
Weiss, R. S. (1991). The attachment bond in childhood and adulthood. In *Attachment Across the Life Cycle.* Parkes, C. M., Stevenson-Hinde, J., & Marris, P. (Eds). New York: Routledge.

Wheelwright, J. (1978). *Women and men.* San Fransisco: C.G. Jung Institute of San Francisco.
Winnicott, D. (1965). *The maturational processes and the facilitating environment.* New York: International Universities Press.
Wolff, T. (1912). On complexes. Unpublished manuscript in C.G. Jung Institute, Evanston, IL archives.

AUTHOR INDEX

A

Aimsworth, M., 74 n.4
Ainsworth, M.D.S., 123, 124, 125, 162
Atwood, G., 19

B

Bach, S., 229 n.6
Bedi, A., 120 n.6
Beebe, John, 229 n.4
Berne, E., 260 n.1
Bowlby, J., 123, 124, 162
Briggs, J., 120 n.10

C

Capra, F., 13, 15, 79

D

Diamond, S.A., 74 n.8, 229 n.7
Dudas, K., 124

E

Erikson, E., 19
Erkine, R., 139

F

Firestone, R., 158, 159
Fish, B., 124
Fordham, M., 32–33, 55, 74 n.2
Freud, A., 19
Freud, S., 120 n.8
Furst, E., 43 n.10, 174

G

Gimbutas, M., 230 n.8
Graves, R., 230 n.8

H

Harding, M. E., 175 n.2
Harlow, H., 124
Hendrix, H., 260 n.1
Hobday, J., 42 n.3, 43 n.4

J

Jacobi, J., 149
Jung, C.G., 4, 5, 6, 15, 42 n.3, 60, 70, 72, 75 n.9, 75 n.10, 76, 79, 107, 135, 178, 260 n.1

K

Karen, R., 74 n. 4, 123, 124
Klein, M., 19
Kramer, H., 62

L

Levin, P., 19, 20, 43 n.7, 260 n.1
Loomis, M., 86, 110

M

Main, M., 123, 124, 162
McCormick, P., 260 n.1
McNeil, J., 139
Moursund, J., 139
Mudd, P., 12, 31, 43 n.9, 74 n.6, 153

N

Nathanson,, 8

P

Perls, F.S., 139
Person, E., 159
Plaut, F., 131
Pon Chao Dong, 119 n.3

R

Racker, H., 61
Ross, E.K., 74 n.3, 110, 230 n.9

S

Sable, P., 122, 124
Samuels, A., 131
Scialli, J., 22
Shorter, B., 131
Solomon, 123

Spitz, R., 74 n.4, 229 n.5
Sprenger, J., 62
Stein, M., 29
Steiner, C., 260 n.1
Stern, D., 9, 19, 36, 69, 76, 77–78, 139
Stolorow, R., 19
Storm, H., 85, 86, 119 n.2

T

Tomkins, S., 6, 7, 40, 90, 91
Trautmann, R., 139

V

Veith, I., 90
von Franz, M.L., 10, 261 n.2

W

Walker, B., 230 n.8
Weiss, R.S., 124

SUBJECT INDEX

A

About Empathy: A Therapy of Contact-In-Relationship, 139
active imagination
  and the anima/animus, 153
  in the clinical setting, 225–226
  concepts about, 261n. 2
  definition of, 263
  performing, 248
  use of, 120n. 7
activity. (*see* doing)
affect
  clinical vignette, 92–93
  definition of, 78, 263
  development of, 6–7, 88–92
  function of, 87
  and memory, 9
  and soul, 79
  theory of, 6–9
affect blockages, 90
affective intensity, 91
affective sequence, 8
affective theme, 8, 9, 66, 88–92, 128–129
affects, innate, 6–8, 7 fig. 1, 90–91
aim of Jungian analysis, 263
air, 98–99
alchemy, 153
ambivalent forms of attachment, 123–124, 125, 162
amplification, 230n. 8, 264
Andersen, Hans Christian, 10–11
anger, 90
anima and animus, 153–158, 264
archetypal/developmental processes
  being (hunger), 20–21, 165–166, 246
  case studies, 186, 195–196, 200–201, 208, 214–215, 223

creativity, 25
and deintegration, 33
doing (activity), 19, 21–22, 166–168, 246
identity (sexuality), 19, 24–25, 170–172, 229n. 3, 247
and the imago, 70
and Jung, 18–19
mediation patterns and ego consciousness, 38 fig. 5, 39–40
and modern theorists, 19–20
and pathological complexes, 40
patterns of mediation. (*see* mediation patterns)
skill development, 246–247
thinking (reflection), 19, 22–23, 168–170, 246
archetypal energy (*see* archetypal structures)
archetypal structures
  the anima and the animus, 153–158
  and the ego/imago axis, 148
  the persona, 149–151
  the shadow, 151–152
archetypes
  creators of complexes, 12–14
  definition of, 4, 6, 9, 264
  dynamic processes, 14–16
Asian medicine, 91
Asperger's disorder, 12–13
assessment, 264–265
association, 131, 265
attachment in children, 123–124
attachment, patterned forms of (*see* patterned forms of attachment)
attachment theory, 123
attuned containment, 30
attuned mediation, 71
attunement, 26, 32, 67–69, 128, 175n. 3
avoidant forms of attachment, 124, 125, 162

281

B

behavior
  clinical vignette, 105–106
  component of ego consciousness, 77, 79
  function of, 87, 104–105
  and patterned forms of attachment, 134–135
being (hunger), 19, 20–21, 165–166, 246
Bipolar II Disorder, 229n. 2
body, 78
body language, 12
body parl, 12
body, physical (*see* physical body)
body, subtle (*see* subtle body)
body work, 119n. 4

C

canalization of the libido, 72
caregiver's role, 37 fig. 4, 43n. 8, 55, 71 (*see also* parenting)
case studies
  active imagination, 225–226
  archetypal/developmental processes, 186, 195–196, 200–201, 208, 214–215, 223
  cycles of nature, 187, 196, 201, 209, 215, 224
  defenses of the Self, 187, 196, 201, 209, 215–216, 224
  ego functions, 185–186, 194–195, 200, 208, 214, 223
  embedded patterns of mediation, 186–187
  enmeshed complexes, 199–200
  fantasy bond, 188, 197, 202, 209, 216, 225
  history of, 184–185, 190–193, 206–207, 211–214, 220–222
  the imago, 188, 197, 201, 209, 216, 224
  negative complexes, 208, 222
  overview of treatment, 189–190, 199
  pathological complexes, 185, 193–194
  patterned forms of attachment, 188, 197, 202, 210, 216, 225
  patterns of mediation, 196, 201, 209, 223
  presenting problem, 183
  therapy dialogue, 188–189, 197–199, 202–204, 216–217
  treatment summary, 205, 210, 226–227
chakras, 95, 120n. 6
chaos theory, 110

children, attachment in, 123–124
Chinese medicine, 90, 94–95
clinical examples
  affect, 92–93
  affective theme, 129
  the anima, 154–156
  the animus, 156–158
  attunement and viewing point, 67–69
  behavior, 105–106
  behavior change and the cycles of nature, 114–115
  the collective unconscious, 83, 101–104
  cooperative patterns of mediation, 29
  creating space between ego/imago axis, 145–148
  denial, 58–59
  directive patterns of mediation, 28
  dreaming as a container, 129
  dreaming body, 97–98
  of the imago, 140–143
  imago in a patterned form of attachment, 136–137
  integration of multiple viewing points, 180–182
  introjection, 61–62
  introjective identification, 64
  layered view of the psyche, 108–110
  memory, 99–101
  movement without change, 110–112
  physical body, 95–97
  projective and introjective identification, 64
  projective identification, 63
  regression in being, 165–166
  regression in creativity, 172–173
  regression in doing, 166–168
  regression in identity, 170–172
  regression in thinking, 168–170
  rigidified memories, 131–134
  of the shadow, 151–152
  soul, 93–94
  splinter personality, 81–82
  splitting, 60
  struggle for power, 159–162
  symbiotic patterns of mediation, 27
  unrecognized regression, 163–164
collective consciousness, 265
collective human memory, 79, 87, 98–99, 130
collective unconscious

Subject Index

clinical vignette, 101–104
definition of, 79, 265
function of, 98–99
and patterned forms of attachment, 130–134
structure in the psyche, 107
companion, evoked, 69–73
compensation, 11, 53–54, 265–266
compensatory process, 11
The Complex Awareness Measure, 231–243, 260n. 1
complex theory, 3–9
complexes
constellation of, 8
creation of, 39–40
definition of, 4, 6, 9, 12, 266
and fairy tales, 10–11
feeling toned, 5
negative (*see* negative complexes)
positive (*see* positive complexes)
rigidified (*see* rigidified complexes)
confirming patterns of mediation, 29–30, 174
conscious, definition of, 266
conscious imago, 136
constellation of a complex, 8, 127 fig. 12, 266
containing patterns of mediation, 30–31, 174
containment, 30–31, 95, 129–130
contempt, 7, 8
control issues, 65–66
cooperation, 29, 66
cooperative patterns of mediation, 28–29, 174
cooperative relationships, 28
creativity, 19, 172–173, 247
cycles of nature
case studies, 187, 196, 201, 209, 215, 224
a viewing point, 110, 111 fig. 10, 113–114

D

daimonic, 74n. 8, 229n. 7
"The Dark Self: Death as a Transferential Factor," 43n. 9
defenses of the Self
case studies, 187, 196, 201, 209, 215–216, 224
denial, 57–59
explanation of, 55–57, 55–57, 74 n.2
idealization, 65–66
identification, 63–64
introjection, 60–62
introjective identification, 64
projection, 62–63
projective and introjective identification, 64
projective identification, 63
splitting, 59–60
summary, 66–69
deintegration
and caregivers, 35 fig. 3, 37 fig. 4
damaged ego consciousness, 39–40
and ego/imago axis, 71
movement toward, 34 fig. 2
process of ego development, 33, 36
denial, 57–59
depression, 85
developmental processes (*see* archetypal/developmental processes)
diagnosis and treatment, 116–118, 117 fig. 11
diagnosis of symptoms, 177–178
Diagnostic and Statistical Manual of Mental Disorders, 177–178
diagnostic template, 179 fig. 15, 228
directive patterns of mediation, 27–28, 174
disgust, 7, 8
disintegration, 39, 39–40, 55, 71, 229n. 5
disorganized forms of attachment, 124
disoriented forms of attachment, 124, 162
dissociative identity disorder, 81
doing (activity), 19, 21–22, 166–168, 246
dream images, 157, 230n. 8
dreaming body
clinical vignette, 97–98
function of, 94–95
and the Medicine Wheel, 87
and patterned forms of attachment, 129–130
structure of ego consciousness, 79
dreams, 14, 15
duration, 7
dynamic archetypal forms, 19
dysfunctional patterns of mediation, 174
dysthymia, 85

E

Earth, 94–95
educating patterns of mediation, 31, 174

ego consciousness
  archetypal aspects of, 89 fig. 9
  archetypal components of, 80 fig. 7
  archetypal structures of, 79–81
  and a constellated complex, 127 fig. 12
  and the cycles of nature, 110
  defenses of, 54–55
  definition of, 107
  formation of, 32–40, 38 fig. 5
  foundations of, 77–78
  and the imago, 71
  and patterned forms of attachment, 126–128
  physical aspects of, 77 fig. 6
ego defenses, 74n. 2
ego, definition of, 266–267
ego development, 18–20, 32–39
ego functions, 185–186, 194–195, 200, 208, 214, 223
ego/imago axis, 71, 72, 137–148, 138 fig. 13
ego, observing, 22, 24, 67
ego/Self axis, 126
emotional balance, 91
empathy, 175n. 3
empowering patterns of mediation, 31–32, 174
empowerment, 32
enactments of the imago, 141–143, 148, 254
encouragement, 31–32
energy, 75n. 9, 87
enjoyment, 90
enmeshed complexes, 199–204
evoked companion, 69–73, 74n. 6, 139
excitement, 90

F

fairy tales and complexes, 10–11
fairy tales and role-playing, 255
fantasy, 159
fantasy bond
  case studies, 188, 197, 202, 209, 216, 225
  and the imago, 259–260
  and the patterned form of attachment, 158–163
fear, 90
feeling tone, 8
feeling toned complex, 5
fire, 104–105

focus, 215–252
Fordham, Michael, 32–39
"Four Powers of the Human Self", 86–87
Freud, 22

G

gender, 229n. 3
Generalized Event Structures (GERs), 9, 36, 69
gestalt therapy, 139
The Goddesses and Gods of Old Europe, 230n. 8

H

Hans Christian Andersen, 10–11
healing processes, 90–92
holding environment, 30
human behavior (*see* behavior)
human experience patterns (*see* complexes)
human memory (*see* memory)
human relationships, 39–40, 162
humiliation, 91
hunger (being) (*see* being)

I

idealization, 65–66
identification, 63–64
identity (sexuality), 19, 24–25, 170–172, 229n. 3, 247
illusion of fusion, 159
imaginary protector, 158–159
imago
  and archetypal energy (*see* archetypal structures)
  case studies, 188, 197, 201, 209, 216, 224
  and the collective unconscious, 75n. 10
  definition of, 267
  enactments of the, 141–143, 148
  and the evoked companion, 70–73
  and parts work, 258–260
  and patterned forms of attachment, 135–137
  skill development, 244–245
  violent, 261n. 4
imago, parental (*see* parental imago)
individuation
  behavior and spirit, 134–135

definition of, 16, 18, 42n. 3, 267
and ego consciousness, 36
and the ego/imago axis, 71
and human behavior, 104–105
"Individuation and the Old Indian Man," 16–18
infrared pole, 79–81, 80 fig. 7
innate affects, 6–8, 7 fig. 1, 90–91
innate defensive responses, 7
innate neurophysiological reflexes, 6
integration, 33, 34 fig. 2, 39–40
intensity, 7
interest, 90
The Interpersonal World of the Infant, 9
introjection, 60–62
introjective identification, 64
introjects, 139
introspection, 95
intuition, 12
invariant forms, 76–81 (*see also* archetypes)
isolation, 74n. 2

J

Journal of Personality and Social Psychology, 6
joy, 90
Jungian analysis, 263

K

Klein, Melanie, 32–33
Kral, Eileen, 96–97

L

libido, 72, 75n. 9
listening, 252–253
"little deaths," 74n. 3, 230n. 9
Little Match Girl, 10–11
long-term therapy, 228

M

Martial Arts, 120n. 9
maternal deprivation, 74n. 4
maturity, 55–56
mediation, attuned, 71
mediation patterns
archetypal/developmental processes and ego consciousness, 38 fig. 5
case studies, 186–187, 196, 201, 209, 223
confirming, 29–30, 174
containing, 30–31, 174
cooperative or mutual, 28–29, 174
directive, 27–28, 174
dysfunctional, 174
educating, 31, 174
empowering, 31–32, 174
symbiotic, 26–27, 43n. 7, 174
mediation quality, 122–123
medicine
Asian, 91
Chinese, 90, 94–95
The Medicine Wheel, 85–88, 86 fig. 8, 106–107, 119n. 2
memories, 69
memory
clinical vignette, 99–101
component of ego consciousness, 78, 79
function of, 87, 98–99
and human affect, 9
and patterned forms of attachment, 130–134
metaphor use, 254–255
mothering (*see* parenting)
multiple viewing points (*see* viewing points)
mutual patterns of mediation, 28–29

N

Native American Medicine Wheel, 85–88
Native American traditions, 43n. 8
negative complexes, 4, 5, 6, 208, 222
negative patterns of attachment, 125
neurophysiological reflexes, 6
numinous, 267

O

Object Relations School, 32–33
observing ego, 22, 24, 67
organizing principles, 19

P

The Parental Image: Its Injury and Reconstruction, 175n. 2
parental imago, 72, 135, 139
parental introjects, 139
parenting, 71, 87–88, 124–125 (*see also* caregiver's role)

partial personality (*see* splinter personality)
parts work, 139, 145, 256–260
Path to the Soul, 120n. 6
pathological complexes
   causes of, 13, 19, 21–22
   definition of, 6
   example of, 44–54
   formation of, 40
   observation of, 24–25
patient education, 31
patient referral, 228
patterned forms of attachment
   affect and soul, 128–129
   archetypal structures (*see* archetypal structures)
   behavior and spirit, 134–135
   case studies, 188, 197, 202, 210, 216, 225
   and ego consciousness, 126–128
   and the ego/imago axis, 137–148
   and the fantasy bond, 158–163
   formation of, 121–125
   formation of an image, 175 n.3
   imaging through enactment, 255–256
   and the imago, 135–137
   memory and the collective unconscious, 130–134
   physical and dreaming body, 129–130
   and regression, 163–173
   viewing points, 125–126
patterns of human experience (*see* complexes)
patterns of mediation (*see* mediation patterns)
patterns of physical/mental disorders, 177
persona, 149–151, 153, 267–268
personal unconscious, 107, 268
physical body
   clinical vignette, 95–97
   component of ego consciousness, 79–81, 80 fig. 7
   connection to subtle body, 229n. 6
   definition of, 15
   and ego consciousness, 89 fig. 9
   function of, 87, 94–95
   and patterned forms of attachment, 129–130
positive complexes, 4, 5–6
power issues, 65–66, 159–162
"Powers of the Four Directions", 86–87
preconscious imago, 136
projection, 62–63, 268
projective identification, 63–64

psyche, 15, 107–108, 108–110
psychoid, definition of, 268
psychoid structure, 13
"The Psychology of the Transference", 135
psychosexual processes, 19
psychotherapy, 91

Q

qi, 94–95

R

rage, 90
reflection (*see* thinking)
reflexes, 6
rigidified persona, 149–151
regression, 163–173
reintegration, 33, 35 fig. 3, 36, 37 fig. 4, 39–40
relational field, 40, 93, 249–250
relationships, 39–40, 162
Representations of Interactions that have been Generalized (RIGs), 69, 139
"A Review of Complex Theory", 4
rigidified complexes, 5, 10–11, 18
rigidified memories, 130–131

S

Sacred Space, 243–244
script theory, 8
secure forms of attachment, 123, 162
Self
   defenses of the (*see* defenses of the Self)
   definition of, 15–16, 269
   explanation of the, 54–55
   and formation of ego consciousness, 32–33
   four powers of, 86–87
   and spirit, 81
self-affectivity (*see* affect)
self-agency (*see* behavior)
self-coherence, 77
self-history (*see* memory)
self-invariants, 19
sexuality (*see* identity)
shadow, 151–152
shame, 8, 91
short-term therapy, 228
simile use, 254–255
skillment

active imagination, 248
archetypal/developmental processes, 246–247
compensation, 243–244
The Complex Awareness Measure, 231–243
development of transitional space, 253–254
enacting the patient, 254
focus, 215–252
group, 248–249
the imago, 244–245
listening, 252–253
parts work, 256–260
relational field, 249–250
triadic role-play (*see* triadic role-play)
use of metaphor and simile, 254–255
somatic awareness, 130
somatic intuition, 12
soul, 79, 93–94, 128–129
spirit, 81, 87, 104–105, 134–135
splinter personality, 81–82
splitting, 59–60
startle, 90
"*Statistical Investigations on Word Associations and on Familial Agreement in Reaction Type among Uneducated persons,*" 43n. 10
subtle body
  component of ego consciousness, 79–81, 80 fig. 7, 82, 84
  connection to physical body, 229n. 6
  definition of, 15
  and ego consciousness, 89 fig. 9
surprise, 90
symbiosis, definition of, 26
symbiotic patterns of mediation, 26–27, 43n. 7, 174
symbols, 15, 269
Symbols of Transformation, 15
symptoms, 177–178

T

temper tantrums, 30
terror, 90
theory of affect, 6–9
theory of complexes (*see* complex theory)
theory, script, 8
therapy, short/long-term, 228
thinking (reflection), 19, 22–23, 168–170, 246
traditions of Native Americans, 43n. 8
transcendent function, 269

transference, 270
transitional space
  creating a, 143–148, 144 fig. 14
  and dream images, 157
  skill development, 253–254
  use of, 31
  use of metaphor and simile, 254–255
treatment of enmeshed complexes, 205
triadic role-play
  development of transitional space, 253–254
  enacting the patient, 254
  explanation of, 251
  focus, 215–252
  listening, 252–253
  parts work, 256–260
The Turbulent Mirror, 120n. 10
typology, 229n. 4

U

ultraviolet pole, 79–81, 80 fig. 7
unconscious, 120n. 8, 266, 270
unconscious human psychic processes, 10–11
unconscious imago, 136
unconstellated complex, 127 fig. 12
undoing, 74n. 2

V

viewing points
  and attunement, 67–69
  into ego/imago axis (*see* archetypal structures)
  into an enmeshed complex, 200–204
  example of integration, 180–182
  and the Medicine Wheel, 87
  into the pathological complex, 73, 116–118, 117 fig. 11, 178, 179 fig. 15
vignettes (*see* clinical examples)
violence, 261n. 4
visualization, 243–244

W

water, 88–92
The White Goddess, 230n. 8
"Winter Talk," 96–97
"The Woman Who Once Walked in Balance," 44–54, 56, 115–116, 149
The Woman's Encyclopedia of Myths and Secrets, 230n. 8
Word Association Test, 43n. 10, 70, 270